INCORRIGIBLES AND INNOCENTS

INCORRIGIBLES AND INNOCENTS

Constructing Childhood and Citizenship in Progressive Era Comics

LARA SAGUISAG

RUTGERS UNIVERSITY PRESS
NEW BRUNSWICK, CAMDEN, AND NEWARK,
NEW JERSEY, AND LONDON

Library of Congress Cataloging-in-Publication Data

Names: Saguisag, Lara, author.
Title: Incorrigibles and innocents : constructing childhood and citizenship in progressive era comics / Lara Saguisag.
Description: New Brunswick : Rutgers University Press, 2018. | Includes bibliographical references and index.
Identifiers: LCCN 2018003851 | ISBN 9780813591773 (hardback) | ISBN 9780813591766 (paperback)
Subjects: LCSH: Comic books, strips, etc.—United States—History and criticism. | Children in literature. | Citizenship in literature. | Literature and society—United States—History. | BISAC: SOCIAL SCIENCE / Popular Culture. | LITERARY CRITICISM / Comics & Graphic Novels. | HISTORY / Social History. | PERFORMING ARTS / Film & Video / History & Criticism. | HISTORY / United States / 20th Century. | SOCIAL SCIENCE / Children's Studies. | SOCIAL SCIENCE / Gender Studies.
Classification: LCC PN6725 .S35 2018 | DDC 741.5/973—dc23 LC record available at https://lccn.loc.gov/2018003851

A British Cataloging-in-Publication record for this book is available from the British Library.

∞ The paper used in this publication meets the requirements of the American National Standard for Information Sciences—Permanence of Paper for Printed Library Materials, ANSI Z39.48-1992.

www.rutgersuniversitypress.org

Manufactured in the United States of America

For my father, Rene, and in memory of my mother, Dulce

CONTENTS

Introduction: Drawing the Lines 1

1 Foreign yet Familiar 24

2 Crossing the Color Line 52

3 Family Amusements 84

4 The "Secret Tracts" of the Child's Mind 114

5 What Would You Do with Girls like These? 142

Conclusion: Naughty Boys in a New Millennium 175

Acknowledgments 187

Notes 191

Bibliography 219

Index 229

INCORRIGIBLES AND INNOCENTS

INTRODUCTION

DRAWING THE LINES

Richard F. Outcault made a living by drawing children. As a cartoonist and illustrator who witnessed and experienced the turbulences and dynamisms of New York City in the Progressive Era, he produced quite an assortment of images of childhood: immigrant and working-class boys and girls who played riotous games in back lots, alleys, and parks; white, middle-class youngsters who threw tantrums and sowed chaos in the parlor; and black children who were, troublingly, modeled after the popular pickaninny caricature. In his newspaper comics—which ran the gamut of single-panel cartoons, large cartoons divided into multiple sections, and multipanel sequential strips—he coaxed readers to sympathize with doleful waifs, admire the resourcefulness of bell boys and street urchins, and chuckle at the sight of city kids who found themselves out of sorts in the countryside.[1] Outcault's persistent fascination with childhood obviously paid off: his work made him a fortune and turned him into a national celebrity. In his lifetime, critics hailed him as "the father of the funnies." His contemporaries sought to replicate his success by launching their own child-centered comics series. Many comics historians and archivists regard Outcault as an innovative, astute artist who helped lay the foundations of the American comic strip.

The case of Outcault demonstrates that the theme of childhood was essential to the emergence and development of comics in the United States in the late nineteenth and early twentieth centuries. But this book does more than just examine Progressive Era cartoonists' exploration of and fixation with childhood. It also reveals that the two strands of comics and childhood were tightly braided with contemporary discourses of citizenship and nationhood. The Progressive Era was a period defined by conflicts—between industrial and agrarian economies, workers and the wealthy, emancipation and white supremacy movements, immigration and nativism, the New Woman and the Cult of True Womanhood—and cartoonists used images of children to explore, dissect, and sometimes defuse these sociopolitical tensions.

As a fledgling cartoonist in mid-1890s New York, Outcault often represented the city's tenements as neighborhoods of bedlam. He filled his frames with caricatures of rowdy immigrant and working-class children. In his cartoon "Golf—The Great Society Sport as Played in Hogan's Alley" (fig. 1), published in Joseph Pulitzer's the *New York World* on January 5, 1896, street children lay claim to a public space and play unruly rounds of golf.[2] Their clumsy attempts at the sport result in several injuries and presumably several broken windows. In this multicolored cartoon that took up half a broadsheet page, Outcault heightens the sense of disorder by forcing readers to take in numerous dynamic actions all at once. As such, Outcault recalls the work of eighteenth-century artist William Hogarth, whose engravings, as Thierry Smolderen puts it, "invite a variable, zigzagging circulation of the reader's gaze."[3]

Turn-of-the-century readers likely apprehended "Golf" as a visual shock as they confronted the cartoon's size, mix of colors, and intricate network of actions. Of course, the themes and techniques of "Golf" were not at all atypical for its time. Like many of his contemporaries, Outcault used images of "swarming" immigrant and working-class youth as shorthand for the tumult and unpredictability of city life. In fact, in drawing "Golf," Outcault walked a path that he had repeatedly tread, as made evident by his earlier work published in the

Figure 1. Cartoon by R. F. Outcault. "Golf—the Great Society Sport as Played in Hogan's Alley." In *New York World* Comic Supplement, January 5, 1896. SFS 58-1-1, San Francisco Academy of Comic Art Collection, the Ohio State University Billy Ireland Cartoon Library and Museum.

humor magazine *Truth* and previous issues of the *World*. But whether readers found "Golf" to be unique or typical, they likely found themselves drawn to a particular character who stood in the middle of Outcault's picture of urban pandemonium. In the foreground, just a little off center, stands a small bald boy wearing a stained yellow nightshirt. As Colton Waugh suggests, the bright hue of the character's garment turns him into a "vivid bull's eye in the whole big page."[4] In a cartoon that is primarily colored with shades of brown and muted blues and reds, the solid-yellow smock is, in Jens Balzer's words, "unusual": the color "[turns] the little boy in the nightshirt into a character that could be identified, setting the urchin apart from the masses around him and multiplying the readers' interest in *Hogan's Alley*."[5]

The yellow nightshirt, however, is not the only thing that makes the character distinct. What is more arresting is his interaction with his audience. Not only does he meet the reader's gaze; he also uses his right hand to instruct her where to look. His expression of amusement also prompts the reader to delight in the various scenes of chaos that play out in "Golf." While most of the figures in the panel remain anonymous, the boy in the yellow smock steps out of the realm of stock characters, emerging as a distinct, memorable individual. Outcault later recognized the commercial potential of his character and made the move to further signal this fictional child's singularity by giving him a name. Outcault christened his creation "Mickey Dugan." The public, however, took to calling him by another name: the Yellow Kid.

Comics historians note that this kid played a definitive role in the development of comics, consumer culture, and journalism at the turn of the century.[6] After the Yellow Kid's debut in "Golf," Outcault turned him into a staple character in his *Hogan's Alley* series. Then, in late 1896, Outcault left Pulitzer's paper—with the Yellow Kid in tow—to work for the *New York Journal*, a rival newspaper published by William Randolph Hearst. In the *Journal*, the character appeared in three consecutive series: *McFadden's Row of Flats* (October 18, 1896–January 10, 1897), *Around the World with the Yellow Kid* (January 17, 1897–May 30, 1897), and *Ryan's Arcade* (September 28, 1897–January 23, 1898). In these various series, Outcault utilized elements that are now considered standard in the modern newspaper comic strip.[7] The Yellow Kid proved the immense commercial value of a distinct, recurring character.[8] Outcault also used the Yellow Kid series to revive the word balloon, a feature that had been commonly used in eighteenth- and nineteenth-century print visual culture but was on the verge of extinction by the time nineteenth-century British caricaturist George Cruikshank utilized it.[9]

The Yellow Kid series also played a vital role in the expansion of consumer culture at the turn of the century. The character's success gave publishers confirmation that the comic supplement was crucial to boosting newspaper circulation. The Yellow Kid also inspired an unprecedented consumer craze in New York City. The character swelled from a two-dimensional figure to a commercial phenomenon as merchandisers used his image to sell a wide variety of licensed and unlicensed products, including postcards, alcohol, cigarettes, and an assortment of decorative items. The Yellow Kid also became intertwined with other forms of mass entertainments: he became a featured character in theater productions, vaudeville skits, and short films. The case of the Yellow Kid illustrates Ian Gordon's description of the dual function of newspaper comics as products and advertisements: they are, on the one hand, goods that readers consume and, on the other hand, sites that promoted other products and normalized the act of consumption.[10]

Because of his extraordinary lucrativeness, the Yellow Kid became a pawn in the well-documented newspaper feud between Pulitzer and Hearst. When Outcault left to work for Hearst's *Journal*, Pulitzer hired the artist George Luks to continue drawing *Hogan's Alley*—and the Yellow Kid—for the *World*. Consequently, for a brief period, two competing series featuring the Yellow Kid appeared simultaneously in two papers, with each publication insisting they owned the rights to Outcault's character.[11] Other enterprising cartoonists and illustrators were also freely "borrowing" the Yellow Kid's image in their editorial cartoons and advertisements.[12] The dispute over who owned the rights to the Yellow Kid was entangled with Pulitzer's and Hearst's aggressive efforts to outsell one another. To expand their readerships, both the *World* and the *Journal* resorted to sensational headlines, stories of crime and scandal, often superfluous use of photographic and drawn illustrations, and heightened slapstick and "ethnic" humor in the comic supplements. In 1897, *New York Press* editor Ervin Wardman wryly observed that the Pulitzer-Hearst rivalry gave rise to a new form of journalism. Ward called their practices "yellow-kid journalism," a term that was eventually abridged to "yellow journalism."[13]

There is, however, a curious omission in the rich body of histories and criticism that consider and debate the significance and impact of the Yellow Kid. Very few scholars have expressed interest in investigating why Progressive Era readers and consumers so avidly embraced a fictional child and why, in the wake of the Yellow Kid's success, child characters proliferated in newspaper comic supplements. Just as the Yellow Kid appeared in the foreground of "Golf," child characters stood front and center in many turn-of-the-century newspaper supplements. Cartoonists such as Outcault, Rudolph Dirks, James Swinnerton, Winsor McCay, and Grace Wiederseim, among many others, built their careers on series headlined by children. Fictional children such as Buster Brown, Hans and Fritz Katzenjammer, Little Jimmy, Dear Katy, Little Nemo, and Dolly Dimple entertained and captivated many Progressive Era readers. Yet comics scholarship—with a few exceptions—continues to overlook the importance of childhood and child characters to the development of newspaper comics in the United States and, more broadly, of comics in their various iterations around the world.[14]

Incorrigibles and Innocents advances existing studies of Progressive Era comics by exploring and emphasizing the cultural form's links to Progressive Era childhoods. In doing so, this book offers new perspectives in histories of childhood and comics. It shows that late nineteenth- and early twentieth-century cartoons and comic strips reinforced as well as interrogated white, middle-class notions of childhood, often upholding the ideal of innocent childhood while also revealing how this ideal was incongruous with children's apparent proclivity for misbehavior. This book also illustrates how the subject of citizenship was interwoven with Progressive Era concerns about childhood; newspaper comics became spaces in which children's citizenship was defined and debated and in which notions of race, ethnicity, gender, and class were used to sort and re-sort children into categories of "future citizen" and "noncitizen." *Incorrigibles and Innocents* demonstrates that American comics at the turn of the century not only theorized childhood but also used child characters to reiterate—and complicate—existing beliefs about who could claim membership in a modernizing, expanding nation. In other words, this book insists that Progressive Era comics are significant cultural artifacts that elucidate how discourses of childhood are inextricably linked with discourses of race, ethnicity, class, gender, nationhood, and citizenship.

In this book, I pay special attention to the ways cartoonists deployed the figure of the child to sustain and/or question stereotypes. In newspaper cartoons and comic strips, images of childhood simultaneously functioned to ridicule and redeem those who were viewed as outsiders or threats. The comics appropriated tropes from late nineteenth-century humor magazines, which often used caricatures to express, perpetuate, and allay anxieties about industrialization, modernization, and the increasing visibility of African Americans, immigrants, and women in social, political, and economic venues.[15] In many late nineteenth-century magazine cartoons, members of minority groups were often depicted as naïve or mischief-making children. Such representations meant to infantilize, diminish, and thus contain those who were deemed "dangerous" and "other." Comics published in Progressive Era newspapers continued this tradition established in magazine cartoons.

Yet many of these newspaper comics series also encouraged readers to view mischief-making children as creative rather than destructive forces. Some texts suggested that young African Americans and immigrant children were potential citizens; they offered pictures of minority children who possessed energy, resourcefulness, and autonomy—qualities that individuals needed to exhibit in order to be welcomed and thrive in a capitalist-democratic society. Moreover, as childhood was increasingly understood as a state of innocence and malleability, associating minority groups with childhood sometimes allowed stereotypes to emerge as sympathetic characters. At the very least, the emphasis on the youthfulness of minority children bolstered the argument that they were pliable enough to be molded into productive members of American society.

But as child characters gained footholds in newspaper comic supplements, many of these figures came to endorse prevailing cultural norms. Comics series gradually upheld the Anglo-Saxon, middle-class, male child as the figure who embodied both exuberance and innocence and was best positioned to be the rightful inheritor of a racial and patriarchal legacy. Cartoonists, perceiving that the white, middle-class boy had universal appeal, framed him as a character who could attract and maintain a wide, diverse readership. With the ascendance of this particular image, fictional children who were "raced," "ethnic," lower class, and female were pushed to the margins of the comic supplements. Overall, *Incorrigibles and Innocents* reveals the ambivalent nature of child characters in late nineteenth- and early twentieth-century newspaper comics: they simultaneously reinforced and undermined boundaries of race, ethnicity, class, and gender. Through the use of images of children, Progressive Era comics became sites of cultural negotiation in which dominant beliefs about childhood and citizenship were at once shored up and interrogated.

Progressivism: Its Visions and Paradoxes

Progressive Era comics featured a varied cast of child characters—well-heeled youngsters who made mischief in the parlor, street urchins who loitered in the streets, and boys and girls who were of Anglo-Saxon, Irish, African, and Chinese descent. It appears that in the late nineteenth and early twentieth centuries, newspaper cartoonists and their readers were fascinated and preoccupied with the experiences of different kinds of children. Such engrossment in childhood, however, did not emerge in a vacuum; rather, this absorption was deeply tied to ongoing discourses of the state of the nation. At the turn of the century, the United States was caught in the fervor of industrialization, urbanization, and expansion. The nation also grappled with shifting ideas about race, ethnicity, class, and gender. The country's rapid economic development and rising global influence inspired optimism and excitement. But the exhilaration over seemingly boundless opportunities was accompanied by much unease and conflict. Even as Americans marveled at and delighted in the technological advancements and profusion of consumer products enabled by laissez-faire capitalism, many were disquieted about the rise of monopolistic corporations.[16] Some expressed dismay over the unprecedented expansion of consumer culture: they worried that as people from all walks of life partook in new pleasures and leisure activities, the values of self-discipline and self-denial would fall to the wayside. Many Americans also observed, with much apprehension, how corporate capitalism hardened, rather than erased, social and economic disparities. Wage workers, laborers, and farmers found their individual rights curtailed by policies enforced by the wealthy, the very ones who preached the creed of individualism.[17] African Americans fleeing the South came face-to-face with deep-seated racism in the North, and immigrants who arrived en masse to fulfill industrialization's voracious appetite for labor found themselves repelled by xenophobic nativist movements. While cities became thriving hubs of industrialization, racial and ethnic minorities, the working class, and the poor often had no choice but to live in squalid conditions.

A remarkable number of Americans mobilized in response to these troubling socioeconomic developments. While many of these "progressives" or "progressive reformers" were white and middle class, they were far from being a monolithic group. Maureen A. Flanagan reminds us that a number of African Americans, ethnic minorities, and members of the working class fervently pressed for the effectuation of progressive reform initiatives.[18] Progressivism was a movement that included a variety of actors and organizations that pursued disparate, though often intersecting, interests and agendas. Reformers championed numerous causes, including the regulation of mass entertainments, temperance, women's suffrage, and rights to adequate housing, health services, and fair working conditions for immigrants and members of the lower classes. Economic progressives vigorously campaigned for workers' rights and increased government regulation of corporate industries. As Michael McGerr puts it, "Progressivism was an explosion, a burst of energy that fired in many directions across America."[19] What united progressives was their vision of a utopic United States and the belief that this vision could be realized through comprehensive reform and active civic engagement.

Their efforts to establish a perfect United States, however, were replete with frustrations and contradictions. Suffragettes and women who took part in reform efforts were often chastised for being "unladylike" and blamed for the alleged breakdown of the (white, middle-class) family. While progressivism pushed for egalitarianism and rejected the competitive, individualistic creed of capitalism, the movement's proponents sought to restrain rather than dismantle liberal capitalism altogether.[20] Racism, sexism, and the pseudoscience of eugenics shaped the views of many economic reformers, who consequently acted to restrict or prohibit the participation of African Americans, immigrants, women, and persons with disabilities in the labor force.[21] As cities became marked by racial, ethnic, and economic ghettoization, reformers generally accepted that segregation could never be entirely eradicated and was perhaps even necessary.[22] Moreover, progressives often approached those they sought to uplift with condescension as much as empathy. McGerr argues that progressivism's mission of transforming the nation was, at heart, an effort to transform others. More specifically, reformers desired to mold immigrants, rural workers, laborers, the poor, and children—in short, those they deemed to be "different"—in their middle-class image:

> To reshape adult behavior, middle-class reformers fought to ban liquor, eradicate prostitution, and limit divorce. To change other classes, the reformers attacked the life-style and fortunes of [the wealthy], tried to improve the living

> conditions of workers, and attempted to modernize the agrarian way of life. To ensure a better future, progressives sought to reconstruct childhood. Together, these campaigns added up to a bold effort to remake Americans, to create new people living by new codes of conduct. Just as the middle class itself had been remade, now other classes would be remade as well.[23]

Put another way, the movement's project of reshaping peoples was primarily a project of universalizing middle-class (and white) conceptualizations of citizenship.

Progressive reformers' fixation with "making good citizens" was especially evident in their work with children. Historian Paula S. Fass sums up the questions that preoccupied these "child-savers": "What kinds of citizens, workers, and family members would [children] grow up to become? How could their futures be directed toward social ends as well as stable, productive adulthoods?"[24] Progressives were not the first to pay attention to children's lives and needs; they built on the work of nineteenth-century child welfare reformers such as Charles Loring Brace. But Progressive Era child-savers differed from their forerunners in urging for the implementation of changes on a national rather than a local level; they also emphatically asserted that government involvement was crucial to solving the social conundrum of how to raise healthy future citizens. Their advocacy resulted in sweeping reforms and initiatives, including the institution of mandatory school and child labor laws; the restructuring of juvenile justice systems; the improvement of public health, housing, and sanitation policies; and the establishment of kindergartens and playgrounds across the country, all of which substantially changed the lives of millions of children in the United States.

Ironically, progressives' concerns about ensuring the "future productivity" of children rendered some young people "unproductive." Viviana A. Zelizer documents how, in the Progressive Era, the image of the "economically useful" child was gradually replaced by the image of the "emotionally priceless" child.[25] As more white, middle-class, urban parents embraced the ideal of childhood as a period of innocence, the model of the patriarchal-hierarchical family gave way to the model of the democratic and demonstrative family. With this new family dynamic, the focus shifted from productivity to playfulness, from discipline to indulgence. Moreover, the notion of adolescence as a "natural" transitional period between childhood and adulthood gained traction among members of the white middle class. This concept of adolescence, avidly advanced by psychologist and educator G. Stanley Hall, dramatically altered young people's lives: it lengthened childhood, delaying children's entry into the workforce and other "adult" spheres. Education, play, and recreation, rather than labor, became the central defining markers of childhood, especially for white, middle-class, urban children.

Thus many young people growing up in the Progressive Era enjoyed an extended period of schooling and leisure and found opportunities to form communities with their peers. But these children paid a price for their new pleasures. The experience of an emotionally priceless childhood came with heightened constraint, scrutiny, and regimentation. Child-savers, subscribing to the notion that children were vulnerable and impressionable, attempted to restrict young people's access to purportedly harmful and corrupting cultural spaces, such as nickelodeons, dance halls, and comic supplements. Many progressives were proponents of child study, a movement spearheaded by Hall that espoused scientific approaches to studying childhood and raising children. Child study, as Steven Mintz points out, "carried profound consequences for the experiences of childhood": "[Child study] identified a series of sharply differentiated developmental stages, each with its own distinctive characteristics and psychology. It isolated certain norms—including norms about weight, size, and cognitive development—that could be applied to children of particular ages. Its standardized norms also altered the way young people were reared by inspiring new kinds of childrearing manuals, written by physicians and psychologists rather than by ministers and moralists, and espousing rational rather than spiritual advice."[26] Many adults also feared that urbanization and growing maternal influence in the family were "softening" and "feminizing" boys. Consequently, male children were often pressured to participate in "vigorous" activities, such as organized sports and camping, so they could exercise and preserve their so-called natural masculinity. Girls, on the other hand, gained opportunities that were not available to their mothers, especially in terms of education, leisure, and participation in consumer culture. But many of these cultural spaces remained highly gendered: sports for girls, for example, emphasized the development of poise rather than strength; popular girls' books, such as Kate Douglas Wiggin's *Rebecca of Sunnybrook Farm* (1903) and L. M. Montgomery's *Anne of Green Gables* (1908), celebrated the image of the spirited girl who eventually chooses family over career and independence.[27]

While the childhoods of white, middle-class boys and girls were marked by contradictions, the more troubling paradox lay in the disparity between white, middle-class ideals and the lived experiences of African American children, immigrant youth, and children who worked in factories and farms. While progressivism, at the outset, was an effort to combat and eradicate social and economic inequalities that were created or exacerbated by industrialization and modernization, the work of child-saving progressives sometimes inadvertently hardened the lines of socioeconomic stratification. For example, eugenics infused white, middle-class child-rearing practices: anxieties about raising "normal" children were tied to the intense desire to preserve a "pure" Anglo-Saxon line and prevent it from being sullied by the "inferior" stock and "vulgar" cultures of African

Americans and immigrants. While reformers declared that universal, mandatory schooling was an equalizing force that would provide education and citizenship training to children from different backgrounds, Clif Stratton chronicles the following reality:

> Textbooks, segregated schools, Americanization campaigns of varying degrees of coerciveness, and policies and narratives of colonialism forged a variegated schooling experience in which certain common threads emerged, especially preparation for different and unequal forms of citizenship.
>
> Ultimately, the paths of citizenship available to many students, particularly foreign-born and nonwhite, were incongruent with the promises of public education as the institutional mechanism of equal social opportunity and as the vehicle of economic mobility heralded by many school reformers at the turn of the twentieth century and beyond.[28]

Some children were also simply written out of narratives of citizenship. Robin Bernstein notes that as the ideal of childhood innocence became exclusively associated with white childhood, the innocent black child became an incongruous, impossible figure. The black child was deemed too "savage" for redemption, too "corrupt" to be accorded (future) citizenship.[29] While some progressives were invested in the uplift of black children, by and large, reformers ignored or failed to prioritize the needs of African Americans, children and adults alike.[30]

Child-savers were more optimistic about the potential of young immigrants. Many reformers pushed back against nativism and xenophobia, arguing that immigrant children were malleable enough to be molded into productive Americans. Lillian D. Wald, writing in 1915, countered the pervasive feelings of distrust and loathing of immigrants by describing young new arrivals as "just little children, forever appealing."[31] Wald argued that the nation had much to learn from immigrant children, stating, "As a nation we must rise or fall as we serve or fail these future citizens. . . . Their appeal suggests that social exclusions and prejudices separate far more effectively than distance and differing language. They bring a hope that a better relationship—even the great brotherhood—is not impossible, and that through love and understanding we shall come to know the shame of prejudice."[32]

Yet the reformers also measured young immigrants against Anglo-Saxon, middle-class ideals, ideals that were often incommensurate with the needs and desires of immigrant children and their families.[33] More specifically, reformers' campaigns to unshackle immigrant children—and, for that matter, working-class and rural children—from the chains of labor were often resisted by the objects of these efforts. For working children, the ideal of a labor-free childhood was one they could not afford—or did not desire—to perform. While industries certainly exploited children, many young people found some pleasure in work. Some took pride in making a contribution to their families, others felt that work gave them a sense of autonomy, and many were especially thrilled by how their income enabled them to purchase goods and partake in amusements.[34] In short, the middle-class dream of an emotionally priceless childhood was not necessarily congruent with the experiences and sentiments of working children.

Comics and Contradictions

Newspaper comics proved to be an especially suitable medium for capturing the paradoxes that shaped Progressive Era childhoods. Charles Hatfield's description of comics as an "art of tensions" is particularly relevant here, as he suggests that a push-and-pull dynamic is embedded in the formal and material properties of comics. As Hatfield observes, readers encounter four tensions when they read comics: they examine the ways verbal and visual codes complement, contradict, and complicate one another; they interpret an image in isolation while also apprehending the image as part of a series; they perform both linear and nonlinear readings, making sense of a panel's part in a sequence and in the larger page layout; and they experience comics as at once a narrative text and as a material (and commercial) object.[35] For Hatfield, these multiple tensions open up "various ways of reading [comics]—various interpretive options and potentialities—[which] must be played against each other."[36]

Progressive Era comics were certainly marked by these tensions. But they also fostered multiple and sometimes oppositional readings in other ways: they utilized the unstable form of the caricature and further destabilized it via sequential panels and serialization, they promoted emergent theories about the function of humor, and they attempted to reach a broad, diverse audience. And as I illustrate below, themes of childhood and images of children frequently overlaid these approaches.

At first blush, it seems impossible to consider caricatures as images that welcome a variety of interpretations. Traditionally, we understand these images to be expressions and tools of aggressive humor: they are one-dimensional representations that use "amplification, distortion, and exaggeration" to denigrate a particular social group.[37] Cartoonists of the Progressive Era copied typographies that were developed and popularized in late nineteenth-century humor magazines such as *Puck*, *Life*, and *Judge* as well as more "genteel" publications such as *Harper's Weekly*.[38] In these magazines, caricatures were often deployed to disparage members of the lower class and racial-ethnic minority groups. These humorous figures not only served to draw a line between "us" and "them" but also stirred and satiated white, middle-class curiosity for "aliens" in their midst. As Henry B. Wonham puts it, "The art of caricature may have been the era's bluntest and most effective means of policing itself in the domain of class and ethnic representation, for caricature's humorous excesses allowed magazines . . . to address a demand for 'real life' while ensuring that undesirable elements of 'reality' remained at a safe distance."[39]

But some scholars suggest that these representations—flat, vicious, and antagonistic by design—sometimes became locations of nuance that encouraged readers to sympathize with the very objects of derision. Martha Banta, building on "Derrida's sly suggestion that art is fatefully complicit, in both painful and positive ways, in the facts of society's inequities," proposes that while the caricature may serve as "the recorder of injustice [and] the tool of injustice," it may also be "the potential annihilator of injustice."[40] Comics theorist Scott McCloud's oft-cited discussion of the function of the cartoon style of illustration is useful to consider here. McCloud offers that an iconic and "cartoony" style of illustration—a style used in caricature—allows a character to be accessible and familiar to its audience. Put another way, a simplified, amplified illustration versus a more mimetic and realistic representation can be more appealing to the reader, as the former serves as a "blank slate" on which the reader can project herself.[41] McCloud states that "when you look at a photo or realistic drawing of a face, you see it as the face of *another*. But when you enter the world of the *cartoon*, you see *yourself*."[42] Of course, it is important to note that McCloud's formalist approach elides the problems of representing race, ethnicity, class, and gender. Still, his theory opens an avenue for considering how the caricature can invite readers to recognize both similarity and difference and can simultaneously reinforce and blur the boundaries between self and other.

The caricature became further destabilized when it transferred from single-panel cartoons to multipanel, sequential comics. As it were, the latter format happened to be embraced by newspaper cartoonists in the Progressive Era. For Jared Gardner, the increasingly common practice of drawing panels in sequence marked the "beginnings of a shift away from cartoon racism toward what we might call 'graphic alterity.'"[43] As he puts it, "A single-panel cartoon gag of an ethnic or racial stereotype is contained by its frame; it does the work of stereotyping as the term originally was defined: printing from a fixed mold. It is static and resists ambiguity, directing the reader to very specific ways of reading."[44] Sequential comics, on the other hand, endow the caricature with more nuance. Citing Scott McCloud's concept of closure, Gardner reminds us that gutters—the spaces that separate panels—require individual readers to fill in and make sense of these empty spaces; the potentially varied interpretive acts that readers perform make "reading [a caricature] in sequential comics . . . a more complicated and unruly enterprise."[45] While Gardner acknowledges that many comics narratives, historically and presently, are shaped by and sometimes purposefully endorse racial hierarchies, he insists that the gutter and the readers' crucial role in interpreting these spaces make sequential comics "resistant to racialist work."[46] I do want to point out here that some single-panel cartoons that appeared in the newspaper supplements could also be read in a "complicated and unruly" fashion. Outcault's Yellow Kid cartoons often were bursting with messiness; as I demonstrate below, a single-panel Yellow Kid cartoon could open up to multiple readings.

Elsewhere, Gardner reminds us of the role that comic strip serialization (as well as syndication and merchandising) played in giving dimension to the caricature and, as such, builds on an argument previously articulated by Kerry Soper.[47] Newspaper strips appeared in regular weekly installments, creating a rhythm of repetition and alteration, and Soper argues that it was this rhythm that allowed familiar caricatures to expand into more complex characters. Although individual comic strip episodes were typically self-contained narratives that followed formulaic plots, some episodes defied readers' expectations by deviating from the usual plot or having the otherwise predictable protagonist behave "out of character." As Soper puts it, "When coupled with ongoing narratives . . . [caricatures] allow for sympathetic meanings and uses to emerge and thrive."[48] Similarly, Gardner maintains that "over time and through the subtle variations that emerge with each new beginning of the same old routine, [the stereotype is accorded] an identity."[49] Soper does provide a measure of caution, reminding us that "even the most progressive treatments of the type were still tied in persistent ways to the ideological claims of the original racist caricature."[50] However, in encouraging us to recognize the ambivalent nature of the caricature, especially as it was deployed in Progressive Era comic strips, Soper reprises Homi Bhabha's claim that the stereotype is an unstable form that expresses how members of dominant cultures regard so-called Others with both "desire and derision."[51] Indeed, as Gardner puts it, "the mass-mediated personality provides no resolution to the scenes of political and racial violence. But it does provide a space for the imaginative embrace—an embrace that could be literalized and commodified in the new phenomenon of licensed products—of the untouchable American, the 'other' in our midst."[52]

I submit that in addition to sequentiality, seriality, and commercialization's roles in making caricatures familiar and welcome figures, another element enabled the elasticity of typographies that appeared in newspaper comics: a frequent association with childhood. Child characters in newspaper comics were perhaps the most potent manifestation of ambivalence for the Other. In the comics, the figure of the child and the metaphor of childhood were apparatuses that, on the one hand, lobbed insults and, on the other hand, elicited compassion. To some degree, alignment with childhood may have redeemed the supposedly inferior members of society; childhood was a metaphor that at once infantilized and humanized them.[53] The images of children running amok in Outcault's "Golf," for example, could be understood as a slur on adult members of immigrant groups and the lower classes; the cartoon may be seen as deriding immigrant, working-class adults, imagining them as irredeemably savage, permanently immature. Yet

"Golf" also used images of childhood to arouse pity for those who lived in tenement neighborhoods. Children gaze out of the building's windows and doorways with forlorn expressions. These "pitiful" images appear to reference the work of photojournalist and reformer Jacob Riis. Riis's book *How the Other Half Lives: Studies among the Tenements of New York* (1890) documented the lives and struggles of the residents of New York's most destitute neighborhoods and helped galvanize the progressive movement. In "Golf," Outcault continues Riis's project by depicting the plight of impoverished children. Yet he places the doleful children in the background, turning them into secondary characters. For Outcault, the deserving stars of his cartoons are the indigent-yet-irrepressible children who command the streets and who seem to transcend suffering.

Without a doubt, comics' representations of rowdy children swarming New York City streets amplified fears that immigrants and the lower classes would sabotage the nation's political, economic, and social systems. But these images also suggested that the young people of the so-called other half possessed vitality and tenacity—values that were understood to be essential in a modernizing nation. The child characters in newspaper comics also express a particularly optimistic view of nonwhite, lower-class children. These characters intimated that there were parallels between children of both halves of society, implying that like white, middle-class children, nonwhite, immigrant, and working-class children bore the markers of innocence. The playful and youthful figures held up the promise that Other children were wholesome as well as pliant enough to be shaped into useful citizens.

The open-ended quality of the comics form—and the child characters that frequently headlined them—was also tied to significant shifts in popular conceptualizations of humor at the turn of the century. Owing to the predominance of Aristotelian and Hobbesian theories of humor, comedy has traditionally been understood as aggressive in function: the subject laughs at the flaws and deformities of the object, and humor thus serves to delineate between the former and the latter.[54] Gregg Camfield, however, outlines how nineteenth-century literary domestic humor encouraged the collapse between subject and object, promoting laughter that was amiable rather than antagonistic.[55] Although Freud's theory of humor as "repressed aggression" enabled the reemergence of hostile forms of comedy in the early twentieth century, Daniel Wickberg insists that the growing "middle-class culture of benevolence, sensibility and sympathy" that first took shape in the eighteenth century allowed sympathetic laughter to become more widespread and highly prized in the centuries that followed.[56] Moreover, the capacity for self-objectification—or the ability to laugh at one's self—was steadily recognized as a sign of maturity and gentility in the early twentieth century.[57] Thus it seems likely that several layers of humor—aggressive, sympathetic, self-deprecating—played out simultaneously in Progressive Era newspaper comic supplements.

Of course, different readers must have laughed at different things. The supplements sought to reach a diverse readership: male and female, native-born and immigrant, adult and child, middle class and working class. Ian Gordon stresses that comics producers worked to broaden their reach by creating "polysemic" characters that a diverse audience would be "[able and willing] to read . . . in multiple fashions [as] it added to a comic strip character's commercial worth."[58] Lisa Yaszek contends that producers' desire to build mass readership for comics enabled "multiple, even contradictory readings."[59] She demonstrates the "multi-accentuality of the 'funnies'" by hypothesizing how readers from varying socio-historical positions may have had divergent interpretations of Outcault's "The Yellow Kid Takes a Hand at Golf," a multipanel episode that appeared in the *Journal* on October 24, 1897. In this episode, the Yellow Kid takes several swings at a ball; with each swing, he misses the ball and instead violently whacks his fellow players. Yaszek suggests nativists may have construed the episode as proof of "the unbridgable gap between middle-class Americans and immigrants"; reformers may have seen it as a pitiful picture that "expose[d] the slums as a liability to the immigrant's progress"; immigrants may have embraced it as a "fantasy space in which revenge can be exacted upon the immigrant's oppressors."[60] In short, this single episode likely activated a variety of responses from different readers, ranging from a sense of superiority, to a pang of sympathy, to an urge for retaliation. Still, Progressive Era comics had the peculiar quality of creating universality in the midst of these polarities. Even while comics offered an assortment of jokes for an assortment of readers, these mass-produced texts enabled readers from coast to coast, from all walks of life, to share in the experience of reading the same text and encountering the same characters.[61]

I do want to highlight the unique relationship between Progressive Era comics and a specific segment of its broad audience: white, middle-class readers. Traditional histories of comics and journalism often note that comic supplements were products meant to draw in immigrant consumers, yet W. Joseph Campbell reminds us that new arrivals were more likely to read papers published in their native tongues.[62] The case of the Yellow Kid is instructive: the Irish, tenement-dwelling character may have been partly designed to entice immigrant and working-class readers, yet the goods and theatrical shows that utilized and reproduced the character's image were aimed at Anglo-Saxon, middle-class consumers.[63] Moreover, as Soper notes, the growing trend of national syndication as well as publishers' desire to appeal to a more middle-class readership resulted in the eventual "gentrification" of the comic supplement.[64] As I demonstrate in this book, Progressive Era comics often heartily endorsed white, middle-class views about citizenship and childhood. As the comics were, in Yaszek's words, "suspended between middle-class producers and mass readerships," they participated in progressive reformers' project of promoting the dominant culture's views of what it meant to be an American and what constituted a "good" childhood.[65]

Of course, I do not mean to downplay the significance of Progressive Era comics' diverse readership. Soper reminds us that comic supplements were filled with series that "explore[d] alternative world views"; as such, they "had one foot in the . . . urban carnival and another in the more sedate world of middle-class white audiences."[66] Put another way, newspaper comics were often disassembling the hegemonic white, middle-class values that they were buttressing. What is remarkable is that the comics' subversive messages, meant to provide immigrants and working-class readers the laughter of relief, were also made available to white, middle-class audiences. In effect, the supplements taught white, middle-class readers to find amusement in texts that simultaneously promoted *and* mocked their culture and ideals.

Progressive Era Comics in Light of Childhood

Throughout this book, I underscore the centrality of childhood to the development of the comics medium. As Charles Hatfield notes, comics scholarship, in its drive to gain legitimacy in academia, has traditionally neglected, even denied, the link between comics narratives and childhood.[67] This book, in illustrating how Progressive Era comics creators repeatedly explored the subject of childhood, pushes back against this act of disavowal. Indeed, R. F. Outcault, the man heralded as one of the founders of the modern comic strip, was deeply fascinated by childhood. From his early work as a cartoonist for the humor magazine *Truth* to his retirement in the 1920s, Outcault did not appear to tire of representing and romanticizing the antics and misadventures of different kinds of children. As I demonstrate in the chapters that follow, he specifically helped perpetuate and make endearing the image of the "naughty-but-nice" child. That in this book I return again and again to Outcault's series testifies to the cartoonist's—and his child characters'—indelible mark on the history of comics.

In considering the intersections between studies of comics and studies of childhood, *Incorrigibles and Innocents* examines the ways Progressive Era comics engaged with contemporary children's literature. Cartoons and strips often borrowed tropes from popular titles such as Lewis Carroll's *Alice's Adventures in Wonderland* (1865) and Mark Twain's *The Adventures of Tom Sawyer* (1876) and *Adventures of Huckleberry Finn* (1884). Like many children's books of the period, newspaper comics disseminated racist imagery, especially the figure of the pickaninny. In other cases, comics complicated the image of "good" children that endured in moralistic books for the young. More broadly, comics reinforced, challenged, and refracted the ways children's books envisioned the child's roles in the family and the nation. As such, comics (and children's books, for that matter) can be understood as cultural forms that introduced young readers to the notion that defining and performing American citizenship are thorny and turbulent projects.

Clearly, both childhood and comics were entangled in volatile debates about citizenship and nationhood during the Progressive Era. This book shows how child characters in the comics were repeatedly deployed to create boundaries between citizens and noncitizens and how, at the same time, these characters revealed these boundaries to be fragile and permeable. Indeed, children in the comics embody what Gary Gerstle calls the "two powerful and contradictory ideals" that repeatedly manifested themselves in the sociopolitical discourses of the Progressive Era: "racial nationalism," which "conceived of America in ethnoracial terms" and insisted that certain peoples "could never be accepted as full-fledged members," and "civic nationalism," which celebrated "the fundamental equality of all human beings."[68] These fictional children implied that figures who are often cast out because of their gender, the color of their skin, their economic status, or their national origin were creative, autonomous, and spirited; the comics proposed that young individuals who appeared to pose a threat to national development could also be potential boons to the nation. Overall, by focusing on and linking childhood and comics—two matters that are often considered ephemeral and disposable—*Incorrigibles and Innocents* not only evinces that these two subjects were meaningful for Progressive Era Americans but also asserts that childhood, children's culture, and popular culture reflect and deeply inform our political, social, and cultural lives.

Chapter 1 focuses on the comics' exploration of the nature and position of the immigrant child. Series such as Clarence Rigby's *Little Ah Sid, the Chinese Kid* and Rudolph Dirks's *The Katzenjammer Kids* suggest that children of immigrants are disruptive forces in both domestic and public spheres, liminal figures who trouble the ways of both the Old World and the New World. Yet the series also celebrate these children for their resourcefulness and malleability, depicting them as streetwise figures who could easily assimilate into white, middle-class culture. By and large, these series hint that immigrant children are able to integrate into American society in ways unavailable to their parents and elders.

Chapter 2 investigates how comics approach the relationship among race, racism, and childhood. It examines the ways various newspaper comics perpetuated—and sometimes interrogated—the pickaninny, a popular caricature of black childhood. This chapter also discusses the recurring trope of racial impersonation in the comics. In these gags, children disguise themselves to "change" their race, and the ease by which they are able to fool adults gestures toward the sameness of children. At the same time, however, these acts of cross-dressing also evoked anxieties about interracial encounters, especially among children.

By the first decade of the twentieth century, nonwhite child characters became less of a presence in the comic supplements, edged out by images of white children. However, as highlighted in the case of the African American character Pore Lil Mose, nonwhite characters functioned as templates for the character who was to become the period's most popular and beloved comic strip child: Buster

Brown. Chapter 3 examines how Outcault's eponymous strip uses humor and the figure of the exuberant child to simultaneously subvert and conserve "outmoded" ideals of domesticity and gender. On one level, *Buster Brown* depicts and celebrates the white, male child as a spirited, independent figure who counters the ossifying effects and the tedium of domestic life. The series' protagonist also serves as a useful tool in exposing the incongruity between the (white) ideal of "pure" childhood and the reality of misbehaving children. Yet the strip also insists that Buster is essentially a "good boy" who recognizes his place in the family and fulfills normative gender roles. Rather than creating or exacerbating family tensions, the amusing naughty boy in *Buster Brown* helps maintain the institution of the (white) family, the purported bedrock of the nation. This chapter also examines a few primary sources that illustrate the complex ways that young readers responded to discourses of childhood that played out in *Buster Brown.*

Chapter 4 discusses how certain comics series transformed the "exuberant" child into the "imaginative" child. Winsor McCay's *Little Nemo in Slumberland* and Lyonel Feininger's *Wee Willie Winkie's World* were published during a period of burgeoning interest in child psychology and of immense popularity of fantasy books for children; both strips propose that dreams and reverie allow the white, middle-class, male child to develop his identity and prepare for his role in a rapidly industrializing, expanding nation. But these comics also dispel the romance of the imaginative child, revealing that the child's fantasy world is often created not by the child but by the adult *for* the child.

While male characters dominated the comics, some cartoonists reproduced the figure of the "naughty girl." Chapter 5 studies W. O. Wilson's *Madge the Magician's Daughter* and Tom Tucker's *Betsy Bouncer and Her Doll,* two series that explore how girls negotiate gender expectations by way of borrowing and reformulating the naughty boy trope. While both strips maintain that their protagonists understood the limits of female misbehavior, their employment of fantasy elements suggests that imaginative play provides girls the ability to test social boundaries and practice participation in public spheres.

Overall, this book tracks several movements in the development of newspaper comics. It illustrates the gradual gentrification of the comic supplement as ethnic, working-class child characters like the Yellow Kid were slowly pushed to the margins and replaced by white, middle-class characters like Buster Brown. But this gentrification did not simply "whiten" the comics. It also enabled an inward movement: series that were predominantly set in public spaces such as city streets and vacant lots gradually gave way to newspaper comics that were set in the interiors of middle-class homes and even the inner spaces of the child's mind. These shifts also likely occurred in response to reformers' campaigns to "clean up" the comic supplement. As I discuss in chapter 3, some progressives charged that the supplement, like the nickelodeon and other mass entertainments, disrupted the project of children's citizenship training. Reformers like Percival Chubb were greatly agitated by comics, claiming that these texts exposed white, middle-class children to the "corrupt" elements of society. In the early twentieth century, many newspapers responded to this moral panic by minimizing or altogether eliminating the presence of fictional street urchins in the supplements. However, this effort to "improve" and "refine" the neighborhood of newspaper comics was not simply a way to safeguard the so-called natural innocence of white, middle-class children; by replacing the figure of the threatening/threatened street child with the playful and spirited white, middle-class child, newspaper comics participated in universalizing the ideal of childhood innocence. In the process, mischief-making, a menacing act when performed by children of the other half, became, in the hands of white, middle-class characters, an expression of natural childhood and a practice of anticipated citizenship.

The Circus of Childhood: *Hogan's Alley* and the Boundaries of Childhood and Citizenship

In his cartoons for the *World*, Outcault predicted how the trends of gentrification and appropriation would shape newspaper comics. An early *Hogan's Alley* episode, titled "At the Circus in Hogan's Alley," was "typical" in its focus on unpredictable, irrepressible immigrant and lower-class children (fig. 2).[69] In the episode, children of the tenements stage a circus in a vacant lot. One boy is dressed up as a clown; other children take on the roles of animal trainer, juggler, and acrobats. The clown announces the presence of the young "Madame Sans Jane der champion bare-(I mean dog-back) rider of der world." The performers are surrounded by what appears to be an appreciative audience, who laugh at and take pleasure in the various ragtag circus acts.

While "At the Circus" highlights the possible threat posed by the "undisciplined" young residents of the tenements, it also encourages viewers to admire these children for their ability to find and invent pleasures in the face of dire conditions. Moreover, this image of an improvised circus suggests that in the tenements, children invoke the rules of the carnival, creating a small, impermanent but still liberating space in which they can upend and mock the social rules established by the dominant white, middle class.[70] Indeed, a number of *Hogan's Alley* episodes show children staging what could be understood as middle- and upper-class pursuits, such as dog shows, elaborate weddings, Easter parades, and, of course, games of golf. Through imitation, they reveal the pretentions and excesses of the more affluent classes of New York. In a sense, "At the Circus" and other episodes in the various Yellow Kid series insist that children of the poor, the working class, and the immigrant class are part of the fabric of urban life. In *Hogan's Alley*, these young people demand to be seen in public spaces and demonstrate their keenness as social observers and commentators. While their economic class, citizenship status, ethnicity, and age often rendered

Figure 2. Cartoon by R. F. Outcault. "At the Circus in Hogan's Alley." In *New York World* Comic Supplement, May 5, 1895. SFS 53-10-1, San Francisco Academy of Comic Art Collection, the Ohio State University Billy Ireland Cartoon Library and Museum.

them impotent, their carnivalesque performances are a means for them to assert themselves.

But while "At the Circus" places othered children in the foreground, and even coaxes viewers to admire such children for their creativity and tenacity, the episode also reinforces the distancing that Riis encouraged in *How the Other Half Lives*. Riis's photojournalistic project was meant to expose white, middle-class audiences to the "realities" of the lives of the poor, the working class, and immigrants and to consequently rouse viewers to recognize and resolve the crisis of urban poverty. But Riis also took on and provided a voyeuristic stance in documenting slum life. Joseph Entin describes how *How the Other Half Lives* "performs a . . . double movement—introducing potentially disturbing scenes, but, through a variety of rhetorical framing techniques, protecting the reader's position of specular distance and security. . . . The poor constitute a spectacle that Riis's viewers observe, inspect, and scrutinize from a distance; he allows readers access to the deepest recesses of the tenements through a rhetoric that paradoxically confirms social separation. The 'other half' remains thoroughly 'Other'; the possibility of an exchange of points of view is avoided."[71] More specifically, Maren Stange argues that Riis employed the "language of tourism" to simultaneously provide his readership the "information needed to transform or control the slums, and the security and privilege of distance that obviates the 'vulgar, odious, and repulsive' experiences that the actual slums would inevitably present."[72] In utilizing the rhetoric of tourism, Riis represents the slum as an exotic, far-off locale and gives permission to viewers to approach his photographs as sources of pleasure and fascination.

In "At the Circus" and his other Yellow Kid cartoons, Outcault repeats this project of turning slum life into an entertaining spectacle. Of course, the photograph and the cartoon are two different mediums. Riis's photographs, as Peter Bacon Hales puts it, "operated by a rhetoric of realism, of verisimilitude: one believed them to be true to life, visual records of a moment in a larger experiential continuum."[73] The cartoon, on the other hand, was, at the outset, not mimetic; it was a form that traded on distortion and exaggeration. But as Rebecca Zurier puts it, the cartoon presented an "odd form of realism."[74] Even as the cartoon presents an "*un*likeness," it was still a form that required the cartoonist to display skills in observation and representation.[75] In other words, even if readers understood the cartoon to be hyperbolic, they did not necessarily apprehend it as a false representation. The cartoon was understood to be "[an] opinionated commentary that constituted a version of real life. . . . [They] proposed their own form of urban visuality by suggesting ways for New Yorkers to regard one another. Presenting city life as amusing rather than perplexing, they depicted strangers as recognizable characters of types whose difference could be seen and read from visual clues."[76] Thus the Yellow Kid cartoons were "authentic" visual representations that alleviated as much as stirred anxieties about the "threat" of undisciplined youth; through humor, these cartoons represent but also isolate a hypothetical social menace.

Nearly a year after the publication of "At the Circus," Outcault restages a similar spectacle in another *Hogan's Alley* episode, one that more forcefully exposes the porousness of social boundaries. This time, the circus is held within the confines of a middle-class home. In "Amateur Circus: The Smallest Show on Earth," scores of well-dressed boys and girls wreak havoc in the parlor. They tumble over pillows, hang from the chandelier, balance on chairs, and dance atop a grand piano (fig. 3).[77] The apparent ringmaster of this amateur circus is a famous child from the slums: the Yellow Kid. He stands in the middle of a makeshift ring, holding a whip. A large paper hat covers his eyes, as if to indicate that he is blind—or chooses to be blind—to the chaotic play he is instigating. The Yellow Kid is accompanied by another young Hogan's Alley resident, who, dressed as a clown, appears to bark instructions at tumbling children.

At first glance, the cartoon seems to confirm white, middle-class adults' suspicions that their children are prone to emulating unruly immigrant, lower-class children. "Amateur Circus" also seems to indict inattentive, indulgent mothers. An alarmed woman stands in the background; she embodies the helplessness of mothers who allow simmering childhood mischief to boil over into absolute mayhem. But the cartoon also implies that white, middle-class children are not

Figure 3. Cartoon by R. F. Outcault. "Amateur Circus: The Smallest Show on Earth." In *New York World* Comic Supplement, April 26, 1896. SFS 58-4-4, San Francisco Academy of Comic Art Collection, the Ohio State University Billy Ireland Cartoon Library and Museum.

necessarily impressionable youngsters who mindlessly imitate the "vulgar" acts they witness. Rather, they appear complicit in staging this raucous spectacle. A sign on the wall reads, "The management has secured the services of the two celebrated clowns from Hogan's Alley and they will remain in the ring for the entire performance." The sign indicates that the Yellow Kid and his companion have not come uninvited; rather, they seem to have answered the summons of the well-heeled children who have cast themselves in the role of "the management." It appears that the young managers wield authority over the clowns from the slums; these white, middle-class children are not naïvely exposing themselves to so-called agents of disorder. As they take pleasure in the buffoonery and otherness of the Hogan's Alley visitors, they practice their roles in supervising, determining, and containing the lives of their lower-class and immigrant peers. While the Yellow Kid and his clown companion commit a transgression by crossing the threshold of a middle-class home, they are penned in a circular arena. Their deviance, it seems, is licensed and limited by the youngsters who comprise the management. In the meantime, some affluent children freely move in and out of the ring, asserting their right to cross the line, to be both performer and spectator, to occupy both incorrigibility and innocence. The amateur circus, then, is a way for them to simultaneously violate and reinforce social norms. It is worth noting that the performances in this little household circus are clearly gendered: with few exceptions, the boys inhabit the roles of clowns and acrobats while the girls watch them from the sidelines.

And yet a few visual and verbal lacunae in "Amateur Circus" propose that the circular border that contains the Yellow Kid can be crossed in other ways. In the foreground lies a paintbrush and an upended can of paint. Presumably, these were the tools used to paint the circus ring. But who created this circle? Who drew the line? Was it the Yellow Kid? The management? The adult? These questions could perhaps be reconstituted as a more encompassing question: What roles do different members of society play in defining, maintaining, and redefining social boundaries? Outcault seems to suggest that he, as the artist, at once draws and challenges such lines. He leaves the ring's perimeter unfinished: the front segment of the circle remains open, as if inviting a response from the reader. Will the reader draw an imaginary arc to complete and close the circle? Or will she keep it open, collapsing the line between observer and participant, allowing restricted social elements some measure of freedom?

A similar open-endedness is enabled by the words inscribed on the Yellow Kid's paper hat. "Little nipper" are words of caution, announcing the Yellow Kid as a petty thief. Yet nipper also means "child."[78] While the label "little nipper" warns against this irredeemable character, it also prods us to acknowledge that he inhabits the circle of childhood, and is thus potentially malleable, potentially pure. The double meaning of nipper suggests that the Yellow Kid is simultaneously naughty and nice, consequently challenging the inflexible binarism of "good children" and "bad kids," of "us" and "them."

"Amateur Circus" hinted at the roles that child characters would play in the pages of newspaper supplements in the years to come. As the comic supplement became a popular form of entertainment, troublemaking child characters became regular presences in the lives of many Americans. While the prevalence of these characters alarmed some adults, many readers—children and adults alike—embraced them. The proliferation of fictional pranksters in the supplements signaled how the notion of naughtiness was increasingly tied to notions of playfulness, creativity, and vitality. This collapse between incorrigibility and innocence, on the one hand, encouraged sympathy for nonwhite and lower-class children and, on the other hand, reveals how so-called uncouth behavior could be usefully appropriated by children of more affluent classes. Overall, images of children in the comics drew and redrew the lines, demonstrating the rigidity and permeability of social boundaries, the intertwinings of hegemony and counterhegemony. They were not simply characters who appealed to a diverse readership; they were also figures who demonstrated that the lines between white and nonwhite, middle class and lower class, male and female, child and adult, were enduring yet also constantly shifting.

CHAPTER 1

FOREIGN YET FAMILIAR

Twenty-first-century readers will likely be appalled by the flagrant racism of John F. Hart's comic strip series *Jap "It"* (1904). The strip's eponymous protagonist bears the traits of the crude "Oriental" stereotype: slit eyes, buck teeth, "broken" English, and traditional clothing—in this case, what appear to be a yukata and geta. "It" is not only a sloppy attempt at conferring the character a Japanese-sounding name; the appellation also announces that the character is less than human, more object than person. In endowing his character with an unusually large head, Hart channels nineteenth-century physician Samuel George Morton, who insisted that cranial volume was correlated to intelligence.[1] Jap It's oversized head expresses and reinforces the pervasive belief that the Oriental is mentally apt and crafty. But the disproportionately large head also infantilizes Jap It: with it, he resembles an outsized toddler. His indeterminate age signals that he is an enigma, impossible to categorize according to "normal" Western conventions; his childlike body further highlights his strangeness as well as implies his arrested mental and moral development. By insisting on Jap It's childishness, Hart references the theory of recapitulation, which posited that "adults of inferior [non-white] groups must be like children of superior groups, for the child represents a primitive adult ancestor."[2]

This image of a stunted Japanese character intertwined with contemporary anxieties surrounding the influx of immigrants into America. Confined to a childish body, the figure of Jap It articulates the fantasy of constraining the immigrant (and more specifically, the East Asian immigrant) and suspending him in a state of dependency and immaturity. Yet Jap It's association with childhood also paradoxically challenges the racial typographies that Hart was reproducing. While the character's uncanny juvenile appearance makes him seem dubious, it also offers reassurance that he is powerless—and it is precisely this intimation that Jap It is a nonthreat that positions him as an underdog. Thus the liminal body that means to diminish and isolate him also serves as a device for eliciting empathy from readers.

Jap "It" was one of numerous Progressive Era strips headlined by immigrant characters. In many cases, these characters were children (or, as in *Jap "It,"* child-like figures). The popularity of the immigrant child motif can be understood as a response to European and East Asian immigration; Progressive Era cartoonists, it seems, found the image of the child to be useful shorthand for communicating the perceived inferiority and physical, mental, and emotional underdevelopment of the nation's new arrivals. But the prevalence of fictional immigrant children in turn-of-the-century newspaper supplements also documented the growing presence of immigrant youth in the country. After all, among the millions who traveled to the United States seeking a new life were children.[3] While *Jap "It"* uses the image of childhood to comment on the nature of immigrant adults, many contemporary strips were keen to explore and fantasize about the essence of young immigrants.

This chapter examines how Progressive Era discourses on immigration, ethnic difference, and childhood played out and intersected in newspaper comics. As demonstrated by Hart's *Jap "It,"* cartoonists often bestowed childish features on ethnic Others in order to infantilize them. But as in the case of Clarence Rigby's *Little Ah Sid, the Chinese Kid* (1904, 1905–1907) and Rudolph Dirks's *The Katzenjammer Kids* (1897–1912),[4] some strips focused on young arrivals and the anxieties—and exhilaration—that their presence inspired. Melissa Klapper reminds us that many commentators and reformers of the Progressive Era viewed immigrant children as the embodiment of both "hopes for childhood" and "fears about immigration."[5] Many newspaper comics of the period expressed this contradiction, reinforcing uncertainties over the nature of young immigrants while encouraging readers to place faith in these would-be Americans. In their strips, Rigby and Dirks offer ambivalent pictures of immigrant children: the main child characters are simultaneously foreign and familiar, suspect and sympathetic, troublesome aliens and future citizens. On the one hand, *Little Ah Sid* and *Katzenjammer Kids* suggest that young immigrants cannot fully assimilate because they are too unruly, too disruptive, too different; these strips pictured immigrant children as, to borrow Klapper's term, "small strangers." Their lives, defined by tomfooleries and accidents, appear incongruous with white, middle-class ideals of childhood. On the other hand, as the characters' misbehaviors occur within the frames of the so-called funnies, they emerge as figures who inspire amusement rather than agitation. Their troublemaking also denotes ingenuity, energy, and autonomy, characteristics that suggest their capacity for effective integration into a modernizing United States. Moreover, the characters' child status implies malleability: they could be potentially shaped to fit the mold of good American childhood. In both *Little Ah Sid* and *Katzenjammer Kids*, children are juxtaposed with calcified immigrant adults to emphasize the former's pliability and openness to acculturation.

As James Marten notes, the turn of the century was marked by a shift in attitudes toward children of the urban poor, many of whom were from immigrant families.[6] Charles Loring Brace, writing *The Dangerous Classes of New York, and Twenty Years' Work among Them* in 1872, considered loitering "street Arabs" as symptoms and agents of social disorder and immorality. Brace was deeply troubled by the thought of "thousands [of] children of poor foreigners [who have been] permitted . . . to grow up without school, education, or religion."[7] He asserted that "all the neglect and bad education and evil example of a poor class tend to form others, who, as they mature, swell the ranks of ruffians and criminals. So, at length, a great multitude of ignorant, untrained, passionate, irreligious boys and young men are formed, who become the 'dangerous class' of our city."[8] By 1890, however, Jacob Riis conveyed a more sympathetic view toward indigent immigrant children in his photojournalistic book *How the Other Half Lives: Studies among the Tenements of New York*.[9] He framed children as wretched victims who needed to be salvaged from the slums. For Riis, "the young are naturally neither vicious nor hardened, simply weak and undeveloped, except by the bad influences of the street."[10] By the early twentieth century, Jane Addams approached her targets of reform with less pity and more optimism. While Addams maintained that young people remained vulnerable in the city—a purported playground for elements of vice—she also celebrated what she called the "spirit of youth": "the spontaneous joy, the clamor for pleasure, the desire of the young people to appear finer and better and altogether more lovely than they really are . . . the unworldly ambitions, the romantic hopes, the make-believe world in which they live, if properly utilized, what might they not do to make our sordid cities more beautiful, more companionable?"[11] Like many reformers, Addams sought to "uplift" children of the underclass. Such "child-saving" efforts were undergirded by the belief that children had a right to a prolonged, protected, "innocent" childhood.[12] This vision of childhood circulated widely among the white middle class, but reformers also endeavored to naturalize and universalize this vision. Of course, this image of childhood—shielded from labor, from the street—was often incommensurate with the experiences and values of many immigrant, working-class, and poor families. Thus members of the lower classes often responded to reformers' work with resistance and suspicion. But it is worth noting that four decades after Brace imagined immigrant children as dangerous and destructive, Addams and her contemporaries maintained confidence in young immigrants' potential to become constructive, productive Americans.

Ethnic Difference and Ethnic Humor

Of course, such hopeful, receptive attitudes toward immigrant children did not mean that new arrivals, whether they were young or old, were met with tolerance and warmth across the board. As the Chinese Exclusion Act of 1882 and the founding of the Immigration League in 1894 attest, immigrants who arrived in the late nineteenth and early twentieth centuries were greeted by native-born whites and "older" immigrant groups with misgivings, resentment, and xenophobia. As John Higham documents, strands of nativism became increasingly entangled with racist thinking, and the resulting "racial nativism" was bolstered by the pseudoscience of eugenics.[13] Eugenicists, who viewed the "[admittance of] 'degenerate breeding stock' [as] one of the worst sins the nation could commit against itself," advocated the "rigid selection of the best immigrant stock [that] could improve rather than pollute endless generations to come."[14]

Newspaper comics participated in recording, exacerbating, and sometimes alleviating the seething tensions that emerged in the wake of mass immigration by deploying what we may call "ethnic humor." The definition of the term is a little slippery, as the descriptor "ethnic" can be associated with the creator, the audience, or the target of the jokes. In other words, ethnic humor could refer to the comedic forms that members of a particular ethnic group produce, that appeal to an audience of a particular ethnicity, or that mock racial and ethnic minorities. For John Lowe, the common theme of ethnic humor is denigration, as it could take the form of "jokes directed against out-group by the in-group, or by one out-group against another, or 'self-deprecating' jokes told by members of the group itself."[15] As such, forms of ethnic humor have a variety of motivations and functions. Jokes about minority groups that circulate among members of a dominant group are assertions of superiority; jokes that one minority group uses against another express competition and aspirations to assimilate into the dominant culture; self-mocking jokes that members of minority groups share among themselves could be taken as attempts to claim and subvert the stereotypes that dominant groups use to repress them.

In perpetuating immigrant and ethnic caricatures in the supplements, newspaper cartoonists continued the tradition established by late nineteenth-century humor periodicals such as *Puck*, *Judge*, and *Life*. These humor magazines, appealing to a white, middle-class readership, were filled with cartoons and marginalia that featured, among other stereotypes, "the shanty Irish" and "coarsely conniving Jewish Shylocks."[16] As Roger A. Fischer puts it, such visual typographies meant to amplify what was perceived to be the "familiar foibles and character flaws of those alien elements in the population deemed hopelessly beyond the pale of assimilation into an American community of citizens."[17] Martha Banta emphasizes the caricature's vicious objectives: it means to "[depict] the abnormal," to "[differentiate] 'we' from 'they.'"[18] Ethnic caricatures printed in humor magazines were born of nativism and xenophobia, reflecting and stoking the hysteria about the presence of "aliens." More broadly, these caricatures extended the project of "federal and state policies and local segregationist practices [that] explicitly intended to isolate those groups deemed 'undesirable' and 'unassimilable' or even a danger to U.S. society and culture."[19]

While series such as Outcault's *The Yellow Kid* and Dirks's *The Katzenjammer Kids* focused on the exploits of child immigrants, many other notable newspaper comics were headlined by adult immigrant characters, including Frederick Burr Opper's *Happy Hooligan* (1900–1932), George McManus's *Bringing Up Father* (1913–1954), and Harry Hershfield's *Abie the Agent* (1914–1931, 1931–1940). Many "ethnic" adult characters also commonly appeared as secondary and background figures in the comics. The New York City of R. F. Outcault's *Buster Brown*, for example, was populated by Irish maids, Irish policemen, and "dago" vendors.[20] At first glance, these series appear to do nothing more than belittle immigrants, young and old; they rebuke immigrant characters for their "deficient" racial/ethnic heritage. But as Banta reminds us, caricature and cartoon—modes by which ethnic humor was developed and delivered in humor magazines and that were later utilized in newspaper comic supplements—are "as susceptible to misreadings as other modes by which cultural exchanges are put into practice."[21] Moreover, as I discuss in the introduction, the newspapers' attempts to appeal to an economically and culturally diverse readership and the comic strips' multipanel format and seriality allowed for various, and sometimes unexpected, responses. Indeed, immigrant readers sometimes embraced the cutting caricatures that were meant to wound them. Lois Leveen points to how the butt of particular ethnic jokes often willingly participate in keeping derisive gags in circulation. Although some humorous gags were "founded on seemingly derogatory stereotypes," members of cultural groups targeted by such disparaging jokes would retell them as "an expression of pride in one's ethnicity."[22] The ethnic humor of the comic strip could thus be both injurious and empowering, divisive and unifying. And as I discuss below, the figure of the "ethnic" child adds further complexity to these jokes, as it can potentially elicit a wide range of (incongruous) responses, including disdain, sympathy, fondness, and delight.

The issue of authorship also complicates the notion that the caricature's project is to unequivocally delineate between "us" and "them." A number of the most well-known cartoonists of the period were immigrants or were born to immigrant parents.[23] Opper's parents had immigrated from Austria, McManus was born into an immigrant Irish family, and Hershfield's parents were Jewish immigrants. Dirks emigrated from Germany to the United States when he was seven years old. The work of these cartoonists brings to the fore the complexities of defining and characterizing ethnic humor, as they appropriate and sometimes destabilize stereotypes of immigrant groups. As Joseph Boskin and Joseph Dorinson put it, "Ethnic humor in the United States originated as a function of social class feelings of superiority and white racial antagonisms, and expresses the continuing resistance of advantaged groups to unrestrained immigration and to emancipation's black subcitizens. . . . In time, ironically, the resulting derisive stereotypes were adopted by their targets in mocking self-description, and then, triumphantly, adapted by the victims of stereotyping themselves as a means of revenge against their more powerful detractors."[24] Of course, newspaper cartoonists sometimes reinforced the social hierarchies prescribed by the dominant white, Anglo-Saxon, Protestant culture. The Austrian American Opper, for example, casts Happy Hooligan in the mold of the shanty Irish caricature; his strip about an unkempt, bumbling Irishman could be understood as an expression of interethnic tensions between different cultural groups. Put another way, *Happy Hooligan* is indicative of the hierarchies that developed among various immigrant populations.

Meanwhile, other cartoonists appear to poke fun at their own ethnic affiliations. In *Abie the Agent*, Hershfield serves up a caricature of a German Jewish salesman and storeowner who spoke in Yiddish-inflected English and possessed an "eagerness to purchase at discount."[25] Yet the cartoonist insisted that his character Abie was a "clean-cut, well-dressed specimen of Jewish humor"; Hershfield intended his creation to serve not as a replication but rather as a forceful rebuttal of the jokes and stereotypes that, as he put it, were "not at all complimentary to Jewish people and not all justified."[26] John Appel records that "[Abie] apparently did not ruffle the sensitivities of the Americanized German Jewish leaders and communal spokesmen who . . . organized the [Publicity or Anti-Caricatural Committees] to monitor and reduce the flourishing mass-culture anti-Semitism they saw spreading after 1900."[27] Rather, Jewish readers likely apprehended Abie as an effective counterpoint to the "big-nosed, calculating, money-mad Hockheimers, Diamondsheens and Burnupskis of turn-of-the-century cartoons and comics."[28] Hershfield's example points to how "ethnic" cartoonists were not necessarily reproducing cultural stereotypes but rather redefining and/or resisting these typographies.

In *Bringing Up Father*, Irish American cartoonist McManus draws his main characters Jiggs and Maggie with simian features, following the tradition of Irish visual caricatures that circulated in nineteenth-century English and American humor magazines. The English illustrator John Tenniel, who is perhaps best remembered by twenty-first-century readers for his illustrations for Lewis Carroll's *Alice's Adventures in Wonderland* (1865) and *Through the Looking-Glass, and What Alice Found There* (1871), was also a highly regarded cartoonist for *Punch* magazine. In his cartoons for *Punch*, Tenniel conceived and developed a caricature of the Irishman as a "swarthy ape."[29] This image of the simian Irish was subsequently adapted by magazine cartoonists across the Atlantic, most notably Thomas Nast and Joseph Keppler.[30] Both Nast and Keppler drew the Irish figure as a "menacing predator," giving him a "small cranium, beady eyes, pug nose and grossly exaggerated baboon mouth and underslung prognathous jaw."[31] Nast was descended from a German immigrant family and Keppler was Austrian-born; their adaptation of the anti-Irish sentiment of Anglo-Protestant groups could be understood as an effort to assimilate into the dominant culture. Certainly, their mockery of the Irish was very much in line with nineteenth-century nativism that was particularly hostile toward Irish immigrants.

At first blush, McManus's *Bringing Up Father* appears to be a public performance of self-loathing, a strip in which an Irish American cartoonist brazenly mocks Irish Americans. In visual terms, the characters Jiggs and Maggie are clearly descended from the caricatures developed and popularized by Tenniel, Nast, and Keppler, though they are not so much predatory as they are inept and crass. In *Bringing Up Father*, McManus chronicles the life and struggles of a nouveau riche Irish family. After Jiggs wins the lottery, he and his family suddenly find themselves hobnobbing with members of the middle and upper classes. But Jiggs is an irredeemable "shanty Irishman." No amount of money can rid him of his vulgarities, and he actively resists his wife Maggie's attempts to refine him. For her part, Maggie is an eager but hapless social climber. Her attempts to adapt the lifestyle and accumulate the trappings of the middle class only reveal her *lack* of class.

It may appear that McManus seeks to claim membership in Anglo-Saxon culture by admitting to—and distancing himself from—the so-called profaneness of Irish immigrants. But as Kerry Soper offers, McManus's characters function as something other than laughingstocks; they may also be apprehended as heroic tricksters.[32] For Soper, the character of Jiggs is especially fluid, as Jiggs is able to "shift among the following comedic positions: the butt of jokes, the put-upon everyman, the wise fool, a romantic other embodying positive qualities absent in the dominant Anglo-American culture, and the wily, subversive trickster."[33] Jiggs's elasticity must also be understood in light of trends of immigration in the early twentieth century. When *Bringing Up Father* first appeared in 1913, immigrants from Eastern Europe had become the new focus of nativist aggression. Audiences regarded fictive (and real) Irish and Irish Americans with more sympathy and less repulsion. Soper suggests that in Jiggs's case, it was ironically his apelike appearance that allowed audiences to find affinity with him: "It was Jiggs's dated ethnic physical shell that gave him license to play . . . various roles. In effect, only a comic outsider [like Jiggs] who had made it to the inner circles of power and wealth in the culture could effectively exploit opportunities to mock both the margin and the center. In sum, because of Jiggs's greater complexity, readers were given more opportunities to laugh with, rather than laugh at, Jiggs."[34] The same can be said of Opper's Happy Hooligan, the disheveled Irishman who was always getting into trouble with the law. The name "Hooligan" was a variant of the Irish name "Houlihan"; when Opper published his strip in 1900, "Hooligan" was widely associated with a fictional Irish family whose boisterousness was memorialized in music hall songs of the 1890s. For his part, Happy, who brandished an empty can on his head as a top hat, tended to generate disorder through ignorance, ineptitude, and insouciance. He was a rabble-rouser because he didn't fit in a nation that prized hard work, discipline, and ambition. Yet as Jared Gardner argues, many Progressive Era followers of *Happy Hooligan* may have embraced its eponymous protagonist as a heroic underdog, recognizing his bungling, troublemaking ways as expressions of antiauthoritarian sentiment.[35]

It is also worth noting that in McManus's *Bringing Up Father*, not all the Irish American characters are drawn with an "ethnic physical shell." Jiggs and Maggie's daughter Nora does not possess her parents' "apeish" features. With her curly hair, small nose and mouth, and waifish figure, Nora resembles a Brinkley Girl (fig. 4).[36] The visual contrast between Nora and her "swarthy" parents is an intimation that Irish immigrant crudeness and inferiority could be erased in a generation. While Jiggs and Maggie's permanent simian features indicate how they resist or fail at acculturation, Nora's "all-American girl" looks evince her success at shedding the "gross" aspects of her Irish heritage.

Nora expresses how real immigrant children negotiated the tensions between their ethnic and cultural heritage, which their parents and adult relatives often wanted to preserve, and the cultural norms of the New World, which they perceived to offer independence, opportunities, and delights. As Klapper puts it, children of immigrants "found that their best chance for achieving success and recognition—even pleasure—during their childhood and adolescence lay in acculturating to mainstream American ideals."[37] Sarah E. Chinn proposes that the conflicts between Progressive Era immigrant parents and their children lay the foundation for what we know today as the "generation gap," and this gap enabled young immigrants to make a claim to an "Americanness" that they were also actively redefining. As Chinn states, "The children of immigrants dissolved the conflation of 'American' and 'Anglo-Saxon'—instead, to be American meant to be sophisticated, to be involved in industrial labor or commerce, to participate

Figure 4. Comic Strip by George McManus. "Bringing Up Father." March 19, 1913. SFC 59, San Francisco Academy of Comic Art Collection, the Ohio State University Billy Ireland Cartoon Library and Museum.

in commercial leisure and consumer spending, and to reject the 'Old World.'"[38] Nora's "Americanized" appearance illustrates such movement away from the Old World. She represents the view that the younger immigrant is more malleable than her elders: she is more receptive to and adept at adapting the language, fashion, and cultural practices of the dominant culture; she can shed the "animalism" of her parents to become a New Woman; she can transform from Irish to American.

The strip's title also shows how the process of assimilation could result in upended familial roles. Although Nora is a supporting character with limited presence in the strip, the title implies that she plays a major role in the family, as she is tasked with "bringing up father." The strip gestures toward the experiences of real immigrant families: children often served as interlocutors, translators, and teachers, "provid[ing] a bridge between their parents and the culture of the United States, which was often undecipherable to the older generation."[39] The title hints that Nora bears the responsibility to raise her father, to correct him when he commits social faux pas, to educate him on the habits and protocols of white, middle-class America.

Yellow Perils and Pleasures: Children from the Orient

While fictional European immigrants abounded in the comic supplements, Asian or Asian American characters were not as commonly featured. Although John Hart's *Little Jap "It"* and Clarence Rigby's *Little Ah Sid, the Chinese Kid* were headlined by East Asian characters, both strips were relatively short-lived. *Jap "It"* lasted for six episodes while *Little Ah Sid* ran from 1904 to 1907, with a year-long hiatus in between. It may be that humorous depictions of the Oriental did not have broad appeal among newspaper supplement readers. The relative absence of Chinese and Japanese caricatures in Progressive Era comics perhaps lay in the fact that European immigrants had a more tangible presence in the urban centers on the eastern coast of the United States, where many cartoonists were based. Immigrants from China and Japan, mostly recruited as railroad contract laborers, landed on the Pacific Coast. Japanese laborers also arrived in Hawaii to work on sugar plantations, though many of them eventually left for the West Coast for higher wages. Fischer suggests that the insularity of the Chinese may have made them appear as not-so-threatening curiosities to European American observers.[40] At first glance, the minimal presence of East Asian characters in the comic supplements suggests that cartoonists and readers were not preoccupied with the phenomena of Chinese and Japanese immigration.

But as the widely circulating label "yellow peril" makes clear, many Americans considered the so-called Oriental dubious and dangerous. In the mid- to late nineteenth century, the "Chinaman" was pictured as an invasive and immoral presence; he was the "coolie" who "stole" opportunities from white working-class men or the sexual deviant who broke the taboos of heterosexual America.[41] The Chinese Exclusion Act of 1882—the first U.S. law that restricted immigration and that targeted people of a particular national-ethnic origin—was meant to satiate native-born whites, who blamed Chinese contract laborers for white workers' unemployment and declining wages. When Japanese immigrants—the Issei—came to fill the void left by Chinese laborers, they were confronted by anti-Japanese movements.[42] In response, both U.S. and Japanese governments took measures to limit Japanese immigration. But even as anti-Asian agitation successfully curtailed the number of Chinese and Japanese immigrants, Lothrop Stoddard, writing in 1920, demonstrated how anxiety over the presence of the Oriental endured in the early twentieth century. Stoddard warned that peoples of "Asiatic" origin constituted "the greatest threat to Western civilization and the White Race."[43] The influx of immigrants from China and Japan alarmed not just native-born Americans but also European arrivals. H. Brett Melendy describes how immigrants from Europe "turned into xenophobes" as they "found these two Asian peoples an unwelcome addition to the mainstream of immigration and worked hard to eliminate them from the United States."[44]

While Asian characters were a rarity in newspaper comics, the Oriental caricature was frequently featured in Progressive Era political cartoons, literature, theater, song lyrics, and film. Performers adapted techniques from blackface minstrelsy and vaudeville in establishing the comic figure of the Oriental in music and theater.[45] British writer Sax Rohmer's Fu Manchu novels, the first of which became available in the United States in 1913, reinforced the image of the villainous Oriental. As Rohmer himself puts it, Fu Manchu was "the yellow peril incarnate in one man."[46] Films such as Cecil B. DeMille's *The Cheat* (1915) and D. W. Griffith's *Broken Blossoms* (1919) "made explicit . . . the Yellow Peril's sexual threat to white civilization. . . . Both [films] constructed and deployed the imagery of sexual relations between Asian men and white women in order to interrogate and ideologically resolve the twin crises of family and nation."[47]

Sympathy for the Other: John Hart's Little Jap "It"

Although most of these images of the Oriental were caricatures of the Chinese, depictions of Japanese characters demonstrate how two distinct East Asian immigrant groups were often conflated. Hart's Jap It, for example, bears the slit eyes and buck teeth often ascribed to the "Chinaman." Such an image would have likely frustrated the educated, elite Issei, who adopted white racialist thinking, aligning themselves with middle-class Anglo-Saxons and apprehending the Chinese as a "degenerate" underclass.[48] But the Japanese immigrant elite were confounded by the racial hierarchy in the United States, a hierarchy that made no distinction between Chinese and Japanese, that withheld the right to naturalization from the Japanese, and that was reinforced and naturalized by comic caricatures such as Hart's infantile Jap It.[49]

Hart's strip also warns that the Oriental's "innocent" countenance is but a mask, hiding his "true" cunning and ruthless nature. In the episode "'It,' the Little Jap, Routs the Enemy with His War Dragon," Jap It's slyness is unveiled (fig. 5).[50] In this episode, Jap It receives a "mysterious box from Japan." A gang of street urchins, intent on "start[ing] a sea fight," decides to play pirate and steal the box. They offer to ferry Jap It and his package across the creek, and the seemingly naïve Jap It accepts their offer. But once the gang moves to attack him, a "chance blow" from one of the boys sets off a trigger in Jap It's package, which turns out to be an oversized jack-in-the-box. A dragon's head springs out of the box, and the terrified boys fall into the water. In the last panel, the dragon's head dangles before the slack-jawed boys, a reminder that the Oriental's guise of harmlessness conceals his "true" vicious nature. The episode suggests that one must approach the Oriental with caution, or risk waking the dragon that lies within him.

In each *Jap "It"* episode, the same gang of boys plots against the protagonist, and they repeatedly fail in their efforts to "make trouble" for Jap It. Although their ethnic origin is indeterminate, they appear to be of European descent. One episode suggests their heritage is Russian, as the boys imagine themselves as "de Rushin Co'socks" ready to wage a "Russo-Jap War" on U.S. soil.[51] In fact, *Jap "It"* repeatedly alludes to the very real Russo-Japanese War. The episode "'It' Has an Encounter with Foreign Dogs, and Wins," for example, overtly references

Figure 5. Comic Strip by John F. Hart. "'It,' the Little Jap, Routs the Enemy with His War Dragon." In *Chicago Sunday Record-Herald* Comic Supplement, April 24, 1904. SFS 43-8-4, San Francisco Academy of Comic Art Collection, the Ohio State University Billy Ireland Cartoon Library and Museum.

the two nations' political and military conflict over "rightful" control of Korea.[52] Jap It, cradling a cat labeled Kor-ee, heads in the direction of a vendor selling "[high bred] foreign dogs," which include a bulldog labeled "English," a dachshund labeled "German," and what appears to be a "French" pointer. One member of the gang spies Jap It and coaxes the other boys to "swipe de cat from It an torment de dorgs wid it." Outnumbered by the boys, Jap It personifies the tiny "Island Empire" that, to all appearances, was vastly outmuscled by Russia. But when Jap It releases the cat "under compulsion," the dogs become agitated. Boys and dogs find themselves in an all-out brawl; only Jap It and the cat escape unscathed. Just as Japan laid waste to Russia's expansionist aspirations, Jap It triumphs over his antagonists.

This episode of *Jap "It"* clearly references geopolitics, documenting Russia's false sense of superiority, Nikola II's underestimation of Japan's military might, and the support that Japan received from European nations, particularly Britain. But overall, the strip focused on the battles that took place in the United States, particularly the ones that emerged between immigrant groups. European immigrants were threatened by the specter of the Oriental, even as they vastly outnumbered immigrants from East Asia. Between 1901 and 1910, 92 percent of immigrants were from Europe while only 1.4 percent originated from Japan.[53] *Jap "It"* displays this imbalance in numbers as the European immigrant boys gang up on the solitary figure of Jap It. To be clear, Hart used his strip to caricature both cultural out-groups. While the strip depicts the Japanese as infantile yet duplicitous, the European immigrant boys are characterized as uncivilized and uncouth. They wear shabby clothes, speak in argot, and while away their time by loitering in the street. As the episode "'It' Has an Encounter with Foreign Dogs" implies, these "shiftless" European immigrants—presumably from Eastern and Southern Europe—are the real "foreign dogs," the idle "mongrels" who fought for scraps on the city streets.

In contrast, Jap It walks the streets with purpose. In "A Story of 'Dough' and 'It' in a Rainstorm," he is pictured as an industrious entrepreneur: he hurries through a torrential storm with a bag of money, trying to keep himself dry with an umbrella.[54] The gang of boys, who are drenched in the rain, accost Jap It, demanding that he hand over "dat umbrella or we'll swipe yur dough." But Jap It has a trick up his sleeve: the umbrella "has a patent handle—which comes off." When the boys wrench the umbrella away from Jap It, they tumble backward and crash into a cart of flour. The boys end up in a literal and figurative sticky situation: they stand covered in dough, too bewildered to run away from the policeman who approaches them. The victimized Jap It emerges as the victor: he becomes the underdog who triumphs over bullies, the mercantilist who distinguishes himself from "loiterers," the productive Oriental who transcends the alleged ignorant and idle European immigrant. What is especially striking is that at the end of each episode, Jap It turns to look and smile at the reader as he points his finger or thumb toward the hapless boys: these gestures are reminiscent of the Yellow Kid's act of meeting and directing the reader's gaze. As I discuss in the introduction, the Yellow Kid's interaction with the reader made him at once object and subject, observed and observer. Similarly, the act of pointing turns Jap It from comedic target to joke-teller, as he redirects the laughter away from the Oriental and toward another ethnic out-group.

Yet while "A Story of 'Dough'" makes clear that Jap It exhibits "American" traits of diligence and savvy—which allow him to prevail over the boys—it also slyly hints that the European boys hold an advantage over him. The image of the boys encased in dough suggests that immigrants from Europe, even if they are indolent and unruly, can potentially pass as white and assimilate into the dominant white culture. Even as their pranks are ill-conceived, they can be rewarded for trying to discipline dubious figures like the Oriental. In the meantime, it was virtually impossible for the Issei to make a similar claim to whiteness and Americanness. As Yuji Ichioka reminds us, U.S. laws categorized Japanese immigrants as "aliens ineligible for citizenship."[55]

Buying into American Culture: Clarence Rigby's Little Ah Sid, the Chinese Kid

A contemporary strip featuring another Oriental figure offers further commentary on East Asians' attempts to assimilate into white America. Clarence Rigby's strip *Little Ah Sid, the Chinese Kid* focuses on the relationship between Grandpa Lee, an elderly Chinese immigrant, and his grandson Ah Sid. The strip depicts the tensions that arise between them as they both seek to participate in mainstream American culture.[56] Grandpa Lee is an avid consumer of toys and other "American goods," which he believes will ease his grandson's—and his own—path toward Americanization. But Grandpa repeatedly miscomprehends and misuses these objects. The episodes conclude with the frustrated elder wrecking the consumer goods while his distraught grandson bears witness to the destruction.

Little Ah Sid, which Rigby drew for the World Color Printing Syndicate, first appeared in March 1904 and was published until November of that year. A year later, Rigby revived the strip, and its second run lasted seventeen months. In naming his child protagonist Ah Sid, the cartoonist appropriated a character that was brought to life by a popular 1880s song.[57] *The American Butterfly: A Comic Song with a Point*, composed by Louis Meyer, describes Ah Sid as a

> Chinee kid, a cute little cuss you'd declare
> With eyes full of fun, and a nose that begun
> Right up the roots of his hair.
> Jolly and fat was this frolicsome brat
> As he play'd thro' the long summer day
> And braided his cue as his father used to
> In Chinaland far, far away.[58]

The song relates how Ah Sid decides to catch a bumblebee, which he has mistaken for a "Milican buttlefly."[59] Although his initial intent is to "catch-ee [the buttlefly] and pull of um wing," he instead shoves the bee into his back pocket.[60] With a "grin / That was brimful of sin," Ah Sid decides to "mash-ee um buttlefly sure."[61] This little Ah Sid of song was the yellow peril in nascent form; he was a young Oriental whose play was laced by a wanton craving to harm the helpless. The song also hints that Ah Sid is sexually effeminate (and thus deviant), as he wears a "loose-fitting dress" and sits in a "style that [is] strangely demure."[62] This representation of Ah Sid was very much in line with late nineteenth-century constructions of Oriental sexuality as "ambiguous, inscrutable, and hermaphroditic."[63]

But Ah Sid ultimately gets his comeuppance. Because he is too ignorant to tell the difference between a butterfly and a bumblebee, he ends up being stung in the behind. "Ka-yi yu-ka-kan! / Hang um Melican man / Um buttlefly belly much hot!" he cries.[64] This comic consequence is a rhetorical move that means to deflate and enfeeble the craven Oriental. While the lyrics maintain that one must remain wary of Ah Sid, who apparently has no qualms about blaming his errors on the "Melican man," the song promises that his ignorance and foolishness prevents him from carrying out his misdeeds and nefarious plots.

The Ah Sid song was widely reproduced in various media. Its lyrics, sometimes with slight alterations, were published in newspapers and children's books. In 1894, the song inspired a humorous poem that appeared in the British humor magazine *Punch*. Although the poem retains the image of Ah Sid as a cruel-yet-ignorant boy, it shifts the setting from America to Japan. *Punch*'s iteration of Meyer's *American Butterfly* also relishes in offering a vicious caricature of the Chinese child, describing him as "lemon-faced . . . [w]ith a visage as old as an ape's."[65] The poem not only calls Ah Sid "pig-tailed," referencing the stereotypical image of the Chinese male with a long, braided queue, but also describes him as "pig-headed," suggesting that he is a willful, animalistic child who will not respond to reason or discipline.[66] The accompanying illustration reproduces pejorative visual typographies associated with the Chinese male: Ah Sid has buck teeth, wears loose-fitting trousers and tunic, and brandishes a long single braid of hair.[67] While the illustration shows a terrified Ah Sid trying to shield himself from a bee, it also insists that this child is a source of terror. His long fingernails resemble claws, prefiguring those of Rohmer's menacing Fu Manchu.[68]

When Rigby appropriated the figure of Ah Sid, the cartoonist was obviously building on a character that already had currency in popular culture. Yet he also eliminated the characteristics that marked Ah Sid as ignorant and insidious. Certainly Rigby used particular visual markers to ensure that his character *appeared* Chinese: the top of Ah Sid's head is shaved, and his remaining hair is woven into a long braid; he wears "traditional" Chinese garments that consist of a cap, a long-sleeved tunic, calf-length trousers, and high-heeled shoes. Yet Ah Sid does not have slanted eyes, buck teeth, or long, sharp fingernails. While some early episodes establish Ah Sid's "foreignness" by having him refer to himself in the third person, he does not speak in "broken" English, nor does he switch his *l's* and *r's*. Although he occasionally engages in mischief, his games are not tainted with malice. In one episode, he playfully aims a pop pistol at a dog, a rooster, and his grandfather's hired man.[69] But he lacks the cruel intent of the Ah Sids of song and the *Punch* poem—the pain he causes is fleeting, more annoying than vicious. Moreover, Rigby's Ah Sid is not sexually ambiguous. Through occasional prankishness, outdoor leisure, and play with "toys for boys," he exhibits boyish exuberance.

In short, Rigby's Chinese boy is an unequivocal departure from the traditional image of Ah Sid. In fact, the character has more in common with Anglo-Saxon comic strip child characters such as R. F. Outcault's Buster Brown, James Swinnerton's Little Jimmy, and the grandsons in Carl E. "Bunny" Schultze's *Foxy Grandpa*. His clothing suggests that he is from an affluent mercantilist family rather than born of the laboring class, indicating that Ah Sid has the refinement—and the money—to enter the realm of middle-class boyhood. Although his name and costume marked him as Oriental, other characteristics imply he is a good, even ideal, American boy. He is inquisitive and active, engages in play rather than labor, and, despite his sense of mischief, is respectful toward his elders.

Moreover, Rigby's Ah Sid is a tender child, one who weeps whenever his grandfather wrecks his toys. This tearful Ah Sid is antithetical to the Ah Sid of song, who, when stung by a bumblebee, furiously and irrationally wishes to exact vengeance against the "Melican man." The comic strip Ah Sid, reduced to tears, not only emerges as a sympathetic figure but also implies that the Oriental child is sensitive rather than cold-hearted and brutal. The ability to cry—the ability to feel and respond to pain—displays Ah Sid's "natural" innocence. As Robin Bernstein notes, nineteenth-century literary and visual cultures associated white children with goodness, benevolence, and vulnerability while imagining racially Other children—specifically black children—as corrupted beings who were "impervious to pain."[70] Ah Sid experiences and exhibits emotional pain, and as such, this fictional character implies that Chinese children could be defined into white childhood. While his tears can signify enfeeblement and feminization, they also confirm that he has more in common with the "suffering" white child rather than the "insensate" black child. Of course, Rigby's alignment of Chinese and white childhoods is misleading, as it cloaks the discrimination that young Chinese faced in the United States. For example, as Iris Chang documents, Chinese children were often refused admission into public schools since the 1870s, and such racist practices were soon buttressed by the Supreme Court's ruling on *Plessy v. Ferguson* (1896).[71]

In any case, *Little Ah Sid* is less interested in comparing and contrasting white and Oriental childhoods than in dramatizing the differences between the Oriental child and adult. The strip finds humor in the oppositional qualities of Ah

Sid and Grandpa Lee, using Ah Sid's linguistic and cultural fluencies to highlight Grandpa Lee's ineptitudes. In other words, the grandfather is cast as the buffoon. He is a caricature of the immigrant adult struggling, and failing, to assimilate. Ah Sid, in the meantime, represents the adaptable young immigrant who assuredly interprets and adapts to the ways of the New World.

Yet Grandpa Lee does not impede Ah Sid's acculturation; in fact, he advocates the Americanization of his grandson and attempts to hasten this process by procuring toys and other consumer goods manufactured in the United States. His actions reflect how immigrant adults, even as they worried that their children were too eager to cast off the customs of the "old country," often "cared enormously about their children's well-being and moral development; many had migrated for the explicit purpose of offering their children better lives."[72] In one episode, Grandpa Lee shows his investment in the project of Ah Sid's assimilation by embracing the Anglo-Saxon holiday of Christmas and, more notably, the emergent American ritual of Christmas shopping (fig. 6).[73] For Grandpa Lee, the holiday provides him the perfect opportunity to shower his grandson with a bundle of toys. He marks time with an "American calendar" and sets up a "Melica Clismas tree" that he adorns with presents for Ah Sid.[74] In another episode, Grandpa Lee expresses his belief that consumer goods will aid

Figure 6. Comic Strip by Clarence Rigby. "Little Ah Sid, the Chinese Kid." In *Courier Journal* Comic Supplement, December 10, 1905. SFS 33-6-2, San Francisco Academy of Comic Art Collection, the Ohio State University Billy Ireland Cartoon Library and Museum.

in de-Orientalizing his grandson. "Glandpa buy Ah Sid Melican hoop—no other Chinee boy havee one," he says.[75] His logic, it seems, is that a hoop and stick will distinguish Ah Sid from other Chinese boys and enable him to find kinship with white American children.

Thus even while Grandpa Lee seems to be an outsider in American society, his constant and pleasurable consumption of goods was his means of participating in American (consumer) culture. By purchasing toys and games for his grandson, Grandpa Lee shows that he has bought into the white, middle-class belief that childhood is a life stage that is characterized by leisure rather than labor. By supporting his grandson's journey toward Americanization, Grandpa Lee is effectively also treading his own path to acculturation. In short, Grandpa Lee practices citizenship through robust consumption.

One episode even suggests that Grandpa Lee is actually well-attuned to American culture and, more particularly, the English language. He purchases alphabet blocks so he can "teachee Ah Sid Melican A.B.C."[76] One may assume that the episode's punch line would reveal Ah Sid to be the fluent child who would edify his illiterate grandfather. But Grandpa Lee proves to be quite familiar with the English alphabet, and throughout the episode, Ah Sid repeatedly asks his grandfather to "tell [him]" what the letters are.[77] The episode suggests that Grandpa Lee is not necessarily the incompetent immigrant who depends on his grandson's translations of the words and ways of the New World. While Steven Mintz documents how, among Progressive Era immigrants, "family and age hierarchies were frequently inverted as immigrant children served as translators, interpreters, and cultural mediators,"[78] the adult immigrant in *Little Ah Sid* is the agent of assimilation, the source of information that his grandson comes to rely on.

The same episode, however, also illustrates the challenges of playing translator and mediator. Grandpa Lee is delighted to witness his grandson's aptitude and enthusiasm for learning English, but his pleasure quickly turns into frustration and annoyance. Ah Sid, in his eagerness to master the alphabet, demands that his grandfather "tell me this [letter]" at the most inopportune moments—when Grandpa Lee is taking a bath, sleeping, or on his way to an "important engagement."[79] "This is too muchee," Grandpa Lee cries. "Glandpa will go crazy."[80] Grandpa Lee eventually sets fire to the blocks. Ignoring his weeping grandson, he is pleased that the blocks "makee velly good bonfire."[81]

Another episode shows how Grandpa's appreciation for American goods transforms into aggravation. Standing at the edge of a pond, Grandpa Lee beams with pride as he regards a small rowboat and sailor suit, his latest purchase for Ah Sid.[82] When a breeze blows his grandson's hat into the water, Grandpa Lee jumps into the boat to recover the hat. But he then falls into the water and ends up ruining both hat and boat. Humiliated, Grandpa Lee blows up the hat, suit, and boat with dynamite. Paying no heed to his wailing grandson, Grandpa Lee dances gleefully.

With his ineptitude with American products exposed, he now takes pleasure not in purchasing or using them, but in destroying them. Through the acts of burning, blowing up, and chopping up the various objects that vex him, Grandpa Lee channels the vicious Ah Sid of song, as he performs a variety of ways to "hang um Melican goods."

As such, Grandpa Lee's tussles with American consumer products signify his failure to effectively assimilate. When he buys a novelty item—an electric thriller that induces a "funny feeling"—his grandson approaches it warily, declaring, "I don't like the looks of it" (fig. 7).[83] Grandpa Lee, lacking Ah Sid's sense of caution, ends up electrocuted. Their neighbor Ping Pong rushes to help, but he ends up electrocuted as well. As Grandpa Lee and Ping Pong have violent "electric fit[s]," their clothes are reduced to rags. With their limbs flailing, they end up tearing a lantern to shreds. The ruined traditional Chinese objects symbolize how the immigrant's interaction with American goods and amusements can effectively "shred" his relationship with his cultural origins. Yet the episode also implies that the adult immigrant who marvels at and purchases American products does not really comprehend these goods. In the meantime, Ah Sid has the good sense to cut the live wire with a hatchet. As the young immigrant who recognizes both the pleasures and perils of consumer goods, Ah Sid temporarily channels one of America's founding fathers: holding the hatchet, the young Chinese boy says, "I did it," calling to mind the mythical image of young George Washington who admitted to cutting down a cherry tree.

While Ah Sid does not suffer bodily harm when he plays with American-made toys and products, he does bear witness to how these goods expose his grandfather to be maladroit and brutish. Grandpa Lee is both guide and impediment to Ah Sid's acculturation. Although Grandpa Lee eagerly attempts to facilitate his grandson's assimilation, he is frequently bewildered and frustrated by the norms and products of the New World. He is alienated from his adopted culture as well as his grandson. *Little Ah Sid* displays the differences between the immigrant adult and immigrant child's experiences of acculturation and the tension that results from such differences; the former faces difficulties while the latter finds ease, and the adult's strained efforts end up obstructing the child's efforts at Americanization.

The Case of the Katzenjammer Kids

As Klapper notes, the differences in the ways that adult immigrants and their progeny experienced assimilation often strained family relationships. Many immigrant adults who migrated to the United States in the late nineteenth and early twentieth centuries were "bewildered and even repulsed by some American social norms [and thus] often set their sights on different goals, more in keeping with their own cultural traditions."[84] On the other hand, their children "found

Figure 7. Comic Strip by Clarence Rigby. "Little Ah Sid, the Chinese Kid." In *Courier Journal* Comic Supplement, December 24, 1905. SFS 33-6-4, San Francisco Academy of Comic Art Collection, the Ohio State University Billy Ireland Cartoon Library and Museum.

that their best chance for achieving success and recognition—even pleasure—during their childhood and adolescence lay in acculturating to mainstream American ideals."[85] This tension is overtly explored in Rudolph Dirks's *The Katzenjammer Kids*, one of the most popular comic strips of the Progressive Era. *Katzenjammer Kids* debuted in the *New York Journal* on December 12, 1897, and it quickly developed a strong following. The strip is still in syndication today, making it the longest running comic strip in history. Dirks, along with his contemporaries Frederick Burr Opper, R. F. Outcault, and James Swinnerton, is often feted by comics historians as a "founding father" of the American comic strip.[86] Although Outcault is often credited as the inventor of the comic strip as it emerged in the United States, Dirks popularized the use of panel borders, word balloons, and recurring characters that are now considered standard elements of the medium.[87]

Katzenjammer Kids also helped establish the figure of the naughty boy as a common comic strip motif. The strip's protagonists, Hans and Fritz, are two incorrigible brothers who plan and execute pranks often directed at adults, particularly their mother. By headlining his strip with child characters, Dirks was following the lead of Outcault, who was, at that point, basking in the popularity of his creation the Yellow Kid. But arguably, it was *Katzenjammer Kids* that inspired the numerous Progressive Era strips that featured fictional troublemakers. In the wake of *Katzenjammer Kids*, newspaper supplements published a good number of strips featuring what Bill Blackbeard and Martin Williams call "demon children."[88]

While Dirks's strip inspired multiple imitations, *Katzenjammer Kids* itself was influenced by tropes in German children's literature. The German-born Dirks was probably familiar with the *schrecklichkinder* ("horrible children") that appeared in German children's books, such as Heinrich Hoffman's *Der Struwwelpeter* (1845) and Wilhelm Busch's books. Many comics historians point to how *Katzenjammer Kids* is particularly indebted to Busch's *Max und Moritz: Eine Bubengeschichte in sieben Streichen (Max and Moritz: A Juvenile History in Seven Tricks*, 1865; first English translation, 1871), a "picture-story" with verse narration. Prior to Dirks, other American artists took inspiration from Busch's work. As Ian Gordon notes, F. M. Howarth's one-off strip "The Revenge of the Persecuted Baker," which appeared in *Judge* magazine in 1891, repeated one of the plots in *Max and Moritz*.[89] In Howarth's strip, two boys steal goods from a baker and then receive their comeuppance—a clear allusion to the "sixth trick" in *Max and Moritz*, in which Busch's bad boys try to steal cracknels from a bakery and end up getting baked into crust.[90] Harry Greening's short-lived *The Tinkle Brothers*, which was published in the *Journal* from September to October 1897, was another nod to *Max and Moritz*.

Two months after the exit of *Tinkle Brothers*, Dirks's *Katzenjammer Kids* entered the scene. An 1898 episode makes a clear allusion to Busch's work, imitating the "seven tricks" structure of *Max and Moritz*. In "Mrs. Katzenjammer Takes a Week's Vacation and the Kids Have a Glorious Time," Hans and Fritz play daily pranks on their hosts, the Zinfandels, over the course of a week.[91] Mrs. Zinfandel transforms from a plump, smiling hostess to an emaciated woman who declares, "I hope I'll never see [the Katzenjammer Kids] again."[92] Meanwhile, Mrs. Katzenjammer, returning from her holiday, appears content and healthy, as if the time away from her wayward sons has done her good.

Although Dirks may have been paying homage to the children's books of his youth, he distanced his work from the moralistic, cautionary-tale tone of Busch, turning instead to humor.[93] Dirks's strip did away with the morbid punishments that Busch exacted upon his schrecklichkinder. In *Max and Moritz*, the eponymous protagonists end up being ground into "coarse-grained feed" that "Master Miller's ducks with speed / Gobbled up."[94] As August Derleth notes, "the verses accompanying Busch's wood-block illustrations . . . were sometimes rather less comic than pegs on which to hang moral lessons."[95] In *Katzenjammer Kids*, the last panel often shows the boys rebuked for their pranks, often in the form of a spanking from Mamma Katzenjammer. Yet week after week, they rebound from punishment, with their naughtiness apparently undiminished. Rather than wagging a finger at boyish misbehavior, Dirks encourages his audience to delight in their persistent mischief-making. The comic strip form itself privileges prank over punishment. As Lisa Yaszek argues, "Given the repetitive nature of *The Katzenjammer Kids*, the conventional ending, a spanking, becomes a mere formality which is easily ignored. Furthermore, very little physical space is devoted to this ending. While [there is a build-up] to the punishment, the spanking itself only occurs abruptly in the last panel."[96] While the spanking became a predictable feature in the series, Hans and Fritz's prank of the week was what likely drew attention because it was the "only element of the comic that varie[d] from week to week."[97]

While many newspaper readers took pleasure in reading *Katzenjammer Kids*, some German Americans were troubled by its humorous depiction of a German family—especially because it was drawn by one of their own. The German American newspaper *New Yorker Staats-Zeitung* bristled at Dirks's use of the naughty boy trope, claiming that "such a German does not exist yet American comic strips perpetuate the model because readers laughed at him."[98] Even though the popularity of *Max and Moritz* proved that German audiences delighted in images of schrecklichkinder, the *Staats-Zeitung* was discomfited by figures of bad German boys in an American setting. For critics of *Katzenjammer Kids*, the picture of the willful German boy effectively functioned as a slur in the New World, projecting an image of Germans as disruptive rather than disciplined and productive. It is also likely that German American readers were not pleased by Dirks's decision to depict German adults as bumbling, ignorant immigrants who could not control their young and lacked fluency in the English language.

The *Staats-Zeitung* complaint did not specifically target *Katzenjammer Kids*. Rather, the paper was broadly addressing the various German caricatures that appeared in popular culture. Hans and Fritz may have struck some readers as a miniature version of the Dutch Act, a staple skit in vaudeville that was especially popular in the 1890s. The most famous Dutch Act featured actors Joe Weber and Lew Fields, who respectively played the German immigrants Mike and Meyer.[99] Their skits revolved around the lean and tall Meyer trying to swindle the short and rotund Mike. Although Hans and Fritz were more conspiratorial with rather than antagonistic toward one another, early iterations of the characters bore a slight resemblance to Mike and Meyer, with Hans drawn as the lean brother of chubby-cheeked, potbellied Fritz. The Dutch Act "relied on heavy German dialect and stereotyped 'national characteristics' for its humor."[100] Actors often wore lederhosen, padded their stomachs to simulate beer bellies, and carried steins to reinforce the notion that Germans were insatiable beer drinkers. Postcards and other forms of visual culture reproduced this vaudeville image, picturing Germans as fat, red-cheeked, greedy consumers of beer and sausages.[101] In some materials and narratives, working-class German men were depicted as lecherous.[102]

While German typographies abounded onstage, in print, and in film during the Progressive Era, Irish, Jewish, and African American stereotypes proved to be more pervasive and enduring. Fischer suggests that as many German Americans found careers as cartoonists and illustrators, they avoided perpetuating stereotypes of their own ethnic group and focused instead on mocking other minorities.[103] Still, Kevin Grace points to how many German stereotypes "were carried over from Germany by immigrants themselves" and even "became a source of cultural identity."[104] Thus caricatures of Germans and German Americans may have lost their vicious edge as they were accepted and embraced by German Americans themselves. As Peter Connolly-Smith suggests, German immigrants may have "made peace with their portrayal on the American stage. They believed perhaps that such stereotypes . . . held positive potential. . . . By laughing at themselves as portrayed as 'Other' onstage, ethnics in the audience defined themselves as non-Other, as 'American.'"[105] In short, even as German American audience members recognized such caricatures, they defined themselves *against* these stereotypical images.

Additionally, perhaps German caricatures were not as brutal or potent as other ethnic caricatures because Germans and German Americans were perceived to embody positive "American" qualities. Native-born whites tended to view German immigrants as possessing values such as "industriousness, thrift, and honesty—admirable virtues in the American value system."[106] A significant number of immigrants from Germany were professional and skilled laborers, and they may have appeared more productive and conscientious than other immigrant groups who were largely made up of unskilled, uneducated laborers. Moreover, upper-class, educated Americans—many of whom were educated in or were familiar with German universities—believed in the "preeminence of German learning."[107]

It is worth noting that the Katzenjammer Kids' German-inflected English is the only element that overtly reveals—and ridicules—the boys' ethnicity. The boys are not costumed in traditional German attire, nor are they depicted as beer-guzzling, bratwurst-devouring characters. Hans and Fritz appear "innocent" of many stereotypical features; perhaps this was Dirks's way of suggesting that the younger generation of immigrants are more evolved, having outgrown the negative qualities of previous generations. Hans and Fritz's prankishness may have discomfited some German American readers, but the boys' antiauthoritarianism was arguably the very characteristic that made them attractive and accessible to a wide, diverse audience.

Moreover, by performing pranks and undermining adult authority, Hans and Fritz were enacting Americanness and, more specifically, American boyhood. Dirks's appropriation of the image of the naughty boy meant to exhibit that the German boy had a lot in common with his American peer. As I discuss in chapter 3, the naughty boy was a much-beloved figure, recurring in various popular cultural forms, including genre painting, visual ephemera, and children's fiction. The American bad boy was not necessarily a figure of incorrigibility; rather, he was a symbol of independence, vigor, and resourcefulness. These virtues aligned with the vision of the nation as a thriving capitalist, democratic republic. Thus the naughty Katzenjammer Kids implied that German immigrant children possessed the qualities that would allow them to seamlessly assimilate into American culture. They symbolized how young people of German descent straddled two traditions, drawing from one cultural heritage in order to thrive in and contribute to their new cultural setting.

As in *Little Ah Sid*, *Katzenjammer Kids* highlights generational tensions between children and adults, implying that the younger generation possesses what the older generation lacks: the flexibility and savvy to adapt to and thrive in unfamiliar cultural terrain. In Dirks's strip, the differences between children and adults result in antagonistic relationships, the most obvious of which is that between the mischievous boys and their exasperated mother. In drawing Mamma Katzenjammer, Dirks reproduced the "obese, unattractive or simple-minded" woman of genre painting, lithographs, and advertisements who was imagined to be a "natural" adversary of young male pranksters.[108] But Mamma proves to be no match for Hans and Fritz. In "Mamma Katzenjammer Plays a Boomerang Trick," she attempts to give the boys a dose of their own medicine (fig. 8).[109] When a pillow, which the boys placed on the top rail of a door, falls on Mamma's head, she decides to play a crueler version of the trick on her sons—she loads the pillow with bricks before placing it on top of the door. Unfortunately for Mamma, her prank "boomerangs": when Hans and Fritz push the door open, the bricks land on *her* head. This injury to the head is also an insult, a reminder

Figure 8. Comic Strip by Rudolph Dirks. "Mamma Katzenjammer Plays a Boomerang Trick." In *Chicago American* Comic Supplement, March 10, 1901. SFS 1-10-2, San Francisco Academy of Comic Art Collection, the Ohio State University Billy Ireland Cartoon Library and Museum.

that Mamma lacks the "cranial capacity" to outfox her foxy sons. Mamma's failed prank not only reveals that she lacks her sons' ingenuity but also exposes her as a petty adult, one who responds to children's mischiefs with a "childish" sense of vengeance.

The Katzenjammer boys are also perceptive enough to recognize—and toy with—adult notions of good behavior. In one episode, they reveal how virtuousness—of the child as well as the adult—is but an appearance. As they set up their prank, one of them remarks, "We got such a lovely ma" (fig. 9).[110] The joke, it seems, is that Mamma will be exposed as a not-so-lovely woman by the episode's conclusion. When she comes to the boys' room to kiss them good night, the two pranksters lie quietly in bed, pretending to be asleep with smiles on their faces. Their performance fools Mamma: she lets her guard down the moment she lays eyes on her "sleeping" children. "Such angel boys," she says. She is so moved by the sight that she makes a New Year's resolution, declaring that she "nefer will . . . whip der darlings again." Mamma takes a seat, presumably to gaze upon the "angelic" faces of her sons. But the bench, having been sabotaged by the boys, collapses. Mamma falls, bum first, into a tub of water. Hans and Fritz

Figure 9. Comic Strip by Rudolph Dirks. "Mamma Katzenjammer Makes a New Year's Resolution." In *San Francisco Examiner* Comic Supplement, December 29, 1901. SFS 1-14-1, San Francisco Academy of Comic Art Collection, the Ohio State University Billy Ireland Cartoon Library and Museum.

end up receiving their just deserts as they get spanked for their deceptiveness. But it is Mamma who is positioned as more disingenuous here—she is the one who breaks her resolution, who reneges on a promise just moments after she makes it. It seems the boys are aware of their mother's propensity for false pledges: the moment Mamma resolves to never again smack her darlings, the two boys exchange knowing winks. *Katzenjammer Kids* not only reinforces the notion of a divide between adults and children; it also implies that in the New World, the gap between generations widens.

A few episodes also comment on how the Katzenjammers contend with other "ethnically Other" children. The title of the episode "The Katzenjammer Kids Rob Happy Hooligan's Nephews of Their Christmas Pie"—which Dirks collaborated on with *Happy Hooligan* creator Frederick Burr Opper, his fellow Hearst cartoonist[111]—suggests that Hans and Fritz have no misgivings about antagonizing their immigrant peers.[112] The boys, spiteful that their mother offers food to the young nephews of the Irish Happy Hooligan, forcibly drag away two of the boys and attempt to assume their identities. This particular installment gestures at the often savage competition for resources that emerged between different immigrant groups. At first glance, it also seems to suggest that Irish immigrant children are no match for their German immigrant counterparts. The aggressive and wily Katzenjammer brothers are easily able to exert their authority over the helpless and passive Hooligan nephews. The latter weep and fall limp as Hans and Fritz drag them away.

But the episode ultimately shows that the nephews' strength lies in their vulnerability and sensitivity, especially in light of the antagonisms of the Katzenjammer boys, who appear less as "boys being boys" and more as selfish bullies. Mamma Katzenjammer sides with the young Hooligans when she uncovers her sons' trick. "Only cowards and moiderers steal pie from innocent babies," she cries, and she punishes her sons with a vigorous spanking. This particular episode thus offers two competing yet coexisting visions of immigrant children. On the one hand, the Katzenjammer boys stir up anxieties about the duplicity and avarice of undisciplined immigrant youth. On the other hand, the Hooligan nephews imply that young immigrants are tenderhearted, whose goodness can be recognized—and presumably fostered—by an adult. Indeed, while the Hooligan nephews, who are recurring minor characters in *Happy Hooligan*, bear the apelike features of their uncle, they are far from being brutish boys. Rather, they are children who seek to abide by the rules of the New World. In *Happy Hooligan*, they collectively serve as the eponymous protagonist's conscience, imploring their uncle to cease his "foolish" behavior. Whenever they witness their uncle being "pinched" by the police, they wail in distress. In his strip, then, Opper flips the script while still pointing to the chasm that lay between generations: the adult Irishman, in his ignorance, misbehaves; the Irish children, in their wisdom, seek to discipline him.

While "Katzenjammer Kids Rob Happy Hooligan's Nephews" encourages readers to commiserate with innocent, suffering immigrant children like the Hooligan boys, episodes of *Katzenjammer Kids* typically attempt to rouse sympathy and even admiration for Hans and Fritz. "The Katzenjammer Kids in School," in particular, is a celebration of the protagonists' assertiveness, autonomy, cleverness, and leadership. The two boys delight their classmates—who, in appearance, are ethnically diverse—by devising an escape from a dull history class (fig. 10).[113] Hans and Fritz lead the other pupils out the window while the teacher, whose nose is pressed against a book, appears to invent ludicrous anecdotes about Napoleon's childhood. Some of the other pupils exchange looks of delight as Hans and Fritz hold out a plank between their school desk and the window; when the Katzenjammers exit through the window, the other boys follow without question. The escape from the classroom is not only a rejection of the institution of the school but also a pointed revolt against a mismanaged classroom and a negligent, hypocritical teacher. This act of resistance, led by the Katzenjammers, is reminiscent of the one that Tom Sawyer and his friends stage against a "severe" schoolmaster on examination day.[114] The one pupil who resists participating in the exodus is the teacher's pet, who desperately waves to the teacher, trying to get his attention. While it seems as if the other boys are blindly following the Katzenjammer brothers, the teacher and his pet are the ones who

Figure 10. Comic Strip by Rudolph Dirks. "The Katzenjammer Kids in School." In *New York American and Journal* Comic Supplement, March 12, 1905. SFS 80-3-2, San Francisco Academy of Comic Art Collection, the Ohio State University Billy Ireland Cartoon Library and Museum.

are truly myopic. Their glasses—supposedly symbols of intellectualism—make their eyes appear blank. The episode concludes with the teacher mistakenly punishing his pet, much to the delight of the other pupils. Here, tattling is portrayed as more egregious than playing hooky. As the teacher's pet gets a whipping, the boys throw up their arms and cheer. Two boys in the back row even hold hands, implying that Hans and Fritz's prank has cultivated a sense of community among the children.

In *Little Ah Sid* and *Katzenjammer Kids*, immigrant youth are liminal figures. Ah Sid and the Katzenjammer boys are simultaneously foreign and familiar, alien and American. Their ethnicity marks them as outsiders, but their child-state insists that they possess resourcefulness and vitality, characteristics that will enable them to make useful contributions to a growing, modernizing society. Moreover, the child characters represent adaptability and openness to assimilation, qualities that immigrant adults purportedly lack. *Little Ah Sid* and *Katzenjammer Kids* arguably express the same optimistic and vigorous defense of immigrant children that Lillian D. Wald articulated in *The House on Henry Street* (1915): "The little hyphenated Americans, more conscious of their patriotism than perhaps any other large group of children that could be found in our land; unaware that to some of us they carry on their shoulders our hopes of a finer, more democratic America. . . . Only through knowledge is one fortified to resist the onslaught of arguments of the superficial observer who, dismayed by the sight, is conscious only of 'hordes' and 'danger to America' in these little children."[115] Ultimately, the "childish" qualities of Ah Sid and the Katzenjammer Kids—their playfulness, malleability, and energy—made them appear fit for the American way of life. These characters represented and fortified the view that immigrant children had the potential to become valuable future citizens.

CHAPTER 2

CROSSING THE COLOR LINE

In a 1906 episode of *Buster Brown*, R. F. Outcault uses the title to pose a question to his readers: "What Would You Do with a Boy like This?"[1] Presumably, the "boy" Outcault is referring to is the series' eponymous protagonist; thus, the title coaxes audiences to wonder, how does one deal with a hellion like Buster Brown? In "What Would You Do," Buster propositions a penniless black boy to help him play a trick on his mother. The African American child readily agrees, and once he dons a Dutch Boy–style wig and trades his tattered clothes for one of Buster's outfits, he transforms into a black Buster. This transformation elicits the reaction Buster hopes for: his mother is horrified by the sight of what she assumes to be her "soiled" son. She drags the little impostor to the bathroom and attempts to scrub off what she thinks to be grime. To her dismay, the dirt "wont [*sic*] come off."[2]

In "What Would You Do," Outcault employs the humorous trope of racial impersonation, a common motif in turn-of-the-century visual culture and theater. Such masquerade expressed contemporary racial anxieties: it articulated and explored the concerns of the white, urban, middle class about the escalating frequency of their encounters with African Americans. "What Would You Do," more specifically, probed the effects of shifting racial demographics on white childhood. Were white children under threat? Could segregation of black and white childhoods be maintained?

Yet the gag of racial impersonation, as employed in "What Would You Do," also undermines the notion that apartheid of black and white childhoods is necessary and natural. Instead, the theme of mistaken identity insists that two children who are "raced" differently also share similarities. By showing the ease with which a black child can put on whiteness, and with which a white child can "conceal" himself under a layer of blackness, the episode gestures toward the fluidity and artificiality of racial identities. More significantly, it insists on the universality of childhood. Even the title wrestles with rigid racial categorizations, offering the possibility that the titular boy could be either Buster or the African American child.

This chapter examines how images of black and "blackened" children that appeared in Progressive Era newspaper comics expressed white ambivalence about the racial Other. It shows how series such as E. W. Kemble's *The Blackberries* reproduced the figure of the pickaninny, a racist caricature that not only cast black children as vulgar and depraved but also implicitly highlighted the "natural" innocence of white children. Other comics, however, challenged this oppositional view of black and white children. Their recurrent use of the gag of racial impersonation, in which white child characters "blacken up" and black children disguise themselves by donning the clothes of their white counterparts, suggested that children of different racial identities are more alike than dissimilar, given the ease with which they are able to switch places.[3] The trope of impersonation, as deployed in newspaper comics, also exposes how unease over racial encounters is primarily an adult preoccupation. Moreover, it typically depicts children as capable of interrogating, rejecting, and mocking adults' racial anxieties. Ultimately, however, cartoonists deployed the gag of "racial trespassing" to privilege the white male child. They utilized this trope to suggest that the white boy who played at being black was engaging in a pleasurable activity that facilitated his ability to perform healthy boyhood. The black child of newspaper comics, on the other hand, proved to be unsustainable, as exemplified by R. F. Outcault's short-lived series *Pore Lil Mose*. The series' eponymous protagonist is a liminal figure, at once based on the pickaninny caricature yet also exhibiting characteristics often associated with white childhood. For two years, Mose supplied a complicated image of black boyhood as he shifted between vulgarity and innocence, between being repellent and being admirable. Yet his crucial purpose, it turns out, was to serve as the prototype for what was to become Outcault's most popular and enduring creation, the white Buster Brown. As a white character who took on the aspects of a fictional black boy, Buster could be understood as a child who constantly engages in acts of impersonation, appropriation, and racial erasure.

Blackness at the Margins

Racial and ethnic caricatures abounded in the pages of Progressive Era newspaper comic supplements. African American typographies, such as Sambo, Mammy, and Tom, circulated in print and performance, in song and silent film; newspaper cartoonists actively participated in disseminating these images in the pages of comic supplements. Yet very few series were headlined by black characters. Often, African American figures appeared in one-off cartoons and marginalia or were cast as minor background characters. In "What Would You Do," for example, the black child remains nameless and does not appear in future episodes. He functions as a prop that enables Buster to exercise prankishness and boyishness.

The marginalization of black characters in the comic supplements obviously mirrored post-Reconstruction efforts to curtail or prohibit African American participation in social, economic, and political spaces. In *Plessy v. Ferguson* (1896), the Supreme Court upheld the constitutionality of racial segregation, ruling that "separate but equal" practices were not in violation of the Fourteenth Amendment. Many white politicians and intellectuals, subscribing to racist pseudosciences that "proved" that African Americans were mentally and morally inferior to those of Anglo-Saxon heritage, argued against blacks' citizenship rights.[4] Others pressed for black exclusion by peddling the notion that blacks were deficient as well as dangerous. The publication of W. E. B. Du Bois's *The Souls of Black Folk* (1903), a testament to black intellectualism, was bookended by the release of Thomas Dixon Jr.'s novels *The Leopard's Spots: A Romance of the White Man's Burden* (1902) and *The Clansman: A Historical Romance of the Ku Klux Klan* (1905). In both novels, Dixon zealously defends segregationist thought and practice by evoking the image of the monstrous black man—and both books became bestsellers. Numbers, not just words, were used to shore up narratives of black criminality. As Khalil Gibran Muhammad reminds us, "Northern black crime statistics and migration trends in the 1890s, 1900s, and 1910s were woven together into a cautionary tale about the exceptional threat black people posed to modern society."[5]

One may assume that turn-of-the-century progressivism, billed by proponents as a movement that served the interests of the oppressed, was at the forefront of efforts to erase the color line. Certainly, a number of leading reformers, including Jane Addams and Florence Kelley, spoke forcefully against segregation, racial prejudice, and lynching and were active members of the National Association for the Advancement of Colored People. But many white progressives were, as David W. Southern puts it, "[acquiescent] in the consolidation of Jim Crow in the South or simply ignored the race problem."[6] In some cases, economic progressives turned to Darwinism, eugenics, and race science to defend and buttress racist views of African Americans.[7] Elisabeth Lasch-Quinn documents how many urban reformers ignored the needs of African Americans who migrated to northern cities, focusing instead on programs for European immigrants.[8] Even as settlement workers like Addams, Louise de Koven Bowen, Frances Kellor, and John Daniels sought to "uplift" their new black neighbors, their actions were ultimately shaped by notions that "the character of blacks [was] somehow maladjusted and their culture as lacking," and that "the harsh system of slavery . . . had obliterated [African American] morality, family integrity, social organization, and even culture and civilization itself."[9]

The relegation of blacks was thus extensive, practiced in both North and South. But the pervasiveness of racial ostracism did not mean that white

Americans were unconcerned about African Americans. On the contrary, widespread discriminatory and exclusionary practices were symptoms of Progressive Era obsession with race. In the newspaper comic supplement, the marginal yet persistent presence of black caricatures signaled such white preoccupation with the subject of blackness. As newspaper comics functioned to deride and diminish those who were perceived to be social threats, they became tools for containing the menace supposedly posed by African Americans.

However, many newspaper comics also expressed white ambivalence for blacks and black cultural practices: aversion for African Americans was deeply intertwined with feelings of desire and captivation.[10] The racist typographies that appeared in the comics meant to repress and ridicule, to highlight the "inherent" vulgarity and depravity of African Americans. But they also conveyed a fascination with black bodies and culture. In Outcault's "What Would You Do," the dark-skinned child is depicted as "dirty"—Buster's mother frantically attempts to scrub off what she thinks to be filth. Yet the panels that show him sitting in the tub and fleeing from Buster's mother make his black body tantalizing (fig. 11). These scenes hint at his nudity, inviting readers to imagine him unclothed.

As "What Would You Do" demonstrates, Progressive Era fixation with race was intertwined with contemporary obsessions about childhood. With the United States caught in the throes of modernization, industrialization, and expansion, the physical, intellectual, and moral well-being of Anglo-Saxon children—the presumed inheritors of the nation—became a much-discussed, much-debated subject. Embedded in Progressive Era discourses of childhood was the notion

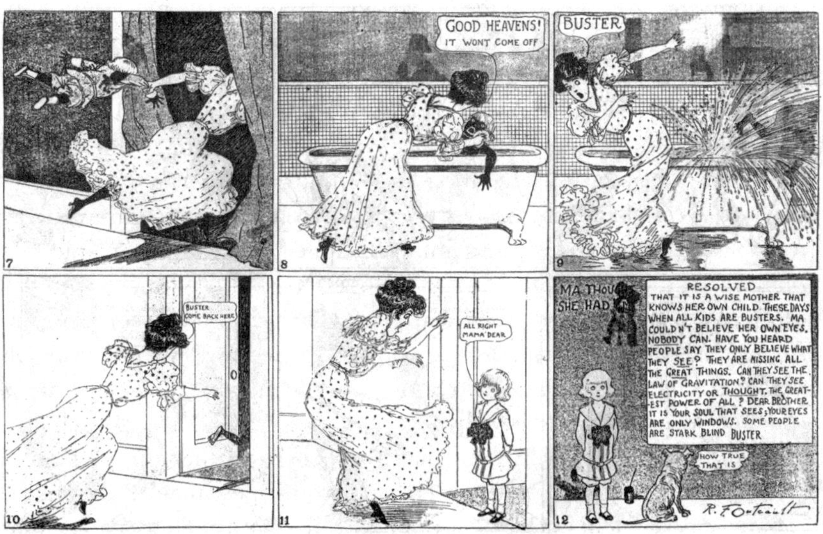

Figure 11. Excerpt from Comic Strip by R. F. Outcault. "What Would You Do with a Boy like This?" Originally printed in *American Journal Examiner.*

that the white child was essentially different from—or, more specifically, essentially superior to—children of other races. This belief had a significant impact on the lives of white, middle-class children: the obsession with healthy childhood meant that their bodies and behaviors were subjected to increased discipline and scrutiny.[11] In order to maintain the "natural" racial order, white children were taught to avoid the "excesses" and "vulgarities" that were supposedly habitual in nonwhite children. In the meantime, African American children, Native American children, and the children of European and Asian immigrants were measured against their white peers, with Anglicization presented as the only viable pathway toward improvement and salvation.

Yet as the comics suggest, white, middle-class children were not entirely segregated from children of other races. For one, the supplements' entry into the white, middle-class home made images of the racial Other frequently visible to Anglo-Saxon children. Even as newspaper comics encouraged white children to recognize the differences between themselves and "raced" children, these texts also arguably allowed their young audience to empathize with children who were "different" and to be enthralled, rather than repulsed, by their otherness. More important, the comics demonstrated to young readers that "risky" racial encounters could aid in defining and fortifying white identity.

The Pickaninny: What the White Child Is Not

Newspaper comics repeatedly deployed a particular caricature that became a powerful instrument in bolstering the notion that white children were superior to African American children: the pickaninny.[12] From the late nineteenth to the mid-twentieth century, the pickaninny was the "dominant racial caricature of Black children."[13] The pickaninny was typically depicted as having extremely dark skin, "nappy" hair, large eyes, and a wide grin and was often placed in a rural setting. Along with happy Sambo and mirthful Mammy, the grinning pickaninny helped some white Americans overlook the problem of racial injustice. Such cheerful black figures became proof positive that African Americans were not suffering. Moreover, these images activated nostalgia for a mythical Old South where "darkies . . . knew their place in society and were content with their servitude."[14] Representations of smiling, playful black children in the countryside effectively advanced the myth of the "good ol' days" in the plantations, when the South was supposedly unblemished by the Civil War and the social, political, and economic upheavals that followed.[15]

The pickaninny's depravity was signaled by his behavior: he engaged in violent acts that brought injury upon himself as well as other pickaninnies, he stole and devoured chickens and watermelons, and he wore ragged clothes or no clothing at all, shamelessly exposing his genitalia and buttocks. The pickaninny was, in other words, a "child coon." He implied the inherent corruption of black children as well as the permanent childishness of African American adults. The caricature also asserted that the black child was a "nonchild."[16] Robin Bernstein reveals how pickaninny imagery implied that young African Americans lacked the capacity to "experience or express pain or sustain wounds in any remotely realistic way."[17] As such, the pickaninny insisted on an intrinsic difference between the white child and the black child: the former is vulnerable, tender, and naturally innocent, while the latter, being insensate, is not innocent. For Bernstein, "at stake in this split [of white and black childhoods] was fitness for citizenship and inclusion in the category of the child and, ultimately, the human."[18] Because of their purported insensitivity and noninnocence, black children could be written out of the categories "child" and "human."

The pickaninny caricature not only defined black childhood; it also reinforced definitions of white childhood by offering an image of what white childhood *is not*. As Mary Niall Mitchell notes, "Images of innocent white children in the nineteenth century, whether sentimental or moralistic, developed largely in relation to their imagined opposite."[19] At the turn of the century, the pickaninny characters in Progressive Era newspaper supplements continued the project of contrasting black and white childhoods, at once naturalizing the image of the insatiable, lustful, and violent black child and setting it up as a figure of excess that "pure" and "disciplined" white children could be measured, and could measure themselves, against.

This picture of abhorrent black childhood did not seem to bother Progressive Era audiences. In fact, consumers, specifically members of the white middle class, embraced pickaninny imagery. This caricature helped sell a wide variety of consumer goods and was itself packaged as a product.[20] It appeared in various forms of consumer culture, including advertisements, postcards, song sheets, trade cards, and memorabilia. Perhaps the most popular pickaninny of the period was Topsy. Topsy initially appeared as a key character in Harriet Beecher Stowe's abolitionist novel *Uncle Tom's Cabin* (1852). In creating the "odd and goblin-like" slave girl, Stowe's intention was to illustrate the harrowing effects of slavery on children.[21] For Stowe, Topsy was not inherently insensate, but rather made insensate by the brutal, dehumanizing institution of slavery.[22] When the character was appropriated by minstrel performers in the late nineteenth and early twentieth centuries, however, she was turned into a "happy, mirthful character who reveled in her misfortune."[23] Onstage, her bedraggled appearance, "woolly" hair, and ineptitude with the English language transformed her from a tragic to a comic character.[24] The theatrical Topsy embodied deviant childhood; she gave audiences permission to mock and reject African Americans. This minstrel rendition of Topsy, comical and repugnant as she was, may have also activated sympathy among audiences. Eric Lott illustrates how antebellum minstrelsy was not simply a venue for ridiculing African Americans; rather, it enabled overlapping feelings of derision and desire for, as well as identification with, black characters onstage.[25] It is not farfetched to conclude that minstrelsy in the Progressive Era continued to encourage similar complex responses among audiences. The theatrical Topsy, then, may have been met with both disdain and affection. Certainly, her emergence on the minstrel stage suggests that black childhood was a subject that intrigued turn-of-the-century spectators.

Always seeking opportunities to boost readership and sell newspapers, cartoonists and publishers capitalized on the popularity of the pickaninny caricature. E. W. Kemble, R. F. Outcault, and other cartoonists recirculated the familiar image of the grinning black child. Kemble even drew a short-lived series headlined by a character named Topsy. Yet in some instances, black child characters in newspaper comics eluded, even just fleetingly, pejorative associations. Given that the comics drew from tropes of contemporary theater, it is likely that the African American caricatures that appeared in the pages of the comic supplement triggered responses that were akin to the ambivalence that minstrelsy inspired.[26] Moreover, the seriality of comics arguably allowed the "vile" pickaninny to become a nuanced, sympathetic character. As Kerry Soper puts it, the serial format of newspaper comics—particularly multipanel strips—allows for both plot and character development: "The formal structure and convention of strips . . . contributed to the medium's potential for ideological complexity . . . since strips used an ongoing narrative, or at least featured the same characters from day to day, the frames of the medium were limiting only in a physical sense; they corralled the contents of an individual frame's words and images and the day's joke, but they were porous when it came to continuity of storyline and to character development."[27] As a serial narrative form that sought to delight its readers, the turn-of-the-century comic strip perpetuated and sometimes complicated the pickaninny stereotype.

The Blackberries: Kemble's Consumable "Coons"

In *The Blackberries*, E. W. Kemble did not express any interest in giving nuance to caricatures of black children. When he launched *Blackberries*, which appeared intermittently in William Randolph Hearst's various Sunday newspaper supplements between 1897 and 1901, Kemble was already an established illustrator and cartoonist. He began his career as an artist for humor magazines and gained nationwide recognition for his illustrations for Mark Twain's *Adventures of Huckleberry Finn* (1884). In *Huckleberry Finn*, Kemble drew the slave Jim with features that were stereotypically associated with African Americans, including bulging eyes and thick lips. By his own account, illustrating *Huckleberry Finn* inspired Kemble to dedicate himself to drawing the "Negro type."[28] Claiming that his "coons caught the public's fancy," he continued to produce numerous cartoons and illustrations that featured African American figures.[29] His work was not always in the vein of caricature. His portraits of blacks living in the

South and in northern cities still essentialized African Americans, though with the purpose of romanticizing rather than ridiculing them. The characters that he drew for an 1892 edition of *Uncle Tom's Cabin* did not stray far from stereotype, though their features were less hyperbolic than *Huckleberry Finn*'s Jim.[30] Yet Kemble seemed to relish drawing African American caricatures, populating his cartoons, strips, and children's books—notably *A Coon Alphabet* (1898)—with slouching Sambos, jolly Mammies, and gluttonous "coons."

In *Blackberries*, Kemble mined the comic possibilities of the pickaninny caricature. The Blackberries are composed of three girls and three boys, yet part of the series' conceit is that the children are virtually interchangeable. Although Kemble assigns his characters gender, by way of dress and the labels "sisters" and "brothers," the Blackberries are void of individual personality. Nameless, nearly identical, and cast as objects of laughter, the Blackberry children are stuck in the mold of comic Other. The characters' lack of individuality implicitly reinforced the white belief that young African American children—or African Americans in general, for that matter—were indistinguishable from one another. Like much of contemporary pickaninny imagery, Kemble depicts the children gathered in clusters and close to one another in terms of age. As Kenneth W. Goings notes, such imagery "gave the impression of 'uncontrolled' breeding among African American[s]. . . . The closeness in age implies that African American women gave birth in litters, like animals, rather than one at a time, like humans."[31]

Blackberries took particular interest in mocking African Americans' relationship with consumer culture. In the Progressive Era, members of the working class, immigrants, and emancipated blacks apprehended consumption as a means of claiming and practicing civic membership. But the image of blacks freely purchasing commodities and partaking in amusements likely struck many members of the white middle and upper classes as absurd and troubling. *Blackberries* encapsulates these anxieties by linking black consumption to childishness. The series portrays black practices of consumerism and leisure as unrestrained, messy, and wrong. "The Blackberries Leave for the Country," for example, dismisses the Blackberries' sartorial choices as ludicrous attempts to "put on" whiteness (fig. 12).[32] The sisters cover their black bodies with long dresses, gloves, and bonnets that signify "proper" white, middle-class womanhood. But their choice of clothing only succeeds in highlighting the contrast between light-colored fabric and dark skin. Their "kinky" hair pokes out from underneath their bonnets, undermining their efforts to conceal their racial identity. One of the Blackberry brothers, in the meantime, wears a Scottish-inspired outfit—he dons a tam o'shanter and a kilt. By wearing tartan fabrics, he appears to make an "impossible" claim to Scottish heritage. He, as well as his brothers, recalls the figure of Zip Coon, the urban black dandy who "put on airs" by dressing up.[33] The presence of the grinning Mammy in the background, however, is a reminder of the "true" genealogy of the Blackberries; she is evidence of the children's "dark" and menial

Figure 12. Cartoon by E. W. Kemble. "The Blackberries Leave for the Country." In *New York Journal* Comic Supplement, May 30, 1897. SFS 60-1-5, San Francisco Academy of Comic Art Collection, the Ohio State University Billy Ireland Cartoon Library and Museum.

roots. Moreover, the awkward use of scale in the episode makes the Blackberry children appear to be the same height as the Mammy, implying that young blacks are too adultish to be vulnerable and innocent. At the same time, the figure of the "stunted" Mammy insists on the permanent childishness of black adults. As Carolyn Dean notes, the "perceived arrested intellect and childlike behavior of the African American" shored up notions of white superiority and dominance over blacks.[34] Images of infantile African American adults "tacitly cast the EuroAmerican consumer as [their] superior and [their] de facto parent."[35]

The series also persistently lampoons African Americans' attempts at play and leisure. Recreation was associated with healthy consumerism at the turn of the century; members of the middle class envisioned leisure—and vacationing in particular—as a privilege earned by those who had, through discipline and hard work, accrued the necessary resources to engage in such activities.[36] *Blackberries*, however, tethered its characters to ignorance and menial work, implying that blacks were incapable of, and had no right to, recreation. It is worth noting that in "Leave for the Country," the walls of the Blackberry household are mostly bare, lacking the portraits and paintings that were often understood as markers of middle-class status in the nineteenth and early twentieth centuries. The sole picture on the wall is that of roosters ostensibly sizing up one another in a cockfight. The Blackberries appear to openly display their propensity for gambling (and perhaps even their appetite for chicken); such commemoration seems to remind readers that the Blackberries are indulgent and have too many vices and thus have no right to recreation. The episode also shows how the children's vacation plans go awry even before they step out the door. The boys, who are frantically packing, have "jes sebenteen minutes" before their boat leaves.[37] Meanwhile, the girls are amused by the spectacle of distress, seemingly unconcerned that they may also miss the boat. They stand shoulder to shoulder at the threshold, blocking the exit, getting in the way of their own holiday. Another episode reinforces the notion that the image of the leisurely black is intrinsically paradoxical and unnatural. In "The Blackberry Picnic Is Interrupted by an Uninvited Guest," a bear that invades the picnic grounds seems baffled and even horrified by the sight of picnicking pickaninnies.[38] Even as most of the Blackberries scatter and abandon their food—which includes a "requisite" plate of chicken—the beast does not revel in its spoils. Instead, it stands frozen with the same expression of terror as the Blackberry girl who cowers in front of him. The episode collapses the boundary between wild animal and black child, showing how each perceives the other to be an uninvited guest.

Yet while *Blackberries* belittled blacks' consumption practices and, by implication, their claims to citizenship in a capitalist nation, the series repeatedly made the figure of the black child an amusing, delightful, even desirable, commodity. That the characters are named after fruit was a way of commodifying African American children; their bodies were implicitly transformed into food that was easy to digest and pleasurable to consume. The association of black children with food was not uncommon during the period. As Dean notes, in visual ephemera, young African Americans were commonly labeled or visualized as dark-colored, edible objects, such as sugar plums, chocolate, and zinfandel grapes.[39] As such, they were "served up to the EuroAmerican audience; often candied and sugar-coated, and always thoroughly objectified, they were offered for consumption."[40] The label "Blackberries" thus turns Kemble's characters into tiny, harmless objects that could be easily plucked and swallowed. These food metaphors were also expressive of white ambivalence over black children: white readers were encouraged to imagine enacting aggression toward young African Americans (as in the act of biting) while also viewing these "edible" children as appetizing rather than toxic or indigestible.

The episode "October = A Blackberry Idyll" similarly expresses white ambivalence over black childhood (fig. 13).[41] Two Blackberries sit on top of a raft, staring into one another's eyes. One of the Blackberry sisters raises her skirt as she dances the cakewalk, exposing her legs to her banjo-strumming companion. These scenes of flirtation insist that black children lack sexual innocence and, therefore, childhood innocence. Kemble remained vague about the exact nature of

Figure 13. Cartoon by E. W. Kemble. "October = A Blackberry Idyll." In *Chicago American* Comic Supplement, circa October 1901. SFS 1-13-5, San Francisco Academy of Comic Art Collection, the Ohio State University Billy Ireland Cartoon Library and Museum.

the relationship between the male and female Blackberries; they may or may not have been siblings. Thus "October" suggests that the characters may be engaging in incestuous liaisons, underscoring their depravity. But these affairs, it seems, will remain unconsummated. A Blackberry boy enviously glares at the couple atop the raft, the razor in his grip denoting his intent to disrupt their flirtation through violent means. A girl baits an alligator with a kitten, putting one of her companions, and likely the entire party, within the reach of the reptile's jaws. Her action insists on the "inherent" cruelty and ignorance of African Americans, indicating a propensity for placing animals and people in harm's way for the sake of amusement. David Pilgrim points out that the image of the pickaninny as easy prey to alligators and other wild animals was a popular trope of the period and "consistent with the many 19th and 20th century pseudo-scientific theories which claimed blacks were destined for extinction."[42] In Kemble's "October," the figure of the black girl baiting an alligator suggests that African Americans are complicit in the annihilation of their race.

"October" echoes the vicious themes of the children's reverse counting song *The Ten Little Niggers*, which McLoughlin Brothers published in sheet music form circa 1878. In this song, fantasies about black extermination are packaged in musical, rhyming couplets, and thus made pleasurable, permissible, and seemingly innocuous. The black characters die in quick succession, often meeting their demise because of ignorance and ineptitude. The lone survivor marries and has a brood of "Little Niggers Nine," whose story, the song promises, will be told "at another time."[43] *Ten Little Niggers* thus makes the perverse suggestion that the black race, despite having short lives that often end in brutish ways, will persist because of their animalistic inclination to overbreed. As such, they supposedly provide a limitless supply of entertainment to white audiences. The book intimates that readers' craving for images of black bodies in distress will always be satiated; even as one generation of African Americans dies off, another generation will take its place, ensuring continual exhibition of black suffering.

Like *Ten Little Niggers*, the "October" cartoon emphasizes that qualities of barbarism, self-destruction, and hypersexuality are emergent in black children. While the episode asserts that African Americans are, at birth, uncivilized and degenerate, it also implies that the inherent corruption of the Blackberry children is further exacerbated by feeble family ties. Purportedly because they lack parental attention, care, and instruction, the Blackberry children prematurely engage in "adult" activities. Overall, "October" plays on the notion that a "Blackberry idyll" is a paradoxical term, pointing to how the Blackberries taint a setting that is meant to be picturesque. They upend a quiet, natural scene with their display of violent, perverse acts.

Yet the spectacle of threatening/threatened childhoods in "October" ironically coaxes readers to view black children as easy and delightful to consume. Kyla Wazana Tompkins observes that in trading cards, which engaged in the business of peddling images of black bodies, "blackness consistently appears being bitten, stung, or pinched, betraying a visual pleasure in black pain that is also a desire to taste it."[44] In the particular trope of black children as "gator bait", "blackness returns as appetizing and sweet; black babies are 'dainty morsels' presented to the viewer in terms of their potential savor."[45] Kemble's cartoons perform similar work as the trading cards. "October," for example, serves the body of the black child in several ways: it turns the black child into a comestible product by way of reproducing the alligator bait motif, it sexualizes the young female African American, and it also turns the Blackberries into souvenirs that could be put on display. In marking the month of October, the episode references the decorative calendar, a popular novelty in the late nineteenth century. Even as the Blackberries perform "abominable" childhoods, they are presented as pleasurable, entertaining characters whose images could adorn the walls of a white, middle-class household.

The rural settings that Kemble uses in *Blackberries* may have also given some measure of enjoyment and comfort to his audience. For readers shocked by and wary of industrialization and urbanization, the image of pickaninnies at play in pastoral settings may have provided respite from the volatilities of city life. By imagining urbanized African Americans returning to the countryside, *Blackberries* also facilitates the fantasy of expelling blacks from metropolitan centers. Notably, the series suggests that urban living has corrupted the Blackberries. These citified black children, dressed in ostentatious clothes, have lost their "inherent" connection to the natural. Consequently, they are alien elements that violate the countryside. Put another way, the picture of Blackberries playing and picnicking in open fields, woods, and riverbanks disrupts contemporary "wholesome" images of romantic pastoral childhood. Nevertheless, *Blackberries* provides a reassuring picture of white cultural dominance: as with much contemporary pickaninny imagery, the image of black children in bucolic scenes not only glorifies a mythical South populated by playful, content blacks but also is a psychic attempt to exile African Americans to a world apart.

Racial Impersonation, Racial Contamination

Notably absent in *Blackberries* are depictions of racial encounters. In placing its characters in rural spaces, *Blackberries* hermetically seals off its characters from the urban "white" world. This banishment of the fictional Blackberry children was a figurative response to the increasing presence and visibility of African Americans in the day-to-day lives of the urban, white middle class.

One of Kemble's fellow Hearst cartoonists, Rudolph Dirks, borrowed a pair of Blackberries to acknowledge, rather than erase, the reality of racial intermingling. In the September 2, 1900, episode of *The Katzenjammer Kids*, Dirks depicts an encounter between Hans and Fritz and two Blackberry boys. As with other episodes of *Katzenjammer Kids*, "The Katzenjammer Kids Change Clothes with the Blackberry Brothers" focuses on the conflict between the prankish Katzenjammer boys and their exasperated mother (fig. 14).[46] In this instance, the young Katzenjammers recruit the Blackberry brothers to participate in their tomfoolery.

In appropriating and interpreting Kemble's characters, Dirks offers his interpretation of the "Negro type." While Dirks employs a simpler and looser style than Kemble, he similarly references the pickaninny stereotype in illustrating the Blackberry boys, drawing them with wide, round eyes; thick lips; and "kinky" hair. Dirks's Blackberries, however, are not urban dandies. Rather, they are "country boys," as suggested by the patchwork shirts, rolled-up pants, and wide-brimmed straw hats that they wear. And while Kemble remained ambiguous about the age of his characters—his Blackberries could be read as adultish children or childish adults—Dirks is straightforward in establishing the child status of the Blackberry brothers. In having the two sets of brothers swap clothes with one another, Dirks suggests that the Blackberry and Katzenjammer boys are of the same (child) size and possess the same sense of youthful mischief.

Still, "Katzenjammer Kids Change Clothes" maintains that black and white children have essential differences. The first panel juxtaposes the upright Katzenjammers, who walk in long, swinging strides, with the more inert Blackberries, who sit idly in front of a bush. In *Blackberries*, Kemble imagines black efforts at recreation as awkward and unnatural; in this first frame, Dirks characterizes the Blackberry boys as too passive to engage in leisure. They are "lazy little coons," more

Figure 14. Comic Strip by Rudolph Dirks. "The Katzenjammer Kids Change Clothes with the Blackberry Brothers." In *Chicago American* Comic Supplement, September 2, 1900. SFS 1-4-5, San Francisco Academy of Comic Art Collection, the Ohio State University Billy Ireland Cartoon Library and Museum.

props than active coconspirators in the Katzenjammer prank. Dean contends that at the turn of the century, visual juxtapositions of black and white children were "substituted for adults [and these images] created a comfortable, allegorical space in which issues such as racial discrimination, violence, and miscegenation could be discussed . . . the discriminatory behavior often displayed by EuroAmerican children in these images is characterized as 'natural' rather than culturally learned."[47] As in contemporary forms of visual humor, Dirks's depiction of interracial relations between black and white children imply the latter's superiority over the former, perpetuating notions of white dominance and racist attitudes toward blacks.

The curious thing, of course, is that the Katzenjammer boys' claim to whiteness is itself questionable. Of German heritage, they had the privilege of belonging to the "superior" Anglo-Saxon race. But their name kept their otherness front and center. "Katzenjammer" deliberately sounds outrageous: literally translated as "howling cats" and German slang for "hangover," the name linked the boys and their mother to disruption and vice.[48] Although early episodes of the series, including "Katzenjammer Kids Change Clothes," were "silent strips" that were devoid of dialogue, Dirks later highlighted his characters' ethnicity by depicting their speech as a rough, German-inflected dialect of English.[49] But in this episode, Mamma's frantic attempt to "scrub the coon kids white" signifies how she identifies as white.[50] She inhabits and performs whiteness through the act of "cleaning" the boys she assumes to be her sons, as the fear of being "contaminated" by blackness was very much a white preoccupation.

The period's visual culture—including newspaper comics—frequently reproduced the gag of "scrubbing off" blackness and, by implication, circulated the belief that blackness was a pollutant.[51] The notion that black skin "connoted filth and ugliness, darkness and disorder, evil and sin, disease and death" fueled anxieties about interactions between whites and blacks in the antebellum period.[52] The association of blackness with dirt and depravity persisted in the late nineteenth and earlier twentieth centuries, sustained by the ascendance of white supremacy movements and racist pseudosciences.[53] The motif of "cleaning" what was perceived to be the filthy black body has, in fact, a long history, one that can be traced to the Aesopic fable "The Blackamoor."[54] In the fable, a man purchases an Ethiopian slave and believes that the slave's dark skin was "due to his late owner's having neglected him."[55] The new slave owner gives the Ethiopian man a "good scrubbing," but "his skin remained as black as ever."[56] Because of the slave owner's misguided attempt, the Ethiopian nearly dies "from the cold he caught."[57] The story is linked to an adage that Dirks alludes to in his title: "washing the Ethiopian (or Blackamoor) white," which means "to labor in vain." As Jean Michel Massing points out, the maxim can also be traced to Jeremiah 13:23: "Can the Ethiopian change his skin, or the leopard his spots? Then may ye also do good, that are accustomed to do evil?"[58] Both the biblical verse and the fable offer this instruction: people cannot change their "true" nature. In the fable, the slave owner comes to understand that his slave's blackness is inherent rather than a result of external conditions. He concludes "that people's natures remain exactly as they first presented themselves."[59]

As Tanya Sheehan suggests, even as the motif of cleaning black bodies was a "symbol of impossibility," it remained a theme that lent itself well to comedy.[60] "Katzenjammer Kids Change Clothes" was only one of a good number of Progressive Era newspaper comics that reproduced the gag of black children being scoured. The image of Mamma Katzenjammer frantically scrubbing two dark-skinned children not only pokes fun at her naiveté but also serves up the Blackberry boys as comical props that help cast light on Mamma's ignorance. "Katzenjammer Kids Change Clothes" also naturalized and validated white women's fears about their children being "adulterated" by blackness. The strip focuses on Mamma's encounter with the Blackberry boys; the Blackberry Mammy's interaction with the Katzenjammer boys, apparently lacking in comic potential, occurs off-scene. Notably, when the Blackberry Mammy drags Hans and Fritz back to their mother, they are still fully dressed, implying she did not strip them down and bathe them. White skin, after all, did not connote grime or infection. Although the episode mocks Mamma's inability to distinguish between her fair-skinned sons and two black boys, the strip also suggests that her error is not so egregious, as dark complexion is shown to obscure distinguishing facial and bodily features, rendering individuals unrecognizable. That the Blackberry mother is the first to discover the prank does not mean she is necessarily more astute than Mamma: she recognizes the Katzenjammer boys because as white children, they are individuals rather than types.

The episode approaches blackness as repulsive, but like Outcault's *Buster Brown* episode "What Would You Do with a Boy like This?" it also encourages readers to take pleasure in viewing the bodies of black children. While the fair-skinned bodies of Hans and Fritz are not put on display, Dirks offers readers a glimpse of the Blackberries' buttocks. The image of the two unclothed Blackberries alludes to Goldie and Dustie, the Gold Dust Twins. These bald, half-naked, black mascots appeared in turn-of-the-century advertisements and trade cards and were used to hawk N. K. Fairbank and Company's Gold Dust Soap Powder. As Pilgrim notes, such nude images of pickaninnies "suggest[ed] that black children, and by extension black parents, are not concerned with modesty."[61] Images of black children exposing their genitalia and buttocks, as recurrent in turn-of-the-century visual and material culture, also "normalize[d] their sexual objectification."[62]

Yet even as "Katzenjammer Kids Change Clothes" maintains notions of racial difference and black inferiority, it also coaxes readers to recognize similarities between the Katzenjammers and the Blackberries. More specifically, the episode depicts its black and white characters as expressing similar emotions. The Blackberries wail and shed tears like their white counterparts, challenging the notion that black children are naturally resistant to pain. The penultimate panel shows the mirror images of Mammy and Mamma embracing their children, revealing that a black mother exhibits the same tenderness and concern for her children as a white mother. Mamma's initial failure to distinguish the Blackberry children from her own highlights her inattentiveness, yet it also gestures toward the universality of childhood: that the Katzenjammer kids and the Blackberry boys are able to swap identities so easily conveys their shared characteristics.

The episode also indicates that a genial relationship develops between the children. In the second panel, the four boys march into the shrubbery with their arms over one another's shoulders. Lined up in a row, white child alternates with black child, and they maintain close physical contact with one another. Yet while the boys do not seem to have interest in drawing the color line, they are aware of racial boundaries as *adults* have defined them. The children foresee that Mamma Katzenjammer would be distraught over the sight of her "blackened" sons. Although their prank eventually results in punishment—the Blackberries are scrubbed vigorously and the Katzenjammer Kids are spanked—the boys share a moment of pleasure as they take advantage of and play upon white adult anxieties about racial contamination.

Like "Katzenjammer Kids Change Clothes," the *Buster Brown* episode "What Would You Do with a Boy like This?" simultaneously shores up and undercuts concepts of racial difference. As in the *Katzenjammer Kids* episode, the white mother is depicted as at once overly fearful of racial contagion and shockingly imperceptive in telling two different boys apart. In the last panel, Buster chides his mother for mistaking a random "colored" child that Buster plucked from the street for her own son. "It is a wise mother that knows her child these days when all kids are Busters," he writes in his resolution.[63] The episode reprimands Mrs. Brown for lacking the "wisdom" to tell black from white, for falling victim to her son's pranks, and for failing to insulate their home from "strange" and "menacing" things that lurked in the street. Buster's mother is unable to fulfill the turn-of-the-century ideal of motherhood, which envisioned the mother as the child's primary guardian, tasked with ensuring that the home was a sanctuary that kept children safe from "dirty" outside elements.[64]

Yet Buster's declaration that "all kids are Busters" lends ambivalence to the episode. The phrase suggests that the difference between black and white is not always clear-cut: it offers the notion that regardless of race, children share common qualities. This view of sameness that Outcault offered was not so radical. As Dean notes, the subject of "parity of [white and black] children" was widely discussed even in the antebellum period: "numerous mid-nineteenth-century thinkers, both pro- and anti-slavery, had argued that African-American offspring were quite different from their elder counterparts as the children possessed an intellect equal to that of their white peers (whereas, the argument goes, adults clearly did not)."[65]

Of course, one cannot ignore that the main joke in "What Would You Do" hinges on the unequal status of Buster and the black boy. The gag begins when Buster, an affluent white child, offers a dollar to an indigent black child. While their apparent economic transaction can be understood as a repudiation of slavery—the black boy seems to participate in the prank out of choice, and he has a promise of compensation for his "labor"—it is worth noting that readers never get to see money change hands. The black boy seems to end up performing the impersonation for free and, figuratively, ends up paying for the prank. He is stripped naked and dunked in a tub, while Buster, who usually is spanked for his mischiefs, remains unscathed. The black child temporarily becomes Buster's proxy, suffering punishment on the white child's behalf. It is disturbing to think that this episode, which turns the image of a traumatized black body into an amusing spectacle, was published a few weeks after the lynchings of Horace Duncan, Fred Coker, and Will Allen in a public square in Springfield, Missouri.

In his resolution, Buster remains mute on the subject of unequal black and white childhoods. "Some people are stark blind," he writes—a statement that becomes ironic in light of his own obliviousness to racial injustice. Even as "What Would You Do" hints at the porousness of the boundary between the black child and the white child, it also hardens this color line. It gestures toward the universality of childhood while ultimately endorsing the "fact" of black inferiority.

Performing Healthy Boyhood: White Boys in Blackface

Like Dirks's "Katzenjammer Kids Change Clothes" and Outcault's "What Would You Do," the April 17, 1904, episode of Carl E. "Bunny" Schultze's *Foxy Grandpa* explores the relationship between white childhood and blackness, but it does so in a different way: both child and adult characters play tricks on one another by donning blackface. In the episode titled "The Little Rogues Pretend They Are Pickaninnies, but a Good-Sized Darkey Gives Them Quite a Fright," Foxy Grandpa's two grandsons attempt to disguise themselves and fool their grandfather by applying burnt cork to their faces and wearing oversized, loud-patterned clothes (fig. 15).[66] Blackface radically transforms the boys. The burnt cork mask changes not only their skin tone but also the size and shape of their facial features. In other words, they turn into bug-eyed, thick-lipped pickaninnies. As in "Katzenjammer Kids

Figure 15. Comic Strip by Carl E. "Bunny" Schultze. "Foxy Grandpa: The Little Rogues Pretend They Are Pickaninnies." In *St. Louis Republic* Comic Supplement, April 17, 1904. SFS 3-4-3, San Francisco Academy of Comic Art Collection, the Ohio State University Billy Ireland Cartoon Library and Museum.

Change Clothes," "Little Rogues" implies that black skin tones—whether natural or artificial—obscure distinguishable characteristics and, in effect, erase individuality.

Foxy Grandpa, remaining true to his name, slyly turns the tables on the boys. He puts on blackface to metamorphose into a "good-sized darkey." At the sight of what appears to be a large black man in their home, the two boys flee in terror. Their reaction contrasts with the Katzenjammer boys' fearlessness in interacting with the Blackberries. Hans and Fritz do not feel threatened by the Blackberries, as perhaps they believe that the Blackberry brothers, being young, and their Mammy, being female, are docile. In juxtaposing the *Katzenjammer Kids* and *Foxy Grandpa* episodes, one can note distinct ways that immigrant and white childhoods are conceptualized in relation to blackness. The "ethnic" Katzenjammers do not perceive they have anything to lose by exposing themselves to dark-skinned strangers. For Foxy Grandpa's grandsons, the stakes are higher: they sense racial interaction as a threat to the sanctity of whiteness. Moreover, the looming "darkey" they encounter recalls the "brute Negro" caricature, a figure that emerged during Reconstruction. In response to emancipation, white supremacists perpetuated the notion that the freed black man would regress into his "natural" animalistic self.[67] Although the black brute was imagined as a figure who defiled "virginal" white women, "Little Rogues" suggests how the caricature was also deployed as a boogeyman that terrorized children.

In the last panel of "Little Rogues," however, the boys' fright turns into delight. After Foxy Grandpa reveals himself to his grandsons, the trio maintain their disguises and put on an impromptu minstrel show. Their performance appears to be loud and rowdy. It takes place outside the home, indicating that the game of "pretending to be black" is too disorderly and unsettling to stage in enclosed domestic spaces. The panel also offers assurance to readers that Foxy Grandpa and his grandsons are *temporarily* trying on blackness. The characters expose their fair hair and skin, reassuring readers they have not abandoned their white identities.

The joyful expressions of Foxy Grandpa and his grandsons communicate that this "transgressive" game of acting black has its pleasures. On the one hand, the characters' staging of a minstrel show could be understood as a performance of what Eric Lott calls "love and theft" of black culture. Working-class whites who frequented minstrel shows in the antebellum period identified with the black characters they saw onstage; while such identification enabled them to develop sympathy for African Americans, they also "stole" the qualities associated with black men—as white actors imagined and depicted them onstage—to assert themselves in the American social order.[68] "Little Rogues" illustrates how white, middle-class boys in the early twentieth century could also turn to and draw from what was perceived to be black culture as a means to explore and assert their boyishness and, in effect, become vigorous young males who would safeguard their Anglo-Saxon legacy.

On the other hand, the minstrel show staged by Foxy Grandpa and his grandsons should also be understood in the context of amateur minstrelsy. Although professional minstrelsy declined by the 1890s, blackface performances staged by amateur actors, including women and children, emerged in the first decade of the twentieth century and thrived in the decades that followed. Susan Smulyan argues that amateur minstrelsy created a sense of nostalgia for the "good ol' days" before Emancipation, the period when professional minstrelsy flourished.[69] Those who participated in amateur minstrel shows understood their performances as pushbacks against the development of film technology and other trends of modernization that were purportedly eradicating "old-time" entertainments.[70] Apprehensions about the effect of radical technological changes on the "art" of minstrelsy paralleled concerns about white children, specifically boys, being "softened" by modern life. In some contexts, amateur minstrelsy was seen as a means to help children recover their "lost" vitality. In early twentieth-century summer camps, for example, young campers performed "cross-racial play," staging minstrel shows under the supervision and encouragement of adults.[71] Implicit in such cross-racial play was a romanticization of black culture and a critique of modernization. African Americans were perceived to possess the "qualities deemed at risk in modern children's busy lives: health, sincerity of feeling, simplicity, play," and the act of borrowing from (an imagined) black culture purportedly enabled young campers to maintain their "natural" vigor.[72] Similarly, "Little Rogues" proposes that the game of minstrelsy ensures the grandsons' physical fitness and, by extension, sustains their moral character.

"Little Rogues" imagines the minstrel show not only as a pastime that revitalized white children but also as a family activity that reinforced the bonds between children and their elders. The performance of a "tried-and-true" form of entertainment allows Foxy Grandpa to strengthen his relationship with his grandsons. Moreover, in instructing the boys to "keep step," Foxy Grandpa intimates that the act of appropriating blackness is a family and racial tradition that allows one to access and practice whiteness. As Leslie Paris suggests, minstrel shows staged in early twentieth-century summer camps "represented a form of intergenerational cultural transmission, socializing white children into modern American citizenship."[73] Amateur minstrelsy was a means for white, middle-class men, women, and children to confirm their position in a racial hierarchy and hone their conceptualizations of racial difference.[74] Performances allowed participants to define what it meant to be white and middle class, often "align[ing] racial stereotyping with good taste and gentility."[75] Moreover, as Smulyan puts it, such shows allowed performers to "[signal] that they could afford to buy things to amuse themselves (because the performances depended on instruction books and other purchased products)."[76] By putting on blackness, Foxy Grandpa and his grandsons work to inhabit the roles they are expected to play as white, middle-class males.

While Foxy Grandpa and his grandsons temporarily wear blackness, a character from another comic strip series exemplifies the consequences of racial impersonation gone too far. Flip, one of the recurring characters in Winsor McCay's popular *Little Nemo in Slumberland*, was perhaps the most visible child-minstrel figure in turn-of-the-century comic supplements. As Edward A. Shannon notes, Flip is reminiscent of actors who appeared in minstrel shows and vaudeville.[77] Flip's whiteness is repeatedly affirmed in *Little Nemo*: his fair-skinned body is revealed in bathing scenes and his genealogy is traced to the white Dawn family. But because he chooses to permanently cover his face in greasepaint, he displays an inability to distinguish between healthy minstrel play and being black. In wearing a seemingly indelible mask, Flip perpetually acts as the racial Other. He is a young amateur minstrel who refuses to bow out of his performance.

Incapable of ceasing or controlling his "act," Flip pulsates with vulgarity and antagonism. In the early episodes of the series, he serves as Nemo's foil. The "little scamp" constantly interrupts Nemo's quest to meet the Princess of Slumberland, purposefully working to "fix [Nemo] and make it hot for him."[78] He unabashedly declares his desire for the Princess, whom he calls "a peach."[79] In inhabiting blackness without restraint, Flip becomes crude and malicious, a threat to fellow white children. His desire for the Princess specifically evokes the figure of the black brute lusting after white women. In short, Flip represents the perils of an undisciplined, unchecked performance of blackness.[80]

A 1908 episode of *Little Nemo* further elucidates the burdens attendant to putting on blackness. In this installment, Nemo and Flip strip down to their shorts to take a dip in a lake.[81] But the "water" turns out to be black molasses, and they emerge to find their white bodies coated with the sticky substance. Covered by molasses from head to foot, the boys resemble pickaninnies, with Nemo's hair even becoming "nappy." The sticky layer makes the children's bodies appear naked yet asexual, expressing a paradoxical view of the relationship between blackness and sexuality. On the one hand, the boys' "exposed" and blackened bodies evoke the notion of blacks' sexual immodesty. On the other hand, the molasses' concealment of their phalli articulates white compulsion to emasculate and desexualize black male bodies. Nemo, worrying that his appearance may upset his female cousin, desperately wants to wash off the molasses. He and Flip try to make their way home and attempt to hitch a ride on a wagon that happens to be carrying flour. The two boys end up covered with the baking ingredient. Nemo and Flip thus become doubly coated figures, two white children dipped in blackness and dusted with whiteness. When they finally appear before Nemo's cousin, she turns away and exclaims, "What are those? Oh!"[82] Unequivocally repulsed by the sight of these near-naked figures, the cousin is a model of virtuous girlhood. She behaves accordingly, offended and frightened by bodies that represent the "unnatural" mingling of black and white. For the cousin, the boys' bodies evoke miscegenation and the figure of the "sullied" mixed-race child. In labeling the black-and-white Nemo and Flip as "those," she categorizes them as objects rather than persons.

Not So Black-and-White: Liminal Lil Mose

While *Little Nemo* demonstrates how Progressive Era comic supplements touted reductive and discriminatory views of African Americans, some contemporary newspaper comics attempted to encourage sympathy for blacks. Such sentiment was perhaps best expressed in R. F. Outcault's series *Pore Lil Mose.*[83]

In 1898, Outcault retired the Yellow Kid, claiming that the character that helped establish his career now suffered from overexposure.[84] Indeed, the Yellow Kid fad had waned at this point. Outcault took the position of in-house artist in James Gordon Bennett Jr.'s *New York Herald*, where he drew spot illustrations for jokes and children's stories and produced numerous one-off gag cartoons, many of which featured Mammies, Sambos, and pickaninnies. Like some of his contemporaries, Outcault obviously capitalized on the popularity of black caricatures.

In December 1900, Outcault launched a series that featured a recurring character. As with his Yellow Kid series, the headlining character was once again an "Other" child. This time around, his protagonist was not an immigrant child but a little black boy named Mose. Early episodes of *Pore Lil Mose* were set in a fictional town in Georgia called Cottonville and revolved around the comic antics of Mose, his pickaninny friends, his family, and a community of "coons." These initial episodes also featured a subplot of Mose gradually forming a gang of animals. Later in the series, Mose and his animal friends strike out for New York City. These latter episodes shift to an epistolary mode, as Mose narrates his urban adventures in the form of letters addressed to his mother.

With his thick lips, large eyes, and extremely dark skin, Mose is reminiscent of Kemble's Blackberries as well as other "coonlets" that appeared in advertisements, song sheets, and marginalia published in the *Herald* and other newspapers. His name associates him with the Uncle Mose caricature, a black butler who faithfully serves his white "massa."[85] The labels "pore" and "lil" also insists on Mose's pathetic, diminutive state. Furthermore, "lil" alludes to Helen Bannerman's *The Story of Little Black Sambo* (1899), the popular children's book in which Bannerman Africanizes an Indian boy by naming him Sambo and drawing him with golliwog features.[86] Other black characters in *Pore Lil Mose* are similarly positioned as objects of ridicule, as Outcault portrays them as bumbling and cowardly. Mose is both protagonist and interlocutor; as he relates stories in stereotypical black dialect, he encourages readers to laugh at him and his fellow African Americans.

Yet Mose is significantly different from the Blackberries. While Kemble's nameless characters are indistinguishable from one another, Mose is not associated with a "litter of coons." He is a distinct individual, the central character and narrator of his own series. While Kemble's little urban dandies constantly return to the countryside, their purported natural habitat, Mose leaves his rural home to explore the city. He also seems to successfully integrate into his urban surroundings. As Alan Havig puts it, Mose finds himself in an "alien, though not hostile, environment," where white characters often treat him with sympathy and kindness.[87] Moreover, when the series shifts to an epistolary narrative, readers are allowed to read Mose's intimate letters and thus encouraged to develop an empathic connection with a protagonist who is racially Other.

Pore Lil Mose unquestionably perpetuates typographies that insist on the inferiority of African Americans. The episode "Poor Lil Mose on the 7 Ages" asserts that the black male's life cycle is essentially an evolution from one caricature to another (fig. 16).[88] In this episode, Mose reinterprets a famous monologue from Shakespeare's *As You Like It*, in which Jaques describes man's seven ages: infant, schoolboy, lover, soldier, justice, pantaloon, and "second childishness."[89] Mose offers a verse in which he "blackens up" Jaques's monologue and he imagines his male relatives representing each of the seven ages. In his verse, he turns the infant into a "tiny picaninn[y]" and the schoolboy and lover into "lazy mokes / Wot nebber does a lick ob work, but jes' lives on dere folks."[90] The accompanying image shows Mose in the role of the schoolboy. He grins at the reader while he stands before a watermelon patch that has a sign that reads, "Help yo-self to water mellyuns."[91] Mose also turns the soldier into a "sol'jer coon"; his pa, in the role of the soldier, marches with a sword and sheath that drag on the ground, metaphors for an oversized phallus.[92] Mose's Uncle Jim appears to fit Jaques's description of the "lean and slipper'd

Figure 16. Cartoon by R. F. Outcault. "Poor Lil Mose on the 7 Ages." In *New York Herald* Comic Supplement, February 3, 1901. SFS 27-2-1, San Francisco Academy of Comic Art Collection, the Ohio State University Billy Ireland Cartoon Library and Museum.

pantaloon / With spectacles on nose and pouch on side," but Uncle Jim's pouch is stuffed with a rooster.[93] The episode also envisions the "seben ages ob de woman" as the black female's movement from a pickaninny to a bare-shouldered coquette to a Mammy whose face increasingly becomes wizened.[94] Here, the black female grows up to fulfill sexual and servile roles. She is literally marginalized, reduced to adornments along the borders of the cartoon.

In imagining the life cycles of black men and women, Outcault reproduces racist notions of the nature of African Americans. However, he also hints at similarities between blacks and whites. "7 Ages" suggests that African American lives inevitably move toward pathos, representing blacks as destined to become white-haired, weary men and women "sans everything."[95] Yet the phrase "sans everything" is quoted directly from Shakespeare's play.[96] This borrowed phrase hints at the shared humanity of blacks and whites, insisting that people, regardless of race, are treading the same path toward what Jaques calls "mere oblivion." Images of enfeebled black men and women may be tragic (as well as reassuring to white observers), but it may also have had a humanizing effect, prompting readers to view African Americans with solicitude.

Outcault's ambivalence toward blackness is most effectively embodied by Mose. This fictional black child is at once a clumsy comic object and a wise observer. Although Mose recounts events in stereotypical black dialect, he writes in legible, cursive penmanship and narrates in the form of rhymed, metered verse. Certainly, his poetic voice is a nod toward the supposed inherent musicality of African Americans, but it also implies his erudition, suggesting that he possesses familiarity with "highbrow" culture and an aptitude for language. In "7 Ages," Mose refers to himself as a "whining schoolboy," yet he displays gentility and wit as he accesses, comprehends, and reinterprets a verse from the English literary canon. He even criticizes "ole Bill Shakespeare" for not "hab[bing] de space" to write about women's seven ages.[97] Mose promptly corrects this error by imagining the life cycle of black women. Of course, the character of Mose also reveals the limitations of the image of a smart, cultivated black boy. While Outcault elevates Mose from the realm of risible stereotype, the character's "redemption" can only come through his adoption of white notions of intellect and culture. In other words, even as Mose demonstrates that black children can be more than just pickaninnies, he does not subvert the dominant white culture that enforced a caste system and dictated standards of sophistication and knowledge.

Pore Lil Mose contains similar contradictory signals about its protagonist's class status. In some early Cottonville episodes, the character is barefoot and dressed in ragged clothes, while in other episodes, he wears a Little Lord Fauntleroy outfit. In the New York City episodes, he wears "tasteful" clothes that suggest cultivation and affluence. He freely partakes of urban amusements and is even able to afford a $750 hat for his mother. In the episode "He Comes to New York," Mose relates that he and his animal cohort skip a meal because "we hadn't any money."[98] But the same episode shows him being welcomed into the

Waldorf-Astoria. The hint of a smile on the concierge's face indicates that the presence of Mose and his animal friends in this extravagant hotel has raised neither questions nor alarm. Of course, the vagueness surrounding Mose's class status is expressive of a refusal to acknowledge and address the very real destitution that many African Americans suffered. Mose's ability to gallivant around the city and consume goods turns him into an iteration of the "happy black." Still, the image of a "refined" and possibly well-off Mose may have also affirmed the possibility that blacks could climb the socioeconomic ladder.

Most significantly, Mose embodies conflicting views about the nature of the African American child. A number of *Pore Lil Mose* episodes set up the protagonist as a liminal character, depicting him as simultaneously corrupt and pure, as a figure who is meant to inspire both disdain and admiration. In "Pore Lil Mose Talks to the Animals," Mose's connection with animals illustrates how he is at once savage and innocent (fig. 17).[99] In depicting Mose's "natural" link with farm animals and wild beasts, with whom he has "long conversations wif . . . nearly every day," the episode anticipates a 1906 postcard, distributed by the New York–based Ullman Manufacturing Company, that bears the caption "Whose Baby Is Oo?" (fig. 18).[100] On the postcard, a black child crawls on all fours, eye to eye with a pig, a juxtaposition that implies that the child is "more animal than

Figure 17. Cartoon by R. F. Outcault. "Pore Lil Mose Talks to the Animals." In *New York Herald* Comic Supplement, February 24, 1901. SFS 27-2-4, San Francisco Academy of Comic Art Collection, the Ohio State University Billy Ireland Cartoon Library and Museum.

Figure 18. Postcard. "Whose Baby Is Oo?" featuring black child and piglet. Ullman Mfg. Co., New York, 1906. From author's collection.

human."[101] Of course, white children were also imagined as sharing connections with animals, as indicated by another Ullman postcard released that same year. This postcard's illustration, signed by Katharine Gassaway, is similarly captioned "Whose Baby Is Oo?" However, it features a white child staring into the eyes of a puppy (fig. 19). Both Ullman postcards link children to beasts and encourage viewers to find pleasure in gazing at half-nude children. But when placed side by side, the postcards express the view that black and white babies have inherent differences. The white child modestly sits back on his legs, as tame as a pet. Meanwhile, the black child crawls on the grass, approaching an animal that is typically perceived to live in and consume filth. These images reveal the disparity between the ways white and black children are viewed. The white child belongs in domestic spaces; he is meant to be sheltered, coddled, and sentimentalized, very much like a pet. The black child is domesticated too—but less as a pet and more as a farm animal. He is linked to beasts who deserve less affection as they are "naturally" meant to provide labor or to be sent to the slaughterhouse.

Like the postcard featuring the pig and the black child, the episode "Talks to the Animals" evokes the image of "beastly" young blacks. Mose develops relationships with "dirty" pigs, "ignorant" mules, "crafty" foxes, and a number of other undomesticated beasts. The episode mocks Mose's ability to talk to animals by bringing it to the realm of the absurd, depicting him holding a conversation with a hare over the phone. Yet in connecting Mose with beasts, the episode also complicates the image of the black child as necessarily animalistic and crude. Mose aligns himself with animals as he believes they "mos'ly always tell de troof," conveying that he prizes integrity and open-heartedness.[102] He is also portrayed

Figure 19. Postcard. "Whose Baby Is Oo?" featuring white child and puppy. Ullman Mfg. Co., New York, 1906. From author's collection.

as a civilizing force: the animals seem to develop manners in his presence. Pigs patiently wait in line for their turn to speak with him; a fox is so deeply engaged in conversation with Mose that it is able to suppress its urge to devour two geese that stand nearby. Another scene places Mose in a naturalistic setting, in which woodland creatures gather around him to "have a pleasant evenin' in a quiet sort o' way / Discussin' all important books an' topics ob de day."[103] Still, the episode reminds readers that the civilized/civilizing Mose is an exception among African Americans. Mose himself implicitly contrasts his peaceful nature with the viciousness of "nigger[s]" and "coons" who, as some of his four-legged friends report, mistreat and indiscriminately butcher animals.[104]

Over the course of several episodes, Mose builds a hodgepodge gang, which includes a monkey, a mouse-hound, a cat, and a baby bear. As a figure who walks among and with beasts, Mose is characterized as a child of nature. That his gang is a mixture of wild and domesticated animals suggests that Mose simultaneously embodies what Chris Jenks calls Dionysian and Apollonian childhoods: Mose is, on the one hand, a wild child who is driven by a "primal force," who "loves pleasure [and] celebrates self-gratification," and on the other hand, "an innocent child who has a natural goodness."[105] In other words, he is both pickaninny and innocent. He is a child "stained" by blackness but also a black figure "purified" by his child status.

Other scholars have noted that *Pore Lil Mose* endorses, sometimes simultaneously, opposing views regarding race and African Americans. Havig argues that in the series, "Outcault presented a dual, somewhat contradictory, vision of blacks."[106] Havig contends that while many of the series' early installments "exploited the comic black image unmercifully," presenting them as "lazy, irresponsible, physically ugly 'niggers,'" explicit racism is absent in later episodes, as the shift to an urban setting transforms the series into a "racially-neutral social satire."[107] In the New York City episodes, Mose's otherness is not the central focus of humor. Instead, these episodes satirize urban life, with Mose serving as a Jonathan figure, an ignorant-yet-wise greenhorn.[108] Readers were encouraged to identify with the little black boy who tries to cope with the stresses and excesses of city life. Sometimes, he is the object of laughter, the oaf who clumsily makes his way through the streets of Gotham. But most episodes depict Mose as successful in his effort to navigate the crowded city streets, even showing him taking pleasure in his urban surroundings. He is a small figure who triumphs over the chaos of the big city; readers who themselves felt alienated by urbanization could thus identify and root for him.

Like Havig, Ian Gordon argues that the episodes set in New York give Mose a "greater depth of character."[109] But Gordon points out that these urban episodes still trade on racial stereotypes. He points to how the episode "He Buys His Mammy a Hat," in which Mose purchases an expensive feathered hat for his mother to replace her bandanna, mocks black extravagance as well as the black woman's supposedly misguided attempts to appear more becoming and cultivated.[110] Moreover, a number of episodes set in New York depict Mose's presence in the city as disruptive. When Mose and his friends ride a streetcar, Mose notes that other passengers "stare / An' gather roun' an' gap[e], at me, and lil Billie Bear."[111] Mose tries to practice proper decorum, sitting upright with his hands on his lap, careful not to invade the personal space of other passengers. But his monkey companion, unable to control himself, hangs on the straps and grabs a fellow passenger's hat. The episode emphasizes Mose's duality, showing how he is at once civilized and uncultivated, simultaneously following and breaking the rules. The monkey signifies the part of Mose that remains undisciplined and unfit for city life. While the boy sits quietly, his simian self refuses to be contained. An inset in the same episode shows three children terrorized by the sight of Billie Bear. For some residents of New York, Billie Bear, and by extension Mose, is a strange and unsettling presence.

Pore Lil Mose, however, also pokes fun at anxieties surrounding racial encounters. The episode "He Visits the Suburbs—and Frightens a Native"—the word "native" here alluding to proponents of the nativist movement—ridicules hysterical responses to the presence of African Americans (and immigrants) in the city. A sign posted on a wall warns residents to take caution: "Beware of Everything. These days all kinds of things are loose. Anything is liable to happen."[112] A woman and her child read the sign, and they appear agitated by the mere *thought* of encountering "all kinds of things." Once they see Mose's gang, they panic, even as the calm demeanor of the black boy and his friends rebuts the image of the criminal black menace. In this episode, the so-called natives become the target of humor. The faces and bodies of the frightened mother and son are comically contorted, and the mother is particularly mocked for her lack of restraint. When she comes across a policeman, she clings to him, then (forcibly) stages a quick courtship by declaring, "Oh George this is so suddent."[113] Outcault does employ visual codes to suggest that mother and child are members of the working class, as she wears what appear to be black work boots as well as a hat adorned with cheap-looking flowers. Here, the episode implies that members of the laboring classes lack the cultivation to respond to the presence of "strangers" in a civil manner. Moreover, it alludes to tensions between the white, working class and African Americans, as the former viewed the latter as potential competition for employment and resources. Order is restored, however, when her son—who has a claim to whiteness whereas Mose does not—asserts his superiority. The young boy overcomes his fear of Mose and his gang. Straddling Billie Bear, the son assures his mother that he is "all right."[114] Billie Bear typically walks upright on his hind legs, but here, he drops to all fours to accommodate the boy. This image gestures to the potential of the white male child to "tame" forces deemed wild and threatening.

Pore Lil Mose vacillates between racist and sympathetic representations of African Americans, particularly African American children. The series blatantly reproduces racial typographies, reinforcing the notion that the black child is a pickaninny, a little buffoon who is inferior to the white child. But the series' constantly developing plot and its ambiguity in characterization also allow its caricature-based protagonist to become more than a one-dimensional, laughable character. In many instances, Mose breaks out of the static mold of the pickaninny, emerging as an agentic child who independently and confidently makes his way through New York City. While Kemble's Blackberries, left unsupervised, engage in "risky" activities, autonomous Mose lives out what appears to be a rags-to-riches story, fulfilling the American ideal of individualism. By uprooting himself from Cottonville and extricating himself from his menial, servile "roots," he transforms into a well-dressed, well-mannered city boy who is able to support himself.[115]

Outcault claimed that "scores of children and many adults . . . wrote letters addressed to Mose containing expressions of kind wishes."[116] Yet even as the series apparently developed a following, it folded in September 1902, less than two years after it debuted. Perhaps its relatively short run was an indication that its nuanced depiction of a black child was too contradictory, too impossible to remain viable. In an era marked by Jim Crow laws and antiblack violence in the South, segregation and discrimination in the North, and the embrace of white supremacy and racist pseudosciences by political and intellectual leaders, comics characters such as Mose, as Gordon puts it, "could not sustain the burden of being innocent and sagelike at the same time. African American characters could have been wise fools, but for them to have been knowingly so would have suggested too much complexity of character and shattered too many typographies."[117]

Denigrating views of African Americans certainly persisted among the *Herald*'s editors and young readers, at least as suggested by the readers' contributions published alongside *Pore Lil Mose*. Ernest Creet, a member of the *Herald*'s Camera Club, sent in a photograph of three black boys on a ship (fig. 20).[118] The photograph bears the title "Three of a Kind Taken on Board the SS New York," reinforcing the message that Kemble made in *Blackberries*: black children lack individualizing features and are indistinguishable from one another. Another photograph features a young white child named Belle Frye wearing a top hat and a patterned suit and whose face was covered in burnt cork.[119] The caption describes Frye as "[doing] the cake walk cleverly."[120] Like the *Foxy Grandpa* episode "Little Rogues," the photograph documents how minstrelsy was becoming a prevalent form of domestic entertainment, of child's play, at the dawn of the twentieth century. Seven-year-old Dorothy M. Yulee submitted a poem titled "Greedy Lil Mose" to the *Herald*.[121] Appropriating Outcault's character, she emphasizes Mose's avarice and clumsiness by having him fall into a tureen full of soup as he rushes toward a jar of jam. Yulee's poem is clearly modeled after Outcault's work, as it is also written in "black" dialect. The short lyric provides a glimpse of how white children were appropriating (and arguably encouraged to

Figure 20. Photograph by Ernest Creet. "Three of a Kind Taken on Board the SS New York." In *New York Herald* Children's Supplement, October 6, 1901. SFS 28-4-1, San Francisco Academy of Comic Art Collection, the Ohio State University Billy Ireland Cartoon Library and Museum.

appropriate) what was perceived to be a black voice and perspective, in the spirit of play and creativity. Outcault apparently approved of the poem, as he adorned it with elaborate illustrations. In doing so, he not only rewarded Yulee for her creative work but also endorsed the racist attitudes expressed in the poem.

Although *Pore Lil Mose* was short-lived, the series served an important purpose in Outcault's career. A year and a half after the debut of *Pore Lil Mose*, Outcault began a new series for the *Herald*. The new comic strip was headlined by a white, affluent boy who curiously bore many similarities to Mose. Like Mose, this child exercised autonomy, freely exploring the city streets. His Little Lord Fauntleroy outfit strongly resembled the clothes that Mose wore during his urban adventures. Like Mose, this character also had an animal companion—a bull terrier named Tige. This little white boy was clearly modeled after a little black child. The link between Outcault's two characters, one white and the other black, is reminiscent of the theme of "Little Rogues": the white male child came to life by drawing from blackness, by appropriating the "natural" energy and spirit of African American culture. The character's name can even be interpreted as a nod to a dark hue of skin: Buster Brown.

In July 20, 1902, Outcault gave Mose a cameo in an episode of *Buster Brown* (fig. 21).[122] In this installment, Buster invites Mose and his animal gang into his home. Unlike the later episode "What Would You Do with a Boy like This?" in which Buster approaches the poor black child as a minor player in one of his pranks, Buster greets Mose as his equal, as an acquaintance whom he wishes to introduce to his father. When Mr. Brown wakes up from a nap, he is startled by the sight of Mose and his animals. Despite the similarities between Buster and Mose—their size, their clothes, their animal companions—Buster's father tumbles backward, shocked by what he believes to be nightmarish elements come to life. Buster tries to calm down his stricken father by insisting that Mose and his animals "are real."[123] By asserting Mose's "realness," Buster takes on the role of the innocent white child who possesses what Jenks calls a "clarity of vision": he sees a black boy as an "authentic" child rather than a pickaninny, as a person rather than an object upon which white fantasies about blackness are projected.[124] Yet even as Buster argues for the authenticity of Mose, even as he calls him his "friend," he is keenly aware that Mose does not belong inside his white, middle-class home. After Mr. Brown falls over, Buster instructs Mose and his animals to leave. Failing to defend his black friend, the white child has no recourse but to exile him.

Mose's exit from "Buster Brown and Pore Lil Mose" was also a farewell to readers. In a matter of weeks, *Pore Lil Mose* ended its run in the *Herald*. There appears to have been very little to-do over the end of the series, as readers found themselves quickly enchanted with Mose's replacement. As Buster Brown found himself on the path to becoming Outcault's most popular and enduring creation, the black boy who served as Buster's template was quickly forgotten.

Figure 21. Comic Strip by R. F. Outcault. "Buster Brown and Pore Lil Mose." In *New York Herald* Comic Supplement, July 20, 1902. SFS 30-1-3a, San Francisco Academy of Comic Art Collection, the Ohio State University Billy Ireland Cartoon Library and Museum.

CHAPTER 3

FAMILY AMUSEMENTS

Perhaps no other comic strip child had as broad an appeal to Progressive Era readers as Buster Brown. R. F. Outcault's eponymous strip first appeared in the *New York Herald* on May 4, 1902, and it quickly developed into a commercial, cultural, and national phenomenon. The series was syndicated and published in newspapers in major cities, including Boston, Chicago, Los Angeles, and St. Louis until 1921. It was also adapted into plays and short films. The strip's popularity extended beyond the shores of the United States, as *Buster Brown* adaptations appeared in newspapers in Brazil, France, and Italy.[1] Today, the character Buster Brown remains strongly associated with the Brown Shoe Company, which, in 1904, began utilizing Buster's name and image to sell children's shoes. In fact, Outcault tirelessly marketed his character, licensing Buster to manufacturers of textiles, musical instruments, food products, and a variety of other goods.[2] Americans avidly consumed dolls, games, and toys associated with the blond, blue-eyed boy whose Little Lord Fauntleroy outfit implied cherubic innocence but who was nonetheless constantly getting into trouble with adults.

Buster's image as an incorrigible mischief-maker has endured over the decades. Progressive Era commentators as well as comics historians and scholars writing in the late twentieth and early twenty-first centuries have largely viewed *Buster Brown* as a subversive series, as it features a prankish protagonist who undermines adult authority and appears to pose a threat to family stability. On the surface, it is easy to regard the title character as an embodiment of anarchy. He is one of the comic strip characters that educator Percival Chubb denounced in a 1911 speech at the Child Welfare Exhibit in New York; Chubb railed against the comic strips for their celebration of "the smart child, proficient in monkey tricks; the cheeky, disrespectful, and irreverent child, who 'guys' his elders and betters; the libertine child of silly, humoring parents."[3] Decades later, comics historians Bill Blackbeard and Martin Williams describe Buster as one of the "demon children" who dominated the pages of turn-of-the-century newspaper comic supplements.[4] For his part, Charles Hatfield contends that Outcault's character functions to upend the rigid rules of white, middle-class America. As Hatfield puts it, the strip "had a superficial varnish of middle-class respectability (Buster being a well-scrubbed pageboy) but still used kids to twit bourgeois mores and manners."[5]

This chapter, however, demonstrates that this subversive series also has a conservative function. While *Buster Brown* questions parental authority, exposes the flaws of adults, and portrays the home as a site of conflict, it also reinforces the family unit and emphasizes the resilience of the Anglo-Saxon middle-class family in the face of internal and external stressors. In particular, Outcault's series presents humor as a useful tool that enables family members to deal with domestic conflict and strengthen bonds of affection. *Buster Brown* practices and encourages genial humor, playfully revealing the flaws in relationships between children and parents with the purpose of guiding family members to view one another with sympathy. In short, *Buster Brown* proposes that laughing at tensions in the household is a way of dispelling these tensions. The strip documents the foibles and troubles of the Brown family as a means to encourage readers, young and old, to come together and share a laugh. As such, the strip is rooted in literary domestic humor, a genre that was especially popular in the mid-nineteenth century and that emphasized that the object of laughter should be viewed with sympathy rather than hostility.[6] By encouraging sympathetic humor, *Buster Brown* expressed as well as participated in promoting a new ideal of the family that emerged in the twentieth century: what Steven Mintz and Susan Kellogg call "the companionate family."[7] This new ideal was a rejection of the strict, hierarchical structure of the patriarchal family and expressed the belief that more democratic, intimate, and loving relationships between family members were more suitable for addressing the challenges of modernization and industrialization.

Buster Brown not only insists that naughtiness in children—specifically boys—is delightful rather than threatening; it also shows that mischief-making is a reassuring sign of healthy boyhood. In decades previous, nineteenth-century genre painting and bad-boy books attached the values of vigor, independence, and resourcefulness to the naughty boy, thus suggesting that he was equipped to meet the demands of a fast-paced, increasingly mechanized society. In the early twentieth century, *Buster Brown* continued the tradition established in these paintings and books, demonstrating that the self-sufficient and energetic "bad boy" had the capacity to prosper in the new century.

In Outcault's strip, the Browns are held up as a model family: they build bonds through jokes, play, and laughter and the parents appropriately cultivate a sense of autonomy and enterprise in their young male child. Audiences apparently embraced the Brown family and delighted in the naughtiness that Buster embodied. Various paratexts—advertisements, correspondence, and photographs that contributed to the Buster Brown phenomenon—illustrate how the doors of middle-class homes were flung open for the prankish Buster. That *Buster Brown* resonated with early twentieth-century readers arguably testifies to its success in assuring its audience that the troublesome ways of children could become a source of household amusement. In other words, the strip was able to effectively sell the notion that poking fun at family matters could fortify the home.

Crisis in the Turn-of-the-Century Family

The Buster Brown phenomenon was not left unchallenged. Many Progressive Era commentators were alarmed by the proliferation of naughty kids in the pages of newspaper comic supplements. Fearful that children would imitate these fictional pranksters, parents, educators, and reformers launched campaigns that called for the regulation and sometimes the outright elimination of the supplement. Percival Chubb emerged as one of the most vocal critics of the naughty kid comics. A leading figure in New York's Ethical Culture Society, an organization that promoted social reform and community service, Chubb also wrote widely on the subject of education, advocating drama and playacting in schools.[8] He often spoke publicly on the subject of comic supplements, which he deplored as a "Sunday debauch in flamboyant color and violent drawings."[9] He was particularly alarmed by the profusion and popularity of naughty child characters in newspaper comics. Chubb's anticomics jeremiads bore many similarities to the criticism voiced by Progressive Era literary critics Ralph Bergengren and Annie Russell Marble. Representatives of what Jeet Heer and Kent Worcester call the "genteel tradition," these critics lamented the crude humor, the poor quality of writing and illustration, and the constant use of working-class and immigrant characters in the comics, claiming that these qualities signaled the decline of Anglo-Saxon culture.[10]

The campaign against the supplements was intertwined with contemporary concerns about the state of the white, middle-class family. The naughty kid strips flourished at a time when many Americans feared that the institution of the family was in a state of crisis, its stability threatened by factors including the rising divorce rate, the declining birthrate among native-born whites, and the increasing number of women becoming involved in politics, business, and social reform. For Chubb, the comics were both the cause and barometer of deteriorating family values. In a speech before the Public Education Association in 1908, he claimed that the strips promoted and reflected the "[disappearance of] our old home culture, and worse still, old home pieties."[11] Arguing that the school and the church were being forced to carry the burden of minding and disciplining the child, he declared, "We have to come back to the old idea of having the parents purge out the moral malaria."[12]

Chubb was especially fearful that naughty kid strips gave readers license to misbehave. At the 1909 meeting of the New York Public School Kindergarten Association, he warned against the purported dangers posed by images of prankish children in the comic strip: "We must get rid of [the 'smart kid' of the comic supplement]. He begins to 'rough-house' in the nursery and hazes the kindergarten. Uncles and aunts, fathers and mothers, are alike made clowns in every comic supplement in order to make attractive to the American youth this ideal of the 'smart kid.'"[13] Underlying Chubb's attack was the belief that the image of the "smart kid" violated the ideal of the innocent, passive child. The smart kid was too smart for his own good and became especially dangerous when he used his knowledge against adults. Chubb also expressed the assumption that children are impressionable and that the strips could easily prod them to become troublemakers. For Chubb, young readers of the supplements were a potential threat to familial and social order, just like the mischief-making characters they encountered in their reading.

Chubb's rhetoric reveals anxiety about the child's impressionability as well as fear that the child had the power to unravel family ties. Yet the reformer believed that parents were ultimately to blame for children's misbehavior. In Chubb's view, parental permissiveness over children's consumption of comic supplements was evidence of moral decay in the family. He implored parents to be steadfast and active in removing the comic supplement from the home: "There is only one word that I can say about reading the comic supplement . . . and that is: 'Don't!' Try to get your children and the parents of other children to 'don't.' The comic Sunday supplement must positively be banished from the American home. . . . Harmless as it may seem, it is one of the most dangerous and degrading influences of our modern child's life."[14] Chubb's stance ran counter to the way newspaper editors and publishers marketed the comic supplements. For newspaper producers, supplements were domestic entertainments that fostered family bonding. The Sunday paper, in particular, purportedly provided "something for everyone," as it included sections that focused on a variety of subjects, such as sports, literature, fashion, high society gossip, real estate, and children's stories and games. The comic supplement itself appealed to a crossover audience, as its pages contained a mix of humor directed at men, women, and children. Many publishers envisioned the comics pages as material that parents and children consumed together and shared with one another. Chubb, however, took a contrary view. He was convinced that the multiple types of supplements only worked to drive wedges between family members. He imagined the newspaper as having an adverse effect on family dynamics: "On Sunday mornings, while the father is buried in the real estate section and the mother in the fashion section, while the sister has run away with the romantic and the brother with the lurid section, the young child begins to cry, and to quiet him we toss the gaudy comic supplement as his portion."[15] Chubb conjures the image of a family composed of isolated individuals who, burying their heads in separate newspaper sections, become uncommunicative and unconcerned with one another. As family members indulge in their own interests, they neglect their youngest, leaving him vulnerable to vulgar and unhealthful material.

Chubb frequently equated the comic supplement with other forms of entertainment that reformers denounced as indecent and deleterious, such as motion pictures, ragtime music, amusement parks, and vaudeville shows. Speaking at the 1911 Child Welfare Exhibit, he described the naughty kid strip as a form of vaudeville that jeopardized the sanctity of the home.[16] Later that year, he founded the League for the Improvement of the Children's Comic Supplement. The organization's name suggests that by then Chubb was more interested in monitoring the supplement's content rather than eradicating it altogether. His effort to "clean up" the supplement echoes contemporary cultural crusades that attempted to regulate various forms of entertainment for children. In 1907, for example, Jane Addams opened a nickelodeon in Hull House. While many reformers alleged that nickel shows encouraged immoral and criminal behavior, Addams screened films in an effort to demonstrate that a medium that appealed to children could be used to teach and rehabilitate them.[17] But while Addams was particularly invested in using entertainments to "uplift" members of the working and immigrant classes, Chubb was focused on preserving what he presumed to be the natural virtue of white, middle-class children. More broadly, his campaign against the supplement was motivated by the belief that the white, middle-class family, supposedly the stronghold of the nation's core values, was in danger of buckling under the pressures of an increasingly corrupt environment and was therefore in need of reinforcement.

Laughter Keeps the Family Together

Some of Chubb's contemporaries, however, did not view the turn-of-the-century family as necessarily in a state of dissolution. Rather, they felt it was important to redefine the institution's ideals and functions in order to meet the challenges of modern life. While Chubb was one of many reformers who contended that the family's survival rested on its ability to resist change, others argued that the family's strength lay in its ability to *adapt* to change. In particular, psychologists, educators, and legal scholars were instrumental in conceptualizing and promoting the ideal of the companionate family, which, as Mintz and Kellogg put it, imagined "husbands and wives [as] friends and lovers and parents and children [as] pals."[18] The ideal of the companionate family was rooted in nineteenth-century domestic ideology, which favored egalitarian and affectionate relationships between family members over a patriarchal-hierarchical structure. In the early twentieth century, this vision of intimate family life became more layered: it began to emphasize romance and sexual intimacy between husband and wife and insisted that children be given "greater freedom from parental control [and] greater latitude in expressing their feelings."[19] This promotion of children's autonomy was yoked to the notion that the family was meant to foster each member's individualism, a belief that, as Joseph M. Hawes and Elizabeth I. Nybakken document, steadily gained wider cultural acceptance from the mid-nineteenth century forward.[20]

In some ways, *Buster Brown* interrogated this new ideal. The strip revealed the challenges that parents faced in indulging their children and granting them independence. Buster, often left unsupervised, creates disorder in the household and causes social embarrassment for his parents. The episode "Buster Brown Has a Birthday Party," for example, depicts giving children free rein as both a feature and problem of modern parenting (fig. 22). When a guest reminds Buster that it is his birthday, the boy throws a tantrum and yells that he "wont [*sic*] be seven."[21] Mr. Brown is perturbed by his son's outburst. But the father's partial presence in the scene, with only his head visible in the first three panels, suggests that he has a marginal role in the household as well as limited reach in disciplining Buster.

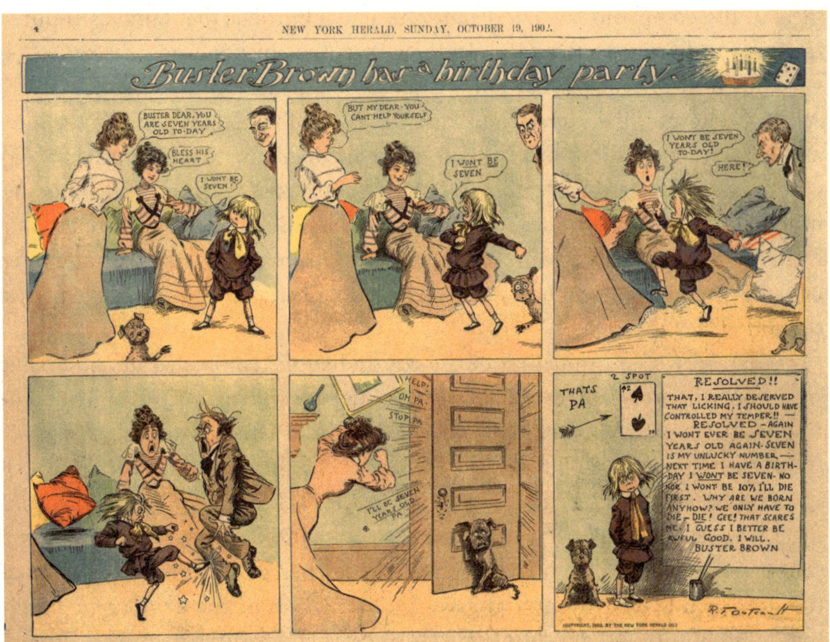

Figure 22. Comic Strip by R. F. Outcault. "Buster Brown Has a Birthday Party." In *New York Herald* Comic Supplement, October 19, 1902. SFS 30-4-3a, San Francisco Academy of Comic Art Collection, the Ohio State University Billy Ireland Cartoon Library and Museum.

Mr. Brown's placement in the episode's first few panels conveys how, as Peter Filene observes, the turn-of-the-century father had a diminished domestic role, becoming less the omnipresent patriarch and more the busy, absent provider.[22] In contrast, Mrs. Brown is placed in the center of most of the panels, signifying that she has more visibility, and perhaps more influence, in the household. Her location signals how the early twentieth-century mother was viewed as the "central and dominant figure within the home . . . wholly responsible for organizing household affairs [and] caring for and disciplining children."[23] Yet Mrs. Brown, instead of admonishing or comforting her son, sits back and smiles, as if amused by the sight of Buster having a violent fit. Buster's tantrum communicates that Mr. Brown's diminished role and Mrs. Brown's complacency are failures in parenting. When Mr. Brown finally decides to assert his authority, entering the frame in full, Buster is beyond reason. He furiously kicks his father in the shin. Mr. Brown responds by violating the ideal of the companionate family. He reclaims the role of the strict patriarch and gives his son a fierce spanking behind closed doors. Mrs. Brown helplessly stands outside the door, an indication of how her inaction and "softness" have caused her to be shut out from any effort to discipline her temperamental child.

"Buster Brown Has a Birthday Party" reveals the incongruity between the ideal of the companionate family and the actual burdens that families endured in trying to live up to this ideal. In this sense, the episode—and the series—is very much in line with what Louis D. Rubin identifies as the raison d'être of American humor: the exposure and examination of the "clash between the ideal and the real."[24] As Rubin writes, "Out of the incongruity between mundane circumstances and heroic ideal, material fact and spiritual hunger, democratic, middle-class society and desire for cultural definition, theory of equality and fact of social and economic inequality . . . between what men would be and must be . . . has come much pathos, no small amount of tragedy, and also a great deal of humor."[25]

Buster Brown's examination of the contradictions embedded in and arising from contemporary domestic ideology also suggests that the strip is rooted in the tradition of nineteenth-century domestic humor. As Gregg Camfield argues, the domestic comedies of writers such as Harriet Beecher Stowe, Marietta Holley, Herman Melville, and Mark Twain "explore and acknowledge the absurd conflicts between ideology and more complicated realities."[26] In the early nineteenth century, sentimental liberalism challenged the patriarchal-hierarchical structure idealized by Calvinism and gave rise to a vision of the democratic family that bonded through affection. The family was conceived as a private sanctuary from an increasingly industrialized society; as Christopher Lasch puts it, the family unit was understood to be a "haven in a heartless world."[27] According to Camfield, however, this new domestic ideology imposed impossible demands on family members: "In an urbanizing, modernizing middle-class culture that demanded that marriages be based on love, men were increasingly forced to spend six days a week, twelve hours a day at work, ostensibly for their wives and children, but alienated from them as a source of emotional satisfaction. Women, declared equal partners, were increasingly denied access to the economic productivity that would make that equality real. Children, freed from the stigma of original sin, were held in even tighter check than before to make sure they would remain 'pure.'"[28] Literary humor of domesticity brought these paradoxes to light; it also suggested that dissecting and confronting these contradictions through a comic approach ensured family bliss and stability. Nineteenth-century domestic humor thus served as a relief valve, poking fun at family matters to facilitate the release of anxieties and tensions that emerged in the household. Moreover, the genre encouraged congeniality and community within the family. Camfield points out that writers employed humor that was amiable rather than aggressive in nature, as they attempted to "[cut] across the grain of obvious antagonisms in order to find common grounds for agreement as well as disagreement."[29] This is perhaps not so surprising: nineteenth-century middle-class culture promoted benevolence and sensibility, often hitching laughter to sympathy. In short, amiable humor meant to bring together husbands and wives, parents and children, rather than alienate them from one another.

Camfield contends that the popularity of genial literary humor about home life waned in the late nineteenth century, as aggressive comedy—often directed at racial and ethnic groups and that likely emerged in response to mass immigration and African American migration to urban areas—reemerged and became the dominant mode of humor.[30] But in actuality, amiable humor continued to flourish in *visual* form. Cartoons, humorous photographs, and comic stereographs about domestic life were widely consumed in the late nineteenth and early twentieth centuries. Humor magazines such as *Puck*, *Life*, and *Judge* published gag cartoons, verbal jokes, and funny stories on the subjects of marriage, child-rearing, children's pranks, and relationships between in-laws.

A humorous genre of studio photography even developed at the turn of the century, one in which actors posed as family members in comic situations. Many of these photographs were mass produced as stereographs (also known as stereoscopic views, stereo views, or stereograms). The stereoscopic viewer, or stereoscope, was initially promoted and used in mid-Victorian American homes as an educational tool, but by the 1890s, it became a means of bringing entertainment—and humor—into the home. A 1905 Sears, Roebuck and Company advertisement for its Comic Series stereographs provides this description:

> *These one hundred pictures are all photographs from life . . .*
>
> *Everybody likes a good laugh*, and every picture in this big set is good for one big hearty laugh.

> Laughable hugging and kissing scenes, humorous scenes of domestic tribulations, amusing bathing scenes, photographs of children engaged in childish occupations—
>
> Funny entertaining and laughable pictures. They will amuse you and help to entertain your friends. (emphasis in original)[31]

In offering up "domestic tribulations" as the object of laughter, the advertisement insists that the mundanities and stresses of family life should be embraced rather than rejected. The stereographs, as the advertisement suggests, holds no enmity for everyday troubles; rather, these images enable viewers to laugh at intimate scenes of family life and, through such laughter, reinforce intimate familial bonds.

Sears, Roebuck and Company also promoted stereographic viewing—whether of humorous or educational images—as a pursuit for the entire family to enjoy. An advertisement in their 1908 catalog emphasizes how stereoscopic views were "a most delightful entertainment" that could bring a family together.[32] The advertisement's illustration shows what appears to be a multigenerational family gathered around a table, sharing stereoscopic views with one another. At first glance, the individuals in the scene appear to be distracted by the stereographs; the father and the grandfather seem to be the only figures who acknowledge one another. Yet the family members form a tight circle around the table. The girl sits on her grandmother's lap as they look at a stereograph; together, they project an image of affection. The advertisement implies that the stereoscope facilitates intimate relationships, as viewing the stereographs becomes a shared experience.

In the pages of the comic supplement, *Buster Brown* performed work similar to that of humor magazines and comic stereographs, providing humorous commentary on the nature of urban, white, middle-class family life. Arguably, Outcault's strip was to early twentieth-century readers what literary domestic humor was to nineteenth-century audiences. The series also supports Daniel Wickberg's observation that humor in the early twentieth century encouraged the "[collapse of] the distance between object and subject by allowing for the possibility of nonderisive laughter *with* rather than *at* another person, and placed a value on the altogether novel capacity of the individual to laugh at himself" (emphasis in original).[33] By displaying the flaws of all members of the family, *Buster Brown* urged readers to be mindful of their own foibles, a practice that could effectively increase their compassion for other family members. Outcault certainly understood that his strip had the capacity to cultivate sympathy between adults and children, claiming that his series (as well as other strips that he deemed "of the better class") did not "[instill] a mischievous spirit" but rather served "to entertain, not only the youngsters, but as well the grown-up people, and to teach them things about human nature that they could never have otherwise acquired."[34] In other words, the cartoonist imagined his strip as a venue in which middle-class families could laugh at, learn from, and move past domestic conflicts.

The medium of the comic strip also proved apt in demonstrating the Brown family's resilience. As illustrated in the episode "Buster Brown Suffers, but Doesn't Get a Beating," the comic strip convention of characters surviving and recovering from physical violence serves to confirm the stability of the family.[35] When Mrs. Brown sends Buster to bed without dinner, he pretends to be pleased by his punishment. "I don't care," he says with a grin. She retaliates by teasing him, claiming she has laid out several dishes that include treats that Buster apparently cannot resist: mince pie, nuts and raisins, plum pudding, tropical fruits, ice cream, cake, and candy. Buster becomes so tormented by the idea that he is missing out on a rich feast that he cries, falls to the floor, violently spins around in a circle, and bangs his head on the wall. In the meantime, Mrs. Brown smiles, as if amused to see her son in a state of distress. Even as Buster progressively becomes upset, she remains in the doorway, maintaining her distance from him. In the last panel, however, the divide between child and parent is bridged. Buster and Mrs. Brown are locked in an embrace and kiss one another. In this final panel, there is no indication that Buster has been physically or emotionally scarred. Although much of the episode depicts the relationship between mother and son as one of manipulation and retaliation, the last panel suggests that Mrs. Brown employed strategies of playfulness and humor in order to ease resentment and ultimately bring about familial reconciliation. Moreover, mother and son appear to have forgiven one another. As Buster writes in his resolution, "Say! With what wonderful intuition Ma handled that affair. Forgiveness is divine. To forgive you simply have to 'forget it.'"[36]

The serial nature of the strip also works to depict the endurance of the Brown family. Comic strip episodes simultaneously function as stand-alone narratives and as installments that are part of a larger series, and this feature, Lisa Yaszek reminds us, opens the comics medium to multiple meanings. In her analysis of *The Katzenjammer Kids*, Yaszek demonstrates how this dual function of comic strip episodes allows both authority figures and young troublemakers to appear triumphant. Each *Katzenjammer Kids* episode concludes with the prankish Hans and Fritz being spanked by an adult. The boys, who bawl as they receive their punishment, thus appear defeated in each denouement. But by the next episode, Hans and Fritz return to gleeful mischief-making. Yaszek interprets this "persistence" of troublemaking as a "joyous celebration of antiauthoritarianism,"[37] which may be why reformers such as Chubb were so alarmed by the proliferation of naughty kid strips. Buster Brown undoubtedly possesses the same persistent naughtiness as the Katzenjammer brothers. Yet in *Buster Brown* (as well as in *Katzenjammer Kids*), it is not just mischief that endures; the family also prevails. Even as Mr. and Mrs. Brown become agitated by their son's endless antics, even as

Buster sometimes feels victimized by his parents' ire, their family emerges intact, week after week. The Brown family is able to withstand the chaos, anxiety, and embarrassment caused by Buster's pranks. The flaws of each family member and the tensions that arise in the Brown household are not strong enough to permanently divide the family.

Buster Brown also implies that familial relationships can be strengthened if parents and children laugh together at the expense of those who do not belong in the family. While the strip encourages members of middle-class families to share moments of amiable laughter, it also directs derisive humor at members of racial/ethnic groups and the working class. The most evident objects of scornful laughter in *Buster Brown* are the family's maids, who are sometimes marked as Irish immigrants. In depicting the Browns' servants, Outcault likely drew from the popular late nineteenth-century Irish caricature "Bridget" (or "Biddy"), a stereotype that expressed the common middle-class notion that the female Irish servant was vulgar, ignorant, and impudent.[38] Roman-Catholic Irish maids were also widely perceived as "aliens" in Protestant households. Although the "swarthy" Irish were slowly "going white" and assimilating into the dominant Anglo culture by the turn of the century, images of Irish Bridgets kept circulating in popular culture. Of course, the presence of servants in *Buster Brown* reveals the extent to which the family attempting to realize the companionate ideal depends on household help. With the maids performing the strenuous and dirty work of maintaining the home, the middle-class family has time for leisure and laughter. Ultimately, however, *Buster Brown* maintains that the maids have a marginal position in the middle-class household. These minor characters often stand partially outside the frame, with only their heads visible. Outcault's depiction of the maids emphasizes that they are not cut from the same cloth as the well-to-do Browns. Their features—such as bulging eyes and thick eyebrows—are in sharp contrast to the delicate characteristics of Mrs. Brown. The servants wear their hair in tight buns, quite unlike Mrs. Brown's pompadour, with its gracefully cascading curls. The maids often laugh with their mouths wide open, displaying their teeth and, consequently, their lack of decorum.

As Margaret Lynch-Brennan notes, one common complaint leveled against Irish maids was that they perceived themselves to be in the same class as their mistresses.[39] In "Buster Brown—Photographer," Delia the maid is particularly mocked for such pretentiousness (fig. 23). Her name is likely a diminutive of Bedelia, which, in turn, is an Irish variant of Bridget. In this episode, Buster invites Delia into the parlor to sit before a camera. Instead of taking her portrait, however, he lights a firecracker that explodes in her face. Delia's blackened face highlights her status as ethnic Other, disrupting her claim to normative whiteness. The prank committed against Delia also serves to foster bonding between Mrs. Brown and Buster. While *Buster Brown* episodes often conclude with the protagonist receiving a spanking, in this particular episode, Buster ends up

Figure 23. Comic Strip by R. F. Outcault. "Buster Brown—Photographer." In *Chicago Sunday Tribune* Comic Supplement, May 8, 1904. SFS 98-7, San Francisco Academy of Comic Art Collection, the Ohio State University Billy Ireland Cartoon Library and Museum.

cuddling with his mother. He lies in repose, with his legs up on the sofa and his torso pressed against his mother's body. The two of them lean in the same direction, their arms around one another. They smile and gaze into one another's eyes as Buster says, "Ma, if you had seen Delia when that fire cracker went off you'd know it was worth it."[40] This image in the last panel recalls the intimate family gathering illustrated in the Sears, Roebuck and Company stereoscope advertisement. In lieu of sharing stereoscopic views, Buster and his mother share a laugh at Delia's deluded belief that she is worthy of a portrait sitting. As such, the episode provides assurance that the maid, even as she is tasked with raising her mistress's child, cannot sever the bond between mother and son. More specifically, Delia's blackening reinforces the unification of her white mistress and young master. In this sense, the episode does not subvert structures of authority but rather allays anxieties about the family's vulnerability.

Complicating Notions of Naughtiness

Buster Brown thus challenges early twentieth-century cultural contributors' view that the figure of the naughty child was necessarily the product and source of moral bankruptcy in the family. The strip associates permissiveness with both perils and pleasures, depicting the challenges as well as the delights of encouraging children, especially boys, to be energetic and independent. *Buster Brown* can be considered a descendant of the naughty boy character who ran amok in nineteenth-century visual and literary culture. As Jadviga M. Da Costa Nunes notes, the naughty boy was one of the stock characters that was widely reproduced in antebellum American genre painting, appearing in the works of artists such as John Lewis Krimmel, William Sidney Mount, and James Clonney.[41] Nunes describes how this child was often "shown in the midst of some prank or mischievous or disobedient act. The child's infraction is never terribly serious or delinquent, but rather the consequence of youthful exuberance or lack of self-control."[42] Genre paintings celebrated the naughtiness of the young boy, intertwining his incorrigibility and mischief-making with the values of autonomy, resourcefulness, vitality, and audacity, which were seen as favorable and necessary qualities in the male child who was expected to manage and ensure the growth of a nascent capitalist democracy.[43]

In imagining how a supposedly angelic child can upend the household, Outcault referenced another artist who specialized in genre painting: Lilly Martin Spencer. Spencer's paintings sentimentalized family life while also picturing how the mistress of the home could be aggravated by her husband, servants, and children. As David M. Lubin proposes, Spencer's ambivalence toward domesticity and children, as expressed in paintings such as *Fruit of Temptation* (1857) and *War Spirit at Home* (1866), resulted from the constraints that marriage and motherhood placed on her career.[44] It is, however, unlikely that the male Outcault experienced frustrations similar to Spencer's; thus, his comics are more exultant—rather than uncertain—about images of naughty boyhood.

Genre painting was in decline by the latter half of the nineteenth century, but the naughty boy made spirited appearances in other forms of popular culture, including lithographs, stereographs, humor magazines, and children's books. Among the most enduring incarnations of this character can be found in "bad-boy books" such as Thomas Bailey Aldrich's *The Story of a Bad Boy* (1869) and Mark Twain's *The Adventures of Tom Sawyer* (1876) and *Adventures of Huckleberry Finn* (1884). As Kenneth Kidd argues, this genre performed "literary boy work," offering descriptive and prescriptive work on boyhood.[45] Kidd contends that *Story of a Bad Boy* and *Tom Sawyer*, in particular, provided a vision of middle-class white boys as "gentle and temporary savages."[46] Bad-boy books encouraged boy readers to imitate and adult readers to foster so-called primitive behavior, suggesting that there was nothing inherently dangerous about the misbehaving boy since he would naturally evolve out of savagery.[47] *Buster Brown* continued similar boy work in the early twentieth century: its protagonist's pranks can be understood as displays of pluck, energy, and self-reliance. Even as *Buster Brown* depicts the family tensions wrought by the mischief-making child, it dispels these tensions by reassuring readers that the protagonist is effectively "being a boy." Buster himself testifies that he is just "following [his] natural instincts to keep busy."[48]

It is worth noting that while Buster is a middle-class, urban boy, most of his predecessors that appeared in genre painting and children's books are barefoot boys growing up in the countryside.[49] Sarah Burns notes that such tales of bad country boys had multiple functions: they idealized rural boyhood, promoted adult nostalgia for childhood, and addressed xenophobic anxieties over the growing presence of working-class, immigrant children in the cities: "[These images of happy country children] symbolize all those longings, overt or submerged, for escape from the pressures of the present, to burrow back into an ideal past, to be a child again, to shed the burden of adult responsibility for a retreat into a sheltered, pastoral never-never land. . . . [They also] functioned as emblems of an ideal to which those multitudes of alien, impoverished, nature-starved [children] of metropolitan tenements must be made to conform."[50] James B. Salazar adds that in the late nineteenth century, the literary bad boy "provided . . . a figurative escape into the pastoral, imaginative life of a premodern, anticapitalist world, while also embodying the enterprising and unsentimental agency of the capitalist himself."[51] In appropriating the bad boy of the countryside and transplanting him into a middle-class home in New York, *Buster Brown* not only provided sentimental attachment to the rural past but also demonstrated that the naughty (white) boy can thrive in the urban present and, potentially, the urban future.

Buster also illuminated the differences between the "wretched" child of the slums and the plucky, energetic, and self-reliant white child. Leslie Paris notes that early twentieth-century educators and psychologists feared that boys were being softened, even feminized, by urbanization;[52] in contrast, *Buster Brown* implies that boys are immune to the enervating effects of city life. Occasionally, Outcault activated nostalgia for the countryside by sending Buster out to a holiday on a farm. In these episodes, Buster is hardly a fish out of water: he confidently navigates the farms and fields in much the same way as he explored city streets. By implying Buster's "inherent" link to the countryside, Outcault invoked not only the barefoot boy but also the New England Yankee, a popular stock character that was especially prevalent in antebellum humor. British audiences laughed at the provincial, coarse Yankee, whom they considered an incarnation of the worst traits of Americans. But American audiences often apprehended the rustic Yankee as a shrewd trickster who embodied the rejection of (British) authority and artifice.[53] As the cosmopolitan heir of the barefoot country boy and the Yankee, Buster is positioned as something more than an inveterate troublemaker. His ties to pastoral innocence, his ingenuity, and his irreverence all testify to his capacity to be a "good" American, one who would preserve democratic ideals, push back against pretension and orthodoxy, and embrace the spirit of modernization and expansion.

That *Buster Brown* and other early twentieth-century naughty kid strips tended to be headlined by male children expresses contemporary beliefs that naughtiness was acceptable, even desired, in boys but not in girls. As I discuss in chapter 5, some comic strips expressed and explored fascination with the figure of the troublesome girl. But naughty girl strips—such as Munson Paddock's *Angelic Angelina*, Penny Ross's *Angel Child*, and Tom Tucker's *Betsy Bouncer and Her Doll*—tended to be short-lived. They were published sporadically and did not gain the following enjoyed by strips with male protagonists.[54] In *Buster Brown*, Mary Jane, a well-dressed girl who wears ruffled skirts and hair ribbons and who becomes Buster's constant playmate, is positioned as a supporting character. With her small nose and mouth and dark curly hair in a well-composed bob, she is a Gibson Girl in the making.[55] Mary Jane does possess a naughty streak, as she delights in and occasionally participates in Buster's tricks. Her participation in them, however, is limited. In "On the Jump!" she is the first to leap from a makeshift springboard that Buster, presumably, has set up (fig. 24).[56] She jumps and awkwardly lands on her head. Upside down with her legs exposed, Mary Jane hardly appears ladylike. But in the next panel, she is standing upright and fixing her hair, as if quickly trying to recover her feminine composure. Although she is entertained by Buster's tricks, she herself never plans or takes the lead in executing mischief. The female child in *Buster Brown* does not possess the same level of boldness and independence as her male counterpart.

Figure 24. Comic Strip by R. F. Outcault. "On the Jump!" In *Boston Sunday American* Comic Supplement, March 17, 1907. SFS 83-3-6, San Francisco Academy of Comic Art Collection, the Ohio State University Billy Ireland Cartoon Library and Museum.

The contrast between Buster and Mary Jane has an antecedent in genre paintings and other forms of antebellum visual culture. While some nineteenth-century genre paintings featured misbehaving girls, more often than not, such works pictured girls as gentle and angelic while upholding the rudeness and impishness of young boys. Mary Lynn Stevens Heininger explains how these different depictions of girlhood and boyhood expressed gender expectations: "The stereotype of the wily, dirty-faced lad directly and accurately foreshadowed his ideal adult role, much as the image of the docile and immaculate little girl foretold hers. While she would become the keeper of home and virtue, apart from commerce and competition, the 'real boy' would need to learn 'the tricks of the trade.' . . . In order to be successful, the enterprising youth would need to dirty his hands with the world's work."[57] In *Buster Brown*, Mary Jane primarily serves as Buster's muse and as witness to his pranks; she is a figure that he must strive to impress. Her presence allows Buster to prove his heterosexuality and assert his masculinity. In "Buster Brown's Valentine," for example, he playfully romances her, sending her flowers and a letter on Valentine's Day.[58] She responds by displaying her budding feminine charms, confirming Gary Cross's contention that in the early twentieth century, the naughty girl was often imagined not as a prankster but rather as a little coquette.[59] In an attempt to reciprocate Buster's feelings, she instructs the messenger boy to "give [Buster] a nice kiss for me" and presses her mouth on the young messenger's lips.

In representing boys as "naturally" naughty, *Buster Brown* denounces maternal attempts to restrain and domesticate them; a central mechanism here is the strip's apparent repudiation of the figure of Little Lord Fauntleroy. With his collared outfit and blond ringlets, Buster recalls Cedric Errol, the protagonist of Frances Hodgson Burnett's *Little Lord Fauntleroy* (1886), as rendered by illustrator Reginald Birch. Lorinda B. Cohoon argues that *Fauntleroy* "explores not the power of badness, but the power of goodness," constructing a vision of boyhood alternative to that embodied in bad-boy books.[60] For Cohoon, Burnett's novel disputes the ideal of the rule-breaking boy, validating instead a "benevolent citizenship" that manifests itself through the functions of generosity, beauty, relationship, and ownership.[61] Moreover, the Fauntleroy costume, as Anne Higonnet notes, "became a symbol of maternal desire to keep sons androgynously childish."[62] Buster, on the other hand, resists the androgyny associated with the costume. Dressed like Cedric but prone to prankish behavior, he exemplifies the triumph of badness over benevolence, of irrepressible boyishness over feminizing influences.

Yet *Buster Brown* also carefully insists that its protagonist, though troublesome, is not immoral. Outcault himself maintained that in creating the series, he "carefully refrained from giving a suggestion that might leave an evil impression on the mind of a child."[63] The strip tempers Buster's mischief-making with scenes that display his compassion toward those he perceives as less privileged than himself. As Soper notes, while comic strips often follow formulaic plots and have one-dimensional characters, episodes that deviate from the formula can turn caricatures into more complex characters.[64] "Buster Brown Helps Santa Claus" thus gives nuance to the figure of the naughty boy, as it shows Buster performing an act of charity.[65] In this Christmas episode, Buster witnesses a landlord browbeating his impoverished tenants. When the landlord drops his pocketbook, Buster decides to take it and dole out the money to the poor. In the last tier, when the landlord confronts Buster, the boy replies that the act of giving "made [the poor] *so* happy."[66] He thus performs an act of justice rather than transgression. A policeman in the background remains oblivious to the exchange. His lack of interference implies that those in positions of authority often fail to address social wrongs; it also signals that the hand of the law is unnecessary in the presence of a plucky, benevolent child.

Another episode shows Buster expressing remorse for his pranks when he grasps that they can harm members of the underclass. In "Buster Brown Plays a Trick in a London Hotel," he frightens a hotel maid with a toy mouse.[67] The maid, in her shock, jumps in the air and flings the breakfast tray she is carrying. Cups, saucers, and tea rain on the hotel proprietor, who threatens to fire the maid, accusing her of being an "awkward simpleton."[68] Buster intervenes without hesitation, admitting to his misdeed. When the proprietor redirects his rage at Buster, his parents and the maid come to his defense, claiming that he is a "good boy" and a "nice child."[69] Here, Buster's willingness to confess to his little crime signifies his mischief-making is not laced with malice. While his propensity for misbehavior signifies resourcefulness and autonomy, the episode also makes clear that he possesses empathy and a sense of justice and fairness.

Buster's relationship with his bull terrier, Tige, also reminds readers of the character's inherent goodness. His conversations with Tige—which adult characters are oblivious to—intimates his psychic connection to nature. Although Tige is sometimes the victim and unwilling participant of Buster's pranks, boy and pet maintain an affectionate relationship, as they often share a laugh and embrace one another. In one episode, Buster and Tige mobilize, respectively, armies of little Busters and dogs to teach a mean-spirited dogcatcher a lesson.[70] While David Rudd reminds us that the association of child with animal has traditionally been used to establish (and permit) the child's "otherly," irrational, and uncivilized behavior, Buster's ardent defense of dogs underscores his "inherent" humaneness and humanness.[71]

Episodes in which Buster displays compassion for the downtrodden and for animals suggest that the strip's protagonist is an interpretation rather than an outright rejection of Cedric Errol. As Beverly Lyon Clark puts it, Cedric "provide[s] . . . a brilliant, albeit contradictory, synthesis of competing ideals of masculinity."[72] Although Cedric is a beautiful child who has inherited his mother's sweetness and tenderness, he is also described as a "very boyish little boy" who easily wins a footrace in the streets of New York.[73] When Mr. Havisham encounters Cedric, he is captivated by the young boy's athleticism, watching the race in which "his lordship's lordly little red legs flew up behind his knickerbockers and tore over the ground as he shot out in the race at the signal word. He shut his small hands and set his face against the wind; his bright hair streamed out behind."[74] For Clark, Burnett's little lord simultaneously represents the competing values of gentility and physicality, service and self-advancement, frugality and materialism.[75] Buster Brown similarly embodies competing visions of boyhood. He is a representation of the child that Cross contends became popular at the turn of the century: "the 'cute' child—willful, even selfish and devious at times, but ultimately good at heart."[76] As a naughty-but-nice boy, a child who simultaneously mocks and mimics Cedric, Buster secures his place in the companionate family. Even as he defies his mother's efforts to beautify and domesticate him, he remains a loving and loyal son. At once spirited and compassionate, Buster appears to be an ideal member of an institution that works to cultivate democratic and sympathetic relationships among its members.

Naughty Boyhood and the Nuances of Family Life

As *Buster Brown* encouraged audiences to recognize its protagonist as a multilayered character, it also gave Buster's mother some dimension. Certainly, many episodes of *Buster Brown* derided Mrs. Brown's child-rearing skills—or lack thereof. Drawn in the image of the Gibson Girl, Mrs. Brown is typically portrayed as a neglectful mother, too distracted by fashion, shopping, house calls, and other leisurely pursuits that she fails to effectively monitor and discipline her son.

The episode "His New Goat Breaks Up Mamma's Tea Party and a Few Other Things" illustrates the clash between Mrs. Brown's leisure activities and her duties as a mother.[77] Mrs. Brown and her female guests play bridge in the parlor. Their gathering, however, is violently interrupted by Buster, who had carelessly tugged the beard of a goat and is now being pursued by the enraged animal. The chase leaves a wide tear on the carpet and a large hole in the wall; the Brown home, supposedly the dominion of Mrs. Brown, now appears scarred by Buster's misbehavior and her negligence. "His New Goat" implies that had Mrs. Brown kept an eye on her son rather than walling herself off in the parlor for a tea party, such chaos and destruction may have been averted. Moreover, the episode highlights how the naughty boy can diminish the woman's influence in the home. Elizabeth Johns notes that in nineteenth-century genre painting, the figure of the bad boy functioned to undermine the mother, arguing that "some [paintings of boyhood] altogether subverted ideals of effective motherhood, pairing young boys' mischievousness with women's helplessness."[78] In *Buster Brown*, Outcault appears to continue this narrative of incorrigible boy and harried mother, using the image of the rambunctious Buster to test—and limit—Mrs. Brown's authority.

Yet Mrs. Brown is not always characterized as a distracted, victimized parent. Many episodes reveal her to be deeply affectionate and demonstrative. For his part, Buster returns her affection, rarely resisting his mother's gestures of endearment. Some episodes also put Mrs. Brown in a sympathetic light by demonstrating how child-rearing can inspire a confluence of contradictory emotions. In "Buster Brown and His Faithful Friend Tige," Buster cuts his face with his father's razor.[79] The horrified Mrs. Brown reaches out to him, as if eager to comfort him and attend to his injury. But instead of nursing him, she paddles him. The episode does not necessarily depict Mrs. Brown as a cruel woman. Rather, it demonstrates the combination of fright, worry, and anger that a mother may feel at the sight of her injured child. That she punishes Buster, rather than nursing him, may even be understood as an expression of her relief: Buster's injury is apparently not severe or life-threatening, and thus she deems it "safe" enough to give him a sound thrashing.

Mrs. Brown's physical appearance may have also invited readers to view her with sympathy rather than ridicule. In contemporary visual culture, women who were positioned as antagonists to young pranksters were typically unattractive and bumbling, as in the case of Mrs. Katzenjammer in *The Katzenjammer Kids*. As I discuss in chapter 5, Mrs. Brown's Gibson-Girl looks may have had a satirical edge, but her appearance also exhibited her refinement and gentleness. And while the Gibson Girl sometimes meant to signal emotional aloofness, as her face is "frozen" in beauty, Outcault gave Mrs. Brown a range of emotions, with her face shifting between various expressions, including distress, embarrassment, ire, and, of course, mirth.

In short, *Buster Brown* presents Mrs. Brown as a layered, sympathetic character. While she is often frustrated and humiliated by her son's incorrigibility, some episodes such as "Buster Brown Suffers, but Doesn't Get a Beating," which I discuss above, reveals her playful side. The episode "Buster Brown Gets Another Joke on the Doctor" also complicates her image as a constantly vexed mother (fig. 25).[80] Here, she responds to her son's troublesome play with tolerance and even amusement. When the doctor drops by for a house call to attend to the purportedly "awful sick" Buster, his young patient sprints back and forth through the parlor, chasing the cat and dog. Buster and the pets run right into the doctor, who is flung into the air. Later, they trample him. He is clearly not amused. In the penultimate panel, the disheveled doctor rolls up his sleeves, as if preparing to give Buster a beating.

The last panel reveals that Buster does receive a good hiding from his father, presumably at the behest of his mother. Buster stares at the reader and asserts that Mrs. Brown is "a cruel woman." He cites her taste for hats adorned with taxidermied birds—or, in Buster's words, birds that have been "brutally murdered"—as proof that she has "no heart." His denunciation of his mother is in sharp contrast to scenes in other episodes, in which he displays tenderness toward Mrs. Brown

Figure 25. Comic Strip by R. F. Outcault. "Buster Brown Gets Another Joke on the Doctor." In *New York Herald* Comic Supplement, May 10, 1903. SFS 31-5-2, San Francisco Academy of Comic Art Collection, the Ohio State University Billy Ireland Cartoon Library and Museum.

through kisses and embraces. Taken together, various episodes display the fluidity of Buster's feelings toward his mother. But Buster may have been too preoccupied with his smarting backside to notice that his mother possesses that same mutability of emotions. In "Buster Brown Gets Another Joke on the Doctor," Mrs. Brown's facial expressions change from panel to panel: her face exhibits surprise then annoyance and eventually becomes contorted in laughter. Her multiple expressions demonstrate that parental response to a child's behavior is nuanced and constantly shifting. The humiliated doctor recommends that Buster be given a dose of prussic acid, a chemical compound that, in diluted form, had been used for medicinal purposes in the early nineteenth century but, in the latter half of the century, was recognized as not only ineffective but also lethal.[81] When the doctor recommends the poison, Mrs. Brown simply laughs. "Doctor, I'm so sorry for you," she says.[82] While she appears to apologize for her son's behavior, she also seems to admonish the doctor for losing his composure and sense of professionalism. In *Buster Brown*, Mrs. Brown is often freed from a rigid characterization as the frustrated and rigid parent; Buster's pranks, in fact, enable her to demonstrate her fondness for and commitment to her son.

Other episodes work in a similar vein, showing how Buster's tricks facilitate and revitalize affectionate relationships in the family. In "Buster Brown Frightens His Parents," Mrs. Brown has withheld Thanksgiving dinner from her son, presumably as punishment for some mischief he committed earlier in the day.[83] Buster, claiming that he is "cruelly and heartlessly treated here at home," pretends to run away. Believing that their son has taken flight, his parents are panic-stricken, and his father immediately runs to the police. Buster, who has been hiding behind a doorway, watching the drama unfold, appears to regret his trick. He reveals himself to his mother and says, "Forgive me, Ma—I did n't run away." Mrs. Brown throws her arms wide open and rushes toward her son. Mr. Brown is wide-eyed with delight when he returns to find his son safe at home. The episode alludes to the parable of the prodigal son: Buster, once "lost," is now "found," and a feast is laid out to celebrate his return. Mrs. Brown offers what she initially withheld from Buster: the Thanksgiving dinner. She even overcompensates. While Buster eats a drumstick, she urges him to "have some more turkey." The theme of the prodigal son, popular in the Victorian period, evidently still resonated with audiences in the early twentieth century; Peter N. Stearns suggests that its appeal may have been its reassurance that children possess a "fundamental goodness [that] could overcome even transitional setbacks."[84] In the episode's last panel, Mrs. Brown rests her head on her husband's shoulder, and they both gaze lovingly at their son, who is tucked into bed, smiling at his parents. The scene emphasizes the theme of giving thanks, showing the members of the Brown family expressing gratitude for one another.

Scenes of heartfelt exchanges between parents and son are in fact not uncommon in the series, although Buster is sometimes confounded by his parents' displays of affection. In "Buster Brown Again. His Parents Fool Him," Buster flagrantly disobeys his father's directive to "go to bed early and be a good boy" (fig. 26).[85] He instead goads the maids and their suitors—a group of policemen—into performing an Irish jig. Like "Buster Brown—Photographer," this episode mocks the household help (as well as the Irish cops), depicting them as vulgar and imprudent. The maids kick up their legs and expose their petticoats; their dance upends the furniture. When Buster's parents return from their night out, the maids flee the scene with their suitors, abandoning the child who is supposed to be in their care. As his parents survey the scene and see the parlor in disarray, Buster thinks he has been "caught with the goods." He bids farewell to Tige, saying, "I'll get killed this time." But Buster and Tige are astonished when his parents simply bid him good night. With his father looking on in approval, Buster's mother bends down to kiss him. "Am I dreaming?" Tige wonders. A doubtful Buster remarks, "I *know*—it is April Fool." The cat explains that Mr. and Mrs. Brown have "been to see a play about a little lonesome boy with cruel parents." It seems that out of guilt, the Browns are making the effort to be more forgiving and understanding of their son, or attempting to make amends for leaving him in the company of irresponsible servants. The reference to the play draws attention to how early twentieth-century parents, anxious about correct child-rearing practices, often took instruction from external sources, in this case a theatrical production. Moreover, the image of the "lonesome boy" speaks to the emotive power of the victimized child. The image of the suffering child alters Mr. and Mrs. Brown's reaction to their son's misbehavior; in turn, the parents' display of fondness seems to transform Buster himself. After being showered with endearments, Buster resolves to "be good."

The episode's title hints that Buster's parents are tricking their son into good behavior, thus exposing how child-rearing, even when arising from love and devotion, often involves strategy and manipulation. Moreover, Mr. and Mrs. Brown's "trick" obviously has but a short-term effect on their son, as he returns to his prankish ways by the next episode. But *Buster Brown* does not necessarily assert that the companionate family is based on guile. Rather, it offers a picture of family members actively negotiating constant shifts in behavior and emotional states. The strip imagines the home as a site in which multiple and even contradictory feelings—misunderstanding and sympathy, frustration and acceptance, anger and affection, guilt and delight—can coexist.

"Every home . . . has a 'Buster Brown'"

The success of *Buster Brown* indicates that early twentieth-century readers were receptive to images of the playful parent and the mischief-making child. Outcault's savvy in licensing his character to multiple manufacturers certainly helped turn Buster Brown into a household name. As Ian Gordon notes, the character

Figure 26. Comic Strip by R. F. Outcault. "Buster Brown Again. His Parents Fool Him." In *Los Angeles Herald* Comic Supplement no. 126 (1904). SFS 70-6-2, San Francisco Academy of Comic Art Collection, the Ohio State University Billy Ireland Cartoon Library and Museum.

"united entertainment and consumer goods": "Indeed, 'Buster Brown' cannot be understood solely as a comic strip. All of his incarnations contributed to the makeup of his character, and each reinforced or advertised the others. Moreover this type of advertising, in the form of entertainment and consumption, allowed Buster's audience to expand their contact with the character by purchasing one of his products."[86] With his "celebrity [growing] out of multiple representations," Buster made his way into many American homes.[87] But the appeal of Buster Brown appears to lie in the fact that audiences perceived him as a realistic portrayal of a boy. In 1904, the *Chicago Tribune* ran "Do You Want to Join a Buster Brown Club?," a puff piece with the following claim:

> Parents have recognized a fairly accurate photograph of their hope and joy in the representation of little Mr. Brown.
>
> The [character] has also been recognized by the boys themselves, who have been shrewd enough to see that certain characteristics of their own were pictured in juvenile Mr. Brown.[88]

The *Tribune* concluded that "it is to be suspected that every home which has a small child between the ages of 6 and 12 has a 'Buster Brown.'"[89] Perhaps undergirding the *Tribune*'s suggestion that Buster was a "real" boy was Outcault's much-publicized declaration that he based the character on his own son.

The *Tribune* piece was prompted by a letter supposedly written by a seven-year-old boy, who claimed that he "dressed like Buster Brown and [my parents] say I act like Buster Brown, and I am going to form a Buster Brown club if I can find any other boys who dress like Buster Brown and act like Buster Brown and want to join the club."[90] Evidently, the young letter writer was not unique in donning a Buster Brown costume. The *New York Herald* documented the popularity of Buster Brown fashion in its feature "A Mass Meeting of the Buster Browns," in which several children, mostly but not exclusively boys, posed for the camera dressed as Buster (fig. 27).[91] The subtitle of the feature, "Brave Little Boys and Even Cute Little Girls Who Think They Are That Wonderful Child and Whose Fond Parents Think So Too," indicates that both children and parents were complicit in the act of "re-creating" Buster. Newspapers certainly helped fuel the fad for the Buster Brown costume. The features "How Mrs. Brown Ties Buster's Tie" and "How to Make a Buster Brown Suit," for example, included instructions on how to dress children so that they resemble the fictional character.[92]

One of the featured photographs in "A Mass Meeting" is that of young Archie Roosevelt, one of Theodore Roosevelt's children. It might appear ironic that a son of the man who advocated "the strenuous life" and championed outdoor sports and masculinity was put on display wearing clothes that were associated with the domestic and feminine. But perhaps the Buster Brown costumes enabled adult and child readers to delight in enacting "naughty" boyhood, to find fun

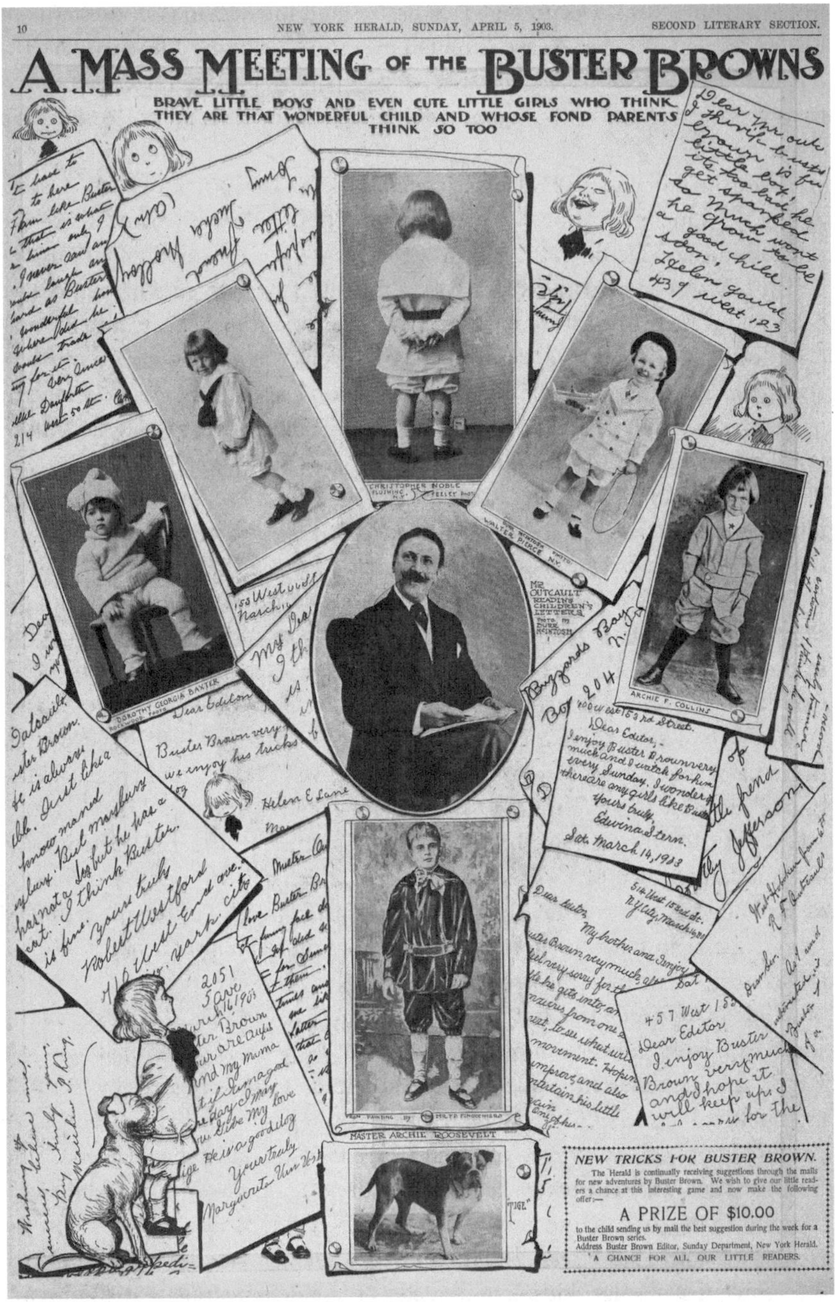

Figure 27. Promotional Material for R. F. Outcault's *Buster Brown*. "A Mass Meeting of the Buster Browns." In *New York Herald* Second Literary Section, April 5, 1903. SFS 31-4-1, San Francisco Academy of Comic Art Collection, the Ohio State University Billy Ireland Cartoon Library and Museum.

in testing boys' resistance to maternal desires and the demands of domesticity. Buster Brown fashion also gave parents a means of exhibiting affection. The *Tribune* and *Herald* features, for instance, coaxed parents to be indulgent and playful by permitting and encouraging their youngsters to dress up as a comic strip character.

Editors' comments in both the *Tribune* and the *Herald* focused on Buster's appeal to young male readers. "Do You Want to Join a Buster Brown Club?" was directly addressed to boys; the subtitle of "A Mass Meeting" implies that Buster's female fans were more the exception than the rule. However, girls appear to have been avid readers of the series, with many of them writing to Outcault, the editors, and Buster himself to claim that they "enjoy Buster Brown very much."[93] Young female readers' response to *Buster Brown* suggests that girls performed or had fantasies about performing mischief. Young Edwina Stern wrote to the editor of the *Herald* "[wondering] if there are any girls like Buster."[94] When the *Herald* encouraged young readers to send ideas for Buster Brown episodes, at least two selected entries were submitted by girls. Margaret Steber contributed the storyline for the May 24, 1903, episode "Buster Brown Just Fixes Up His Mama's Hair Tonic"; her name, address, and photograph were published underneath the title to acknowledge—and reward—her effort (fig. 28). Marjorie Lachmund sent in the idea for the December 27, 1903, episode "Buster Brown Helps the New Cook to Bake a Cake." Steber's and Lachmund's entries indicate that little girls are as capable of dreaming up mischief as little boys. Although *Buster Brown* depicts the female child as passive muse rather than active prankster, the open solicitation of ideas for Buster's antics provided young female readers a space to fantasize about and practice being bad and boyish. In other words, girls' participation in the Buster Brown phenomenon complicated the strip's restrictive definition of girlhood. As the examples above attest, young female readers participated in a comic strip phenomenon as a way of rewriting a cultural narrative that tended to place them in the periphery.

While many young readers used *Buster Brown* to indulge in fantasy pranks, some expressed concern about its protagonist's waywardness. Ballard Dole Wood, a nine-year-old reader from Honolulu, was distressed by Buster's mischief-making ways: "Why do you make so many mistakes?" he asked. "I like you and dont [*sic*] want to see you get whipped."[95] A reader named Helen Gould was also discomfited by the punishment that Buster received. "Its too bad he get spanked so much won't he grow up to be a good child soon," she wrote to the *Herald*.[96] While Chubb feared that children would imitate the misbehavior of the supplements' smart kids, letters such as these demonstrate that child readers were not so impressionable. It appears that some of them did not always approve of Buster's behavior and made distinctions between delightful play and disobedience, between the slapstick, hyperbolic humor in the strip and the rules of real life. Wood's and Gould's letters suggest that children were active

Figure 28. Comic Strip by R. F. Outcault. "Buster Brown Just Fixes Up His Mama's Hair Tonic." In *New York Herald* Comic Supplement, May 24, 1903. SFS 31-5-4, San Francisco Academy of Comic Art Collection, the Ohio State University Billy Ireland Cartoon Library and Museum.

readers: they did not necessarily imbibe the anarchic themes of the strip, but rather understood that "being like Buster" was an act they had to shed outside the sphere of play.

It is certainly worth questioning the authenticity of these letters purportedly written by child readers. Newspaper publishers may have manufactured such correspondence as an advertising ploy, attempting to build and maintain readership by publishing "proof" of other children caught up in the Buster Brown frenzy. There is evidence to show that children were active newspaper contributors who sent in letters, story ideas, poems, and illustrations, but it is not farfetched to conclude that editors carefully selected and revised the materials that young readers sent in. Still, these examples of correspondence, whether authentic or fabricated, published as is or heavily edited, can be understood as performances of childhood. These paratexts supported the notions that childhood is a period of play and delight, that both fictional and real children can inspire amusement.

Overall, it seems that both parents and children participated in welcoming Buster Brown into their homes. This cross-generational embrace of Buster illustrates how the ideal of the companionate family was being adopted by white, middle-class families across the nation. As Shirley Wajda notes, play became a "place" where turn-of-the-century Americans "displaced their ideals and where the tensions inherent in the shift to modernist . . . culture could be articulated and negotiated."[97] *Buster Brown* served as one such venue for play, providing parents and children a space in which they could find and share enjoyment. Through the strip, children received permission to make mischief. Parents, particularly mothers, willingly dressed up their boys in Buster Brown costumes, feminizing their sons while also condoning naughty behavior. By drawing inspiration from a comic strip, parents indulged in humor and found delight in the serious business of raising a boy.

Buster Brown recorded and participated in what Mintz and Kellogg term a turn-of-the-century "domestic revolution," during which the concept of the companionate family gained ground and replaced the ideal of a patriarchal-hierarchical structure. The strip championed the family as an institution that thrives in the face of internal conflicts and external pressures. *Buster Brown* became a source of leisure in the home, functioning as a domestic comedy that demonstrated and encouraged play, humor, and sympathy between parents and children. In the genial comedy of *Buster Brown*, however, there was also a not-so-hidden hostility directed at racial/ethnic and working-class groups whose values and habits were conceived as incommensurate with what Chubb called the "old home culture." While the strip fostered intimacy and inclusiveness in the white, middle-class family, it also excluded the supposed inferior entities that threatened to sully this "sacred" institution. Amiable laughter, as deployed in the strip, ultimately served to shore up Anglo-Saxon culture.

As the next chapter shows, some of Outcault's contemporaries entertained readers by focusing more on elements of fantasy rather than humor. Influenced by popular fantasy books and the burgeoning interest in child psychology, cartoonists such as Winsor McCay and Lyonel Feininger created protagonists who were preoccupied less with mischief-making and more with imaginative world-building. But in proposing that dreams and reverie allow the white, middle-class boy to develop his identity, assert his masculinity, and prepare for his role in a modernizing, expanding nation, McCay's and Feininger's strips undoubtedly echoed Outcault's celebration of exuberant boys like Buster Brown.

CHAPTER 4

THE "SECRET TRACTS" OF THE CHILD'S MIND

The child is here and he reigns, he commands, and oh how happy are we to follow his commands, for does he not reign in the land of joy, happiness and love? Indeed then are we happy to be subjects in this beautiful Fairyland.[1]

With these words, Augusti S. Earle opened his rapturous review of the Klaw and Erlanger theater production of *Little Nemo in Slumberland.* The play was based on Winsor McCay's eponymous strip, a popular series published in the *New York Herald* that chronicled a young boy's adventures in the realm of dreams.[2] In his review, Earle expressed his ardent wish for "every child from 'seven to seventy' [to] witness this performance, which words are inadequate to describe, for it is a memory and a pleasure it were hard to estimate."[3] Earle seemed to be enthralled not only by the "gorgeous production" of *Little Nemo* but also by the figure of the child that was represented in the play.[4] For Earle, *Little Nemo* accurately captured the image of the child as the sovereign of a world of fantasy and delight. He believed that this child was a deserving object of adult admiration and adoration.

In upholding the child as the monarch of Fairyland, Earle echoed a concept that was gaining traction among parents, educators, writers, artists, and psychologists during the Progressive Era: the concept that the child had an inherent attachment to fantasy. The play as well as the weekly strip upon which it was based were both popular and widely lauded, testifying to how the image of the imaginative child had become naturalized, celebrated, and even revered in the early twentieth century. This notion of childhood materialized beyond the stage and the newspaper page. Between 1860 and 1920, the period that literary historians often refer to as the Golden Age of Children's Literature, numerous children's books such as Lewis Carroll's *Alice's Adventures in Wonderland* (1865), L. Frank Baum's *The Wonderful Wizard of Oz* (1900), and J. M. Barrie's various *Peter Pan* narratives (published between 1902 and 1911) depicted the child as a born fantasist who accesses, and sometimes creates, fabulous realms that adults cannot readily enter. Around the same time, psychologists and practitioners associated with child study, a movement that took place on both sides of the Atlantic and was to become the foundation of what we know today as developmental psychology, argued that imaginative play and reverie were natural and healthful childhood activities.[5] Child study proponents advised parents and educators to take an active role in cultivating the imagination of children.

Little Nemo and other fantasy comic strips were clearly in conversation with contemporary children's literature as well as written texts produced by the child study movement, specifically as the movement developed in the United States. Using Winsor McCay's *Little Nemo in Slumberland* (1905–1911) and Lyonel Feininger's *Wee Willie Winkie's World* (1906–1907) as case studies, this chapter illustrates how fantasy comic strips drew from and built on literary and scientific discourses of childhood, becoming a third space in which the nature of the child and the workings of the child's mind were theorized. Like children's books and psychology tracts produced in the late nineteenth and early twentieth centuries, these strips perpetuated the image of the highly imaginative child and insisted that his perception and experience of the world was shaped by an "intrinsic" proclivity for fantasy. Moreover, these strips suggested that the child's "inherent" connection with fantasy made him a complex and sometimes inscrutable figure.

These strips not only reinforced but also complicated existing theories of the imaginative child. For one, they gave a *visual* dimension to the ideas offered by the field of psychology, providing readers a *picture* of what occurred in the child's mind and how the child saw the world. As Katherine Roeder notes, Progressive Era visual culture, such as paintings, lithographs, and children's book illustrations, already venerated (and commodified) the imaginative, dreaming child.[6] The narrative and serial quality of fantasy comic strips, however, offered readers a more expansive view of the child's interior world as well as invited them to look *through* the child's eyes. More significantly, these strips called attention to two related paradoxes of studying childhood: first, the strips demonstrated how theories of childhood insisted upon and even romanticized the elusiveness of the child while simultaneously making claims of knowing this child; second, the strips showed how the imaginative child who supposedly reigns and commands did so under the watchful eye of the adult.

McCay's *Little Nemo* and Feininger's *Wee Willie Winkie* participated in theorizing childhood while also exposing that this act of theorizing was fraught with contradictions. *Little Nemo* suggests that the child's power of imagination bestows him with autonomy. In accessing and constructing an elaborate dream world, the character Nemo not only fulfills the ideal of childhood innocence but also exercises agency and thus activates both longing for the (imagined) past and optimism about the future. Similarly, *Wee Willie Winkie* features a creative and independent protagonist who, despite or because of the lack of adult supervision, is able to transform his environment, turning natural and man-made objects into sentient beings. Yet both fantasy series also use metacomic elements to remind readers of the presence of the adult artist who is constructing and controlling the putatively inaccessible realm of the child. Thus both *Little Nemo* and *Wee Willie Winkie* can be understood as fantasies of childhood, in two senses of the term. On the one hand, these strips depicted the fantasies supposedly created by the child. On the other hand, these texts also revealed that the image of the dreamy, creative, and playful child was itself a fantasy, a figment of the adult imagination.

Intersecting Studies of Childhood: Children's Literature and the Emerging Field of Developmental Psychology

In her examination of intersections between literary works for children and scientific inquiries into childhood in the late nineteenth century, Juliet Dusinberre argues that research into the origin and development of the species not only "focused attention on the child" as a subject of inquiry but also "simultaneously produced for those children a literature which revealed as clearly as possible adult hopes for the new generation."[7] Holly Blackford similarly historicizes the relationship between children's literature and child psychology, suggesting that this relationship was more reciprocal than unilateral: as imaginative writers were influenced by contemporary psychological studies for children, psychologists were themselves "deeply influenced by the growing canon of children's literature . . . [and] cited writers and artists remembering childhood as evidence of child thought."[8] Blackford outlines parallel developments between the work of children's book writers such as Lewis Carroll and Robert Louis Stevenson and the writing produced by scientists and psychologists such as Charles Darwin, Bernard Perez, and James Sully, showing how, in the late nineteenth century, both literature and science actively investigated the differences between child consciousness and adult consciousness.

In his essay "Child's Play," first published in 1878, Stevenson argued that the child's perception of the world is necessarily different from the adult's because the former's "experience is incomplete":

> [Adults] know more than when they were children, they understand better, their desires and sympathies answer more nimbly to the provocation of the senses, and their minds are brimming with interest as they go about the world.
>
> This is a flight to which children cannot rise.[9]

In his 1893 tract *The Contents of Children's Minds on Entering School*, the psychologist G. Stanley Hall, who was to become the leading advocate of child study in the United States, echoed Stevenson's contention that the child's lack of experience shaped his consciousness and thus made him essentially different from the adult. Hall came to this conclusion after a decade-long study conducted among four hundred schoolchildren in Boston. Using a "questionnaire method"—interviewers asked their child subjects a fixed set of questions—Hall sought to "[obtain] an inventory of the contents of the minds of children of average intelligence on entering the primary schools."[10] By measuring children's grasp of concepts and comparing the results across racial, gender, and spatial lines, Hall intended to improve pedagogical practices. He noted that children had many misconceptions of natural phenomena and other common occurrences, such as beliefs that "meat [is] dug from the ground," "potatoes [are] picked from the trees," and "cheese is squeezed butter."[11] He warned that "in the absence of corrective experience," the child may end up creating and perpetuating "the most fantastic and otherwise unaccountable distortions of facts by shadowy word-spectres or husks."[12]

Yet Hall did not prescribe the reining in of children's imaginative-yet-inaccurate explanations of the world around them. Rather, he declared that children's "distortions" were natural and, given their lack of knowledge and inexperience, inevitable. Just as Stevenson claimed that "'making believe' is the gist of [the child's] whole life," Hall argued that children were predisposed toward daydreaming and imaginative play and that parents and educators must work to nurture rather than restrain such activities.[13] Contemporary writers for children echoed Hall's theories. In his introduction to *Wonderful Wizard of Oz*, Baum naturalized the image of childhood that Hall promoted, writing that "every healthy youngster has a wholesome and instinctive love for stories fantastic, marvelous and manifestly unreal."[14]

Hall even romanticized the purported complexities and mysteries of the child's mind. Convinced that there were "secret tracts in [children's] minds," he felt that the "most intelligent adults quite commonly fail to recognize sides of their own children's souls."[15] Hall's image of secret tracts is quite similar to the description of the child's mind in Barrie's *Peter and Wendy*. In the novel, Barrie characterizes the mind of the child as one that cannot be easily mapped, as it "keeps going round all the time.... It is all rather confusing, especially as nothing will stand still."[16] Hall, however, believed that there was an effective strategy to understanding the child: careful observation and interviewing of children could allow adults to comprehend and, in effect, theorize their young subjects.[17]

Many Progressive Era women responded, quite enthusiastically, to Hall's theories and methods. Emily Cahan goes as far as to say that "mothers and teachers... became zealots... for child study."[18] Hall took advantage of women's interest, turning to clubs and organizations to vigorously recruit women to the movement and persuade them to monitor and take notes on their children. In essence, he envisioned the home and the classroom as laboratories where one could collect empirical evidence on young people. Hall's methods and teachings were roundly criticized in academic circles, but his ideas were embraced by parents, educators, and other child workers.[19] Women involved in the child study movement wrote numerous magazine articles and advice books on child-rearing and classroom management, endorsing observation as a tool for measuring and ensuring child development. For example, in *The Kingdom of the Child* (1918), Alice Minnie Herts Heniger argued that the most effective way to understand the child was to "observe his methods while he is enjoying perfect freedom in undirected play."[20] Under child study, children became research subjects to be scrutinized, assessed, and interpreted. As Steven Mintz puts it, Progressive Era children, especially those from white, middle-class homes, were placed "under the magnifying glass."[21]

Psychologists practiced and promoted the method of observation as a tool for understanding the child's mind, an approach that contemporary children's book writers were already utilizing. British stories familiar to Progressive Era readers—for example, Carroll's *Alice's Adventures in Wonderland* and *Through the Looking-Glass, and What Alice Found There* (1871) and Barrie's various *Peter Pan* narratives (chapters published in the 1902 *The Little White Bird*; the play *Peter Pan; or, The Boy Who Would Not Grow Up*, first staged in London in 1904 and in New York in 1905; the 1906 children's book *Peter Pan in Kensington Gardens*; and the 1911 novel *Peter and Wendy*)—were purportedly inspired by the authors' interactions with and observations of real children.[22] Carroll and Barrie often acknowledged the presence of the "real" child in their books: *Through the Looking-Glass* ends with an anagrammatic poem about Alice Liddell,[23] and in his dedication to the published version of the *Peter Pan* play, Barrie reminisces about meeting the Llewelyn Davies boys.[24] By emphasizing the presence of "real" children in their books, these authors suggested that their texts could be understood as true records of childhood and that their exchanges with children allowed them to accurately represent these "elusive" subjects in text.

Psychology and literature thus concurrently expressed the belief that careful examination of the child would enable the adult to perceive, recreate, and write about the child's secret tracts. Both fields canonized childhood's attachment to fantasy. Although many child study tracts insisted that the child was not fully capable of distinguishing between the imaginary and the real, they also glorified childhood as, in James Sully's words, "the age of imagination."[25] At the same time, fantasy children's books became widely available. These texts showed child characters accessing worlds such as Wonderland, Neverland, and Oz; interacting with fairies, mermaids, and other mysterious entities; and transforming inanimate objects into sentient beings. Coded in these texts was the assumption that child readers would easily suspend their disbelief and embrace fantastical elements and narratives.

The fantasy comic strips published in early twentieth-century newspapers were shaped by and contributed to these parallel developments in psychology and children's literature. They reiterated and perpetuated theories that the child was a natural fantasist who had secret tracts that adults could not easily penetrate. But these fantasy comic strips also offered a visual theory of childhood, in the sense that they presented pictorial representations of the contents of children's dreams and processes of children's imagination and perception. In other words, they made tangible and accessible the parts of the child that were not readily visible and available to the adult. McCay's *Little Nemo in Slumberland* and Feininger's *Wee Willie Winkie's World* demonstrate how fantasy comic strips served as spaces in which childhood's supposed inherent connection with fantasy was depicted, promoted, and exalted.

A Fantasy of Childhood: Winsor McCay's *Little Nemo in Slumberland*

Winsor McCay's *Little Nemo in Slumberland* debuted in James Gordon Bennett Jr.'s *New York Herald* on October 15, 1905, and had a successful run in the newspaper for six years. In 1911, McCay accepted an offer to work for William Randolph Hearst's *New York American and Journal* (before 1902, the paper was called *New York Journal*). He continued to draw the strip under the *American*, retitling it as *In the Land of Wonderful Dreams*.[26] After three years, *Wonderful Dreams* ended its run as McCay, under pressure by Hearst, shifted his focus to producing editorial cartoons.[27] He attempted to revive *Little Nemo* in the late 1920s, but the series did not come close to matching the commercial success of the original version.

The strip revolves around the adventures of Nemo, a boy with perpetually tousled hair, as he explores the world of dreams. *Little Nemo* provides very few glimpses of Nemo's waking life, although it establishes that his family abides by middle-class beliefs about child-centered spaces and objects: his parents provide him a separate bedroom as well as a bed and clothing specifically designed for children. For the first few months of its run, the series' plot focused on Nemo's slow approach toward the Palace of Slumberland, where the Princess, who "crave[s] a playmate," patiently waits for him.[28] Nemo soon meets and befriends the gentle Princess as well as the cigar-chomping Flip and the dark-skinned Imp. These three supporting characters become his constant companions in the land of dreams. Together, they wander around the seemingly borderless realm of Slumberland. In the last panel of each episode, Nemo abruptly wakes up, his dream disrupted. But by the next episode, he effortlessly slips back into Slumberland and resumes his adventure. The series thus moves with the rhythm of dreaming and waking, movement and interruption.

In creating *Little Nemo*, McCay seemed to take his cue from popular children's books of the period. For one, he also coded a "real" child in his strip: it was widely reported that the series' protagonist was based on McCay's son, Robert Winsor. The name Slumberland also clearly paid homage to Carroll's Wonderland and Barrie's Neverland. While the title of the series was clearly a nod to British fantasy literature, *Little Nemo* was arguably also inspired by the success of Baum's *Wonderful Wizard of Oz*, published in the United States a few years earlier. McCay's strip was also building on trends in newspaper comics. By the time *Little Nemo* debuted, newspaper supplements—especially ones produced by publishers who consciously appealed to middle-class readers—had already been expounding on fantasy's association with childhood. The *New York Herald* was particularly invested in publishing narratives about dreamy, imaginative children. After leaving William Randolph Hearst's *New York American and Journal*, R. F. Outcault, then most well known for the Yellow Kid, began his stint at the *Herald* by producing spot illustrations for a fiction series in which a young boy's toys came to life. In 1903, the *Herald* launched artist Henry "Hy" Mayer's illustrated series *Will O' Dreams and the Sandman*. *Will O' Dreams* was short-lived, but it can be considered a precursor to *Little Nemo*, as it centered on the adventures of a young boy who encounters talking beasts and mythical creatures in his dreams.

It was the popular and long-running *Little Nemo*, however, that testified to Progressive Era enthusiasm for fantastical narratives for the young. A number of critics, alarmed by the proliferation of strips that featured rowdy, mischief-making children, upheld McCay's strip and his image of the dreamy child as welcome antidotes to the "noisy, explosive, garrulous pandemonium" in the comic supplement.[29] The literary critic Ralph Bergengren, who dismissed the comic supplement as having a "perverse and cynical intention . . . to prove the American sense of humor a thing of national shame and degradation," praised *Little Nemo* for providing a moment of "rest and refreshment."[30] He singled out McCay as a "man of genuine pantomimic humor, charming draughtsmanship, and an excellent decorative sense of color, who has apparently studied his medium and makes the best of it."[31] Bergengren also imagines *Little Nemo* as creating a safe *interior* space for the child: "out of the noisy streets, the cheap restaurants with their unsteady-footed waiters and avalanches of soup and crockery, out of the slums, the quarreling families, the prisons and the lunatic asylums, we step for a moment into the world of childish fantasy, closing the iron door behind us and trying to shut out the clamor of hooting mobs, the laughter of imbeciles, and the crash of explosives."[32] In Bergengren's view, *Little Nemo* allowed young readers to retreat inward, to move into the cloisters of their minds, away from the profanities of the slums and the streets.

For McCay, however, dreaming was not exclusively the province of childhood. In his adult-geared series *Dreams of the Rarebit Fiend*, which ran concurrently with *Little Nemo*, he focused on picturing adults' dreams. Bennett, the *Herald* publisher, was keen to protect McCay's image as a "child-friendly" artist, and he instructed McCay to draw *Rarebit Fiend* under a pen name.[33] McCay thus signed the strip as "Silas," and Bennett published *Rarebit Fiend* in another newspaper, *The Evening Telegram*. But it was not simply the artist's signature and site of publication that spelled the difference between the two series. In juxtaposition,

Rarebit Fiend and *Little Nemo* insist on the distinct natures of adults' and children's dreams, desires, and preoccupations.

In *Rarebit Fiend*, the realm of dreams functions as a space where dreamers confront their anxieties about "adult" concerns: career, love, marriage, sexual intimacy, money, and mortality. The adult characters tend to experience terrifying nightmares rather than pleasant dreams. In each episode's last panel, the dreamer wakes up, often in a panic. He or she immediately places the blame on the rich meal—often a cheesy Welsh rarebit—that he or she consumed before going to bed. The dreamer promptly vows to never eat rarebit again. As one character puts it, "that mince pie with melted cheese does some funny things with you but I'm done. No more for me."[34] In declaring "no more for me," the adult dreamer apprehends the dream world as a dreadful place that is not worth another visit.

Little Nemo also uses the conceit of waking up in the last panel. Some episodes conclude with Nemo startled awake by strange events that transpire in the dream; in other episodes, he wakes when he falls out of bed. Whether he wakes up frightened or befuddled, his parents and adult relatives often rush to his bedside to comfort him. In one dream, Nemo rapidly ages, becoming an old man with a long white beard. He wakes up and cries out, "Am I an old man? Mamma! Oh!" His mother tries to alleviate her son's distress, minimizing his dream by saying, "You were only dreaming, Nemo."[35] In another episode, when Nemo wakes up "trembling with rage," his father instructs him to "go to sleep . . . and stop that dreaming."[36] Here, Nemo's father views dreams as an impediment to a good night's sleep. Like the adult characters of *Rarebit Fiend*, the adults in *Little Nemo* view the dream world as a place that one can, and perhaps should, refuse to enter. In a sense, *Little Nemo* recalls Lewis Carroll's notion that the deep connection with dreams, characteristic of childhood, is severed in adulthood. At the end of *Alice's Adventures in Wonderland*, Carroll shows how the adult dreams "after a fashion." Alice's older sister only "half believe[s] herself in Wonderland":

> She knew she had but to open [her eyes] again, and all would change to dull reality—the grass would be only rustling in the wind, and the pool rippling to the waving of the reeds—the rattling teacups would change to tinkling sheep-bells, and the Queen's shrill cries to the voice of the shepherd-boy—and the sneeze of the baby, the shriek of the Gryphon, and all the other queer noises, would change (she knew) to the confused clamor of the busy farm-yard.[37]

Alice's sister envies her younger sibling's ability to tumble headlong into a fantastic realm, yet she herself dispels her dream while in the very act of dreaming. Like *Alice's Adventures*, *Little Nemo* insists on the differences between children's and adults' understanding of dreams: what is a tangible space for Nemo is, for adults, "only" a dream.

The designs of *Rarebit Fiend* and *Little Nemo* also envisage stark differences between the contents of adult's minds and children's minds. *Rarebit Fiend* was, for much of its run, a black-and-white strip; a significant number of its episodes had nearly empty backgrounds (see fig. 29).[38] *Little Nemo*, on the other hand, was a full-color strip in which McCay attended to minute details. For example, he painstakingly drew the stripes of several zebras, the feathers of two peacocks, and the radiant rays of the sun—all in a single episode (fig. 30).[39] While many episodes of *Rarebit Fiend* picture the adult's dream world as desolate and monochromatic, *Little Nemo* imagines the child's realm of dreams as rich and vivid.[40] Sigmund Freud, in *The Interpretation of Dreams* (1899; first English translation, 1913), describes children's dreams as "innocuous," as "simple wish-fulfillments [that are] of no interest at all compared with the dreams of adults."[41] In *Little Nemo*, McCay pushes back against Freud, offering pictures of children's captivating, intricate dreams.

As Roeder observes, *Little Nemo* put McCay's skilled use of perspective and knowledge of architecture on full display; he often utilized "unusual visual angles" that reflected how technological advancements in transportation, such as elevated trains and amusement rides, were offering new vantage points from which to view the city.[42] The spectacular settings of *Little Nemo* were also likely inspired by the theater. Before he began his cartooning career, McCay designed signs, posters, and backdrops for the Vine Street Dime Museum and Palace Theater in Cincinnati.[43] Even when he enjoyed success as a cartoonist, McCay remained an active patron and participant of the theater, often joining the vaudeville circuit as a lightning sketch artist. John Canemaker also observes that in drawing *Little Nemo*, McCay took inspiration from the circus and amusement parks.[44] With his elaborate and colorful illustrations of garments and the interiors and exteriors of palaces and other grand structures, *Little Nemo* may have reminded early twentieth-century readers of costumes and stage designs of the theater and the circus. But the backdrop of *Little Nemo* changed week to week, as Nemo encountered new characters, new structures, and new geographical features in each episode. One episode's "set" was built, utilized, then taken down to make way for the following episode's set. With relentlessly shifting settings, McCay implies that Nemo's mind, so inextricably tied to the dream realm, is itself in a state of continuous metamorphosis.

That *Little Nemo* featured a recurring protagonist—an element absent in *Rarebit Fiend*—also points to differences in the nature of adults' and children's dreams. *Rarebit Fiend* was episodic, featuring different, often nameless protagonists in each installment. The series depicted the adult's encounter with the dream world as brief and lacking in continuity. In *Rarebit Fiend*, the lack of recurring characters suggests that adults rarely experience recurring or serial dreams. *Little Nemo*, on the other hand, suggests that the child's dreams develop into an

Figure 29. Comic Strip by Winsor McCay. "Dreams of the Rarebit Fiend." In *San Francisco Call* Comic Supplement, January 23, 1906. SFC 34, San Francisco Academy of Comic Art Collection, the Ohio State University Billy Ireland Cartoon Library and Museum.

Figure 30. Excerpt from Comic Strip by Winsor McCay. "Little Nemo in Slumberland." Originally printed in *New York Herald* Comic Supplement.

extended, sustained narrative. Even as Nemo finds himself ejected from Slumberland at the end of each episode, he effortlessly returns to the dream world in the following episode, almost at the same point where the previous installment ended. The first few months of the strip, for example, illustrates Nemo's rather laborious journey toward the Palace of Slumberland. Nemo's progress is interrupted each time he wakes up, but the next episode puts him right back on track. In this pattern of forward movement and brief suspension, waking life is depicted as interfering with Nemo's adventure. However, it is worth noting that the image of a wide-awake Nemo is typically relegated to the episode's narrow, final panel. The last panel, showing Nemo's small bed and bare bedroom walls, appears bland and insignificant when juxtaposed with the colorful, vivid, and detailed panels that precede it. As Scott Bukatman reminds us, "The mundane life our Nemo led during the day [was a life] to which the reader was never privy."[45] Perhaps such absence hints that the life that Nemo lives out in slumber and dreams is infinitesimally more intriguing, more deserving of dramatization and visualization.

Nemo as a Link to the Past and the Future

Given McCay's attention to scenery, objects, and the peoples and creatures that populate the land of dreams, Slumberland, rather than young Nemo, may appear to be the true star of the series. McCay suggests that Slumberland is a borderless realm that is inhabited by fairies, elves, giants, mermaids, "exotic" animals, and "primitive" races, and is marked by unique geological formations. McCay seemed more invested in giving depth and dimension to the strip's setting rather than its protagonist. Indeed, the descriptor "little" insists on Nemo's diminutiveness, implying that he is destined to be absorbed by Slumberland rather than stand out in it. Some readers may even interpret him as a passive character, one who unquestioningly follows the lead of the Princess, Flip, the Imp, and other Slumberland residents. "Oh!" is his signature cry, an interjection that expresses his constant awe and surprise at encountering different characters, objects, structures, and landscapes. It is as if Nemo's role is to stand back and witness the strangeness and wondrousness of Slumberland. Sometimes, he even appears to be at the mercy of the dream world. In one sequence of episodes, he falls victim to a violently changing landscape, tossed about by shifting tides and stumbling as the earth shakes and cracks beneath his feet.[46]

Nemo, then, appears to have no control over Slumberland. The series hints that this dream realm existed before and will continue to exist beyond Nemo, in much the same way that Neverland in the *Peter Pan* narratives predates and will outlast Wendy Darling. But Nemo's ability to effortlessly enter a preexisting, ancient realm aligns with G. Stanley Hall's belief that childhood was attached to the primal and mythological. A proponent of recapitulation theory, Hall likened the child to a member of a primitive tribe, claiming that there were "deep roots in the childish heart" that were anchored in superstition and folktales.[47] In his preface to *Aspects of Child Life and Education* (1907), Hall further linked the child to the primitive, arguing that children's acts of daydreaming can be understood as "[rehearsals of] the experiences of our remote forbears."[48] Nemo's connection with the "ancient" world of Slumberland makes manifest the child's "deep roots."

In attaching the child to the past, the strip activates nostalgia. *Little Nemo* evokes a fairy tale aura of "once upon a time" and "far, far away"; the monarchy of Slumberland, with its king, princess, and royal court, may have appeared to twentieth-century readers as a world long gone, or at least a world left behind. In *Alice's Adventures*, Alice's sister mourns her lost childhood as well as the childhood Alice will eventually lose. Similarly, *Little Nemo* intimates the tragedy of impermanence: monarchs belong to a different age, and children will grow up and cease to dream fabulous dreams. The series allows adult readers to indulge in yearning for their lost childhoods as well as "relive" childhood's (imagined) pleasures. *Little Nemo* also instructs child readers to recognize the transience—and pricelessness—of their abilities to fantasize, to make believe.[49]

But even as *Little Nemo* sentimentalizes the ephemeral quality of childhood, it also paradoxically attempts to provide an antidote to growing up. It does so by preserving the image of the dreamful child in the recurring, unchanging character of Nemo. While Carroll ended his narrative by wistfully admitting that

Alice will, "in the after-time, be herself a grown woman," McCay kept Nemo in his child state through years' worth of episodes.[50] In *Peter and Wendy*, Peter also remains perpetually in his child state but becomes distressed when he realizes that Wendy has grown up to become a "tall beautiful creature."[51] He is made to witness such transformations repeatedly as Wendy's daughter and granddaughter (and presumably future descendants) fly with him to Neverland until they become "common grown-up[s]."[52] In *Little Nemo*, the protagonist is more Peter than Wendy—he does not grow up, despite the passage of time. McCay occasionally marks time in his strip, most visibly in his New Year's Day episodes, in which the cartoonist utilizes the motif of an old man welcoming and making way for a newborn. Yet the series' young protagonist himself does not age: Nemo wakes up in (or out of) the same child-sized bed Sunday after Sunday.

This is not to say that Nemo is in a state of complete stasis. The strip asserts that his capacity to dream and fantasize, which keeps Nemo childlike, is also the quality that allows him to move forward and eventually outgrow childhood. In *Little Nemo*, Slumberland functions as a space where the protagonist is able to manage the unknown, assert autonomy, and practice resourcefulness. In other words, while the strip works to immortalize childhood innocence and evoke nostalgia, it also uses the concept of childhood imagination to celebrate progress and innovation and promote optimism about the future.

In her examination of modernist picture books for children published after World War I, Margaret R. Higonnet discusses how modernists helped establish the image of the innocent child as "an emblem of the future, and therefore, of modernity."[53] Higonnet identifies a "duality of the Modernists' symbolic child: not only an image of origins, nature, and archaic expressiveness, but also an image of an increasingly technological and mechanically innovative future."[54] The modernists' child metaphor was thus at once "deploy[ed] with nostalgic, backward-turned strain" and a "forward-looking revolutionary vision."[55] *Little Nemo* arguably prefigured the children's books of modernist artists such as El Lissitzky, Kurt Schwitters, and Mary Liddell. Nemo embodies the dualisms of past and future, inertia and movement, passivity and agency. On the one hand, Nemo is rooted in the romantic ideal: he is an imaginative innocent, whose dreams linked him to the primitive and prerational. On the other hand, his imagination is also a sign of energy and ingenuity, allowing him to be a child who could easily adapt to a rapidly changing world. His ability to make-believe suggests he has not yet been ossified by the rationalities and responsibilities that mark adulthood.

While the series sometimes depicts Nemo as an inert and sometimes incapacitated figure, it also implies that Slumberland both predates Nemo and arises from Nemo himself: this intricate, mysterious world is partly a product of his active, enigmatic mind. Slumberland is a world that Nemo expands and populates by drawing from the fairy stories he hears and reads; the plays, pageants, and parades he watches; the holidays he enjoys; the images he sees in photographs; and the spectacles he witnesses in the city. The dreaming child in *Little Nemo* is intensely aware of his surroundings, capable of appropriating elements from waking life and utilizing them in his private fantasies. As such, the strip recalls some of Robert Louis Stevenson's poems in *A Child's Garden of Verses* (1885). For example, in "Young Night-Thought," a child drifts off to sleep and has this vision:

> Armies and emperors and kings
> All carrying different kinds of things,
> And marching in so grand a way,
> You never saw the like by day.
>
> So fine a show was never seen
> At the great circus on the green;
> For every kind of beast and man
> Is marching in that caravan.[56]

In both strip and poem, the child seems to adopt images and narratives that he has seen, heard, and read to generate his own narratives and adventures. Both texts also show how the child who lies asleep in bed, a seemingly passive figure, has a wildly active imagination that takes him to a world outside the walls of his nursery.

Little Nemo also repeats the martial and imperial imagery in Stevenson's "Young Night-Thought." While Stevenson's poem alludes to the "glories" of the British Empire, McCay's strip, published in the first decade of the twentieth century, can be understood as expressing the United States' nascent fantasies of expansionism. In one series of episodes, children from all over the world present themselves to Nemo, who sits above and apart from the parading children, a visual statement of his more privileged position as a white American boy (fig. 31).[57] The parade is reminiscent of a real pageant that took place on August 2, 1904, at the World's Fair in St. Louis. The day was designated as "Children's Day," and the fair's young and presumably white visitors were given free entry to the fair as well as treated to a procession of "strange children" from China, Ceylon, Japan, the Philippines, and Native American reservations.[58] At the World's Fair, the parade—as well as the ethnological exhibits featuring live subjects—accentuated the boundary between self and other, between observer and observed, between (white) Americans and members of "inferior" races and nations.[59] Children's Day provided an elaborate spectacle that trained young white Americans to view foreign and nonwhite children as their subjects.

That *Little Nemo* intertwined imperialism with childhood imagination is not surprising. Hall and other child study practitioners, who obsessively gathered data on children and sought to create standards of "normal" child development, were driven by the belief that they were nurturing the (Anglo-Saxon)

Figure 31. Excerpt from Comic Strip by Winsor McCay. "Little Nemo in Slumberland." Originally printed in *New York Herald* Comic Supplement.

heirs to a growing American empire. Encouraging activities such as reverie and imaginative play purportedly secured the white child's mental fitness, kept him on the path toward healthy adulthood, and prepared him to inherit the nation-empire. In 1917, Baum made a similar connection between fantasy, health, and progress, stating in his introduction to *The Lost Princess of Oz* that "the imaginative child will become the imaginative man or woman most apt to create, to invent, and therefore to foster civilization."[60] At first glance, it may seem as if Nemo is too inactive a character to become the "imaginative man" who would protect the civilized world. As Roeder puts it, Nemo is largely a passive figure who "embodies the transition from a society of producers to a society of consumers."[61] His practice of citizenship initially appears to be limited to the acts of spectatorship and consumption. But the themes of exploration, conquest, and white supremacy coded in the strip shows how a white, middle-class American boy uses the dreamscape to rehearse the roles of soldier, leader, and colonizer. It is worth noting that even after the heyday of *Little Nemo*, there was much to-do when the then-adult Robert McCay, the cartoonist's son and model for the fictive Nemo, received "the British military medal" for his service in World War I and involvement in the Hundred Days Offensive.[62] Several newspapers published a photograph of the young sergeant in uniform with his famous father.[63] The photograph's title "Little Nemo Home with War Honors" seems an eager validation of the promise of youth, a celebration of what could result from childhood whimsy and reverie: here was the real-life Nemo, a dreamer who grew up to be a valiant soldier. Much scholarship has discussed the pressures placed upon Anglo-Saxon women in the early twentieth century, as they were condemned for attending more to leisure than domestic responsibilities, for "feminizing" their sons, for committing "race suicide."[64] The interrelated discourses of child study, children's literature, and fantasy comic strips, however, remind us that anxieties about racial and imperialist legacies were also projected upon white children in the early twentieth century.

In *Little Nemo*, the eponymous protagonist seems to understand his responsibility to the future. Although he is often overwhelmed by the dream world's strange features and is dependent on the guidance of the residents, he is also viewed and treated as the lord of Slumberland. Many residents of Slumberland acknowledge his presence with a bow, welcoming him to a kingdom that seems to have always belonged to him. Interestingly, the image of the "child's kingdom" was commonly invoked during the Progressive Era, as demonstrated by Earle in his review of the *Little Nemo* play and Heniger in the title of her child study book. The notion of the child's kingdom not only insists that the child has a realm that is distinct from the world of the adult, but also suggests that the child, empowered by his natural imagination, governs this space and exercises authority over the characters he invents. For Nemo, these "made-up" figures include tribal peoples and slum dwellers, indicating that those deemed Other are nothing more than fantasy figures that he could bring to life as his subjects.

In essence, Nemo's juxtaposition with three child (or childlike) characters—the Imp, the Princess, and Flip—puts him in stark relief against images of the primitive, the feminine, and the untameable, uncouth troublemaker. *Little Nemo*, in other words, defines the Anglo-Saxon boy by way of contrast. Moreover, while the series clearly maintains that Nemo is a child, the other characters' ages are more ambiguous, hinting that characters that are savage, female, and vulgar are immature, are *like* children.

The Imp clearly referenced contemporary infantilizing caricatures of the so-called primitive.[65] The editorial cartoon "Holding His End Up," published in the *Philadelphia Inquirer* in 1898, commented on the United States' ambitious project of empire-building by depicting Uncle Sam as an acrobat who skillfully performs a balancing act with the spoils of the Spanish-American War, represented here as dark-skinned, "kinky"-haired, and nearly naked children who carry U.S. flags labeled "Cuba," "Porto Rico," "the Philippines," and "Ladrone I" (or Ladrones Islands).[66] The child who stands atop Uncle Sam's head wears short pants labeled "Hawaii." The Imp, a brown, bug-eyed, gibberish-speaking island dweller who wears a grass skirt, is similarly expressive of the entanglements of colonialism and racism. In one episode, McCay mocks the Imp by equating him with primates. Nemo, Flip, and the Imp open a giant picture book that contains their images drawn in the style of caricature. The picture book versions of Nemo and Flip have exaggerated features, but nonetheless bear a strong resemblance to their subjects. Meanwhile, the Imp is portrayed as a furry, tailed, and thick-lipped creature balancing on a tree branch (fig. 32).[67] The picture book caption reads, "So you are a Jungle Imp? You look more like a Baboon!"[68] Flip exclaims with a laugh, "That's the best picture of the Imp I ever saw. Haw! Haw!"[69]

While the Imp is made into an object of ridicule, the Princess is characterized as the object of Nemo's desire. Even as she pines for Nemo's company, she exercises little effort to move toward him. Instead, she waits in the palace, sometimes in tears, functioning as the prize that Nemo must earn. The Princess also represents the fantasy of the female as simultaneously exuding both purity and desirability. In one episode, she literally gleams like a jewel. When the Imp turns off the lights in the palace, the characters are swallowed by darkness, with only their faces visible. The exception is the Princess, who remains visible from head to toe.[70] As Richard Dyer argues, "at the heart of the conception of whiteness as virtue [is] absence,"[71]; the glowing body of the Princess signifies that she is immaculate, untouched by vice and vulgarities. Despite contact with the "profanities" of the masculine and the Other, she remains virginal and sacred. Paradoxically, it is her chasteness that ostensibly seduces Nemo, Flip, and the readers of *Little Nemo*.

Figure 32. Excerpt from Comic Strip by Winsor McCay. "Little Nemo in Slumberland." Originally printed in *New York Herald* Comic Supplement.

Nemo's relationship with Flip is perhaps the most complex in the series. Their relationship is initially antagonistic. Flip, a "bad and brazen brat," becomes Nemo's "first enemy in Slumberland" as he works to obstruct Nemo's journey toward the Princess.[72] Enraged by Flip's tricks, Nemo declares that he would "like to get a hold of that Flip, oh!"[73] But Nemo is soon enthralled by Flip, a character who is cousin to the bad boys and tricksters that appeared in numerous contemporary comics such as H. C. Greening's *The Tinkle Brothers*, Rudolph Dirks's *The Katzenjammer Kids*, and R. F. Outcault's *Buster Brown*. Nemo helps save Flip from execution, and thereafter, the two become constant companions. The relationship between the two is a figurative representation of the allure of trouble and troublemaking, especially for boys.

Overall, Nemo's attachment to the Imp, the Princess, and Flip expresses Progressive Era anxieties about boyhood being sullied by aspects that are uncivilized, feminine, and disruptive. But *Little Nemo* also soothes these anxieties, showing how the male child, despite constant interaction with and even attraction to "wrong" or "inferior" elements, is able to maintain his distance from them. Notably, it is in a sequence set in a slum area called Shantytown, where Nemo is without the guidance of these three supporting characters, that he is able to fully play the role of leader and savior (fig. 33).[74] The only help he receives is from a fairy, who bestows Nemo with a wand—an object that Nemo later calls a "wish-stick."[75] Aghast by the poverty and suffering that he sees in Shantytown, Nemo proceeds to transform the "ramshackle city" into a "paradise."[76] He uses the wish-stick to turn the residents' rags into "the best of clothes," convert a dump into a park, replace a jailhouse with a candy store (which he then turns into a church), and heal the blind, the crippled, and the sick.[77] At the end of one of the Shantytown episodes, Nemo cries out to the residents, "Follow me and you'll all be happy!!!!"[78] The Shantytown sequence, as M. Thomas Inge points out, was published to commemorate Easter.[79] These episodes clearly allude to the miracles of Jesus; Nemo's revitalization of the slum could be understood as a reference to Jesus's resurrection, the most magnificent of miracles. But the Shantytown sequence also reminds readers of the image of Jesus as the Holy Child. "[He's] a strange beautiful boy," says one of the mesmerized slum dwellers.[80] Indeed, the slum residents appear to be astonished by Nemo, in much the same way that visitors at the temple were awestruck by the prodigious twelve-year-old Jesus.

The sequence set in Shantytown also clearly alludes to the work of white, middle-class Progressive Era reformers who sought to "uplift" immigrants and the working class and beautify their surroundings. It may be that the sequence dismisses the efforts of such reformers as fantasy, as impossible projects that can only occur in the world of dreams. But the sequence also suggests how *imagination* may be key to the project of "saving" those who lived in squalor. It also assumes that the white, middle-class, and male child has unique potential. Depicted as leader and redeemer, Nemo is set apart from the helpless, ragged, and

Figure 33. Excerpt from Comic Strip by Winsor McCay. "Little Nemo in Slumberland." Originally printed in *New York Herald* Comic Supplement.

"ethnic" residents of Shantytown. As the one who bears the wish-stick, Nemo is allowed to freely impose his fantasies and values on the slum dwellers, giving them the gift of order, cleanliness, and religion as he fulfills his vision of paradise. The sequence suggests that ultimately, the transformation of the slum benefits Nemo more than the residents. In the realm of dreams, he is able to practice the roles of leader, visionary, and messiah. In the meantime, the miraculous changes to the residents' environment cannot change their nature. Even as they wear fancy clothes, some of them still speak in a rough dialect, a sign that they have yet to transcend their so-called coarseness. Nemo's miracles have not necessarily empowered or transformed them, and their purpose seems to be to follow Nemo and bear witness to the deeds that this "wonderful" boy is performing.[81]

The Child as Solitary Daydreamer: Lyonel Feininger's *Wee Willie Winkie's World*

As the *New York Herald* celebrated the critical and commercial success of *Little Nemo*, the *Chicago Tribune* scrambled to hire artists who could create similar fantasy comic strips that could bolster the paper's appeal to children (and their parents).[82] The newspaper also sought to broaden its readership, especially among the city's German immigrant population. The paper's publisher and editors were aware that many German immigrants read *The Katzenjammer Kids*, created by the German-born Dirks. They engaged in a campaign to hire eminent German caricaturists and succeeded in securing the services of Hans Horina, Karl Pommerhanz, Victor Schramm, and the American-born Lyonel Feininger.[83] By the time he joined the *Tribune* in 1906, Feininger was studying art in Germany, his parents' homeland.[84]

The *Tribune* considered the hiring of Feininger, whom they labeled "a famous German artist," to be quite a coup. To drum up interest for his strip *The Kin-der-kids*, the *Tribune* set up a robust advertising campaign. Touting Feininger as "the most popular cartoonist in Germany's capital," the paper declared that "his drawings have worldwide circulation" and that "there is no better draftsman in the world than Mr. Feininger."[85] Just before the release of the strip, the *Tribune* published a portrait gallery of an oddball cast of characters, including the three Kin-der brothers: Daniel Webster, a "mental gymnast and Infant prodigy"; the insatiable Pie-mouth, who "never [had] been known to refuse his victuals"; and Strenuous Teddy, a "phenomenally constituted lad" who served as a mild parody of Theodore Roosevelt and his glorification of "the strenuous life."[86] In the series, the brothers set off to see the world in the family bathtub. The tub is propelled by a clockwork automaton named Little Japansky, a figure cast in the mold of the slit-eyed Japanese caricature. Through Japansky, Feininger equates the "Oriental" to a mechanical, dutiful object.

Kin-der-kids' theme of exploration was certainly not unique. Spurred by the success of *Little Nemo*, other artists tried their hand at titles that celebrated the image of child-as-adventurer. Notable titles include Harry Grant Dart's The Explor*igator* and Muriel Mitchell's *The Adventures of Nip and Tuck*. But what arguably set *Kin-der-kids* apart from contemporary fantasy comic strips is a curious subplot. The intrepid boys are pursued by Aunt Jim-jam and Cousin Gussie, who believe the Kin-der-kids are misguided for mounting their expedition. They deem it their mission to correct the children with a dose of castor oil. Aunt Jim-jam and Gussie, drawn as caricatures of Puritans, signify authoritarianism, restraint, and dogmatism. They are threats to the spirit of adventure, innovation, and, more pointedly, boyhood. That the Kin-der brothers successfully elude them seems to assure readers that young boys are capable of casting off Puritanical orthodoxy.

Despite the *Tribune*'s avid campaign, *Kin-der-kids* failed to gain a following. Overall, the paper's "German experiment" was a commercial failure, as the featured work of celebrated German caricaturists did not translate into a larger readership for the *Tribune*. *Kin-der-kids*, which first appeared in May 1906, was pulled from circulation by December that year. Another Feininger strip, *Wee Willie Winkie's World*, which appeared in the fall of 1906, had an even shorter lifespan, lasting only twenty episodes.

The short-lived *Wee Willie Winkie*, however, is a useful text to examine alongside McCay's *Little Nemo*. In this series, Feininger explores the imaginative power of the child—but unlike Nemo, Willie is wide awake.[87] As in *Little Nemo*, *Wee Willie Winkie* depicts the child as constantly engaged in transforming the world. But while *Little Nemo* gives readers glimpses of the child's perpetually shifting internal world, *Wee Willie Winkie* portrays a view of the *external* world altered by a child's perception. Focusing on the act of *day*dreaming, *Wee Willie Winkie* does not explore the world within the protagonist, nor does it visualize the contents of the sleeping child's mind. Rather, it shows how the child revises his outside environment through his imagination.

Willie's environment, specifically, is the countryside. It is a place of expansive fields, rolling hills, and twisting lanes that lead to little towns with rising church steeples. The setting may have reminded readers of European towns and landscapes. For a European immigrant audience, the strip may have even evoked nostalgia for the Old World. As in *Little Nemo*, the imaginative child in *Wee Willie Winkie* is attached to the past, particularly to the world that immigrants left behind. The strip's setting, however, also implies that the child belongs in a natural/rural landscape, showing that the child's mental health is shaped by his physical environment. The series suggests that in the country, Willie exercises both mental and physical muscles, engaging in imaginative acts while walking about and getting fresh air. Certainly, the protagonist of *Wee Willie Winkie* often seems to be swallowed by the setting, as was Nemo in McCay's strip. And just as Nemo is made "little," Willie is marked diminutive by the label "wee." With Willie often a miniscule figure in the panels, the setting seems to be the focus, the object of fascination, of the series. But as the strip's title suggests, Willie also *owns* this world. Although he is small in size, he often gazes out at the landscape like a child-king surveying his kingdom. Moreover, the strip insists that this is a world worth seeing and contemplating because the viewer perceives it through Willie's eyes.

And through the eyes of this wide-awake child, natural and man-made objects become strange beasts and sentient beings. A bridge becomes a centipede; tree roots become birds' claws; a house's façade becomes a face, one that "opens one sleepy blinking eye" when it senses the first rays of sunlight.[88] Sometimes, Willie casts nature as the antagonist in his adventure. When he encounters two poplars, for example, they appear to him "like sentinels, with arms held forbiddingly on high. . . . It was rather intimidating, especially as there were some big clouds in the sky, who certainly looked queer."[89] Confronted by the sentinel-like trees and peculiar clouds, Willie declares, "To the courageous belong the world."[90] He then "pushed bravely on. . . . [He] passed the poplars and even stuck his tongue in his cheek at the clouds."[91]

It is notable that the intrepid Willie is also a solitary child. Willie is depicted as an independent little boy who wanders about fields, roads, and villages without adult supervision. In effect, Feininger links the imaginative acts of the child with autonomy. The strip suggests that the child who is untethered from the adult is best able to actively and imaginatively engage with the world. Lacking adult supervision, Willie frolics by the seaside, where he pictures the rocky beach as a menagerie of aquatic animals (fig. 34).[92] In the absence of adults, Willie is free to "create," to give life to inanimate objects, to reenvision the world. The strip's celebration of the unsupervised child shores up Hall's contention that childhood reverie "is generally a natural function and should usually be allowed free course."[93]

In one episode, however, Willie has a noteworthy adult companion, a figure who is meant to represent Feininger himself. The artist draws his likeness standing alongside Willie, and the two stand at the base of a cliff (fig. 35).[94] Paper and pencil in hand, the gangly figure of Feininger is presumably sketching the landscape that stretches out before him. Meanwhile, Willie holds out his left arm, pointing and directing the gaze of Feininger and, in effect, the reader. Here, Willie's gesture of pointing recalls the image of the Yellow Kid in "Golf, the Great Society Sport as Played in Hogan's Alley." The accompanying text confirms that the character of Feininger is taking direction from Willie: "Willie Winkie took me down to the cliff to see the giants . . . and Williewinks would give me no rest until I had sketched some of the strange shapes he pointed out."[95] Later in the episode, when Willie exclaims, "Look at ze big ol' dragon-rock an' ze pretty lady!" the artist verifies what the boy sees: "And there, sure enough, was a tall piece of cliff standing out from the rest, and it had the exact form of a friendly-looking hippogriffin with outstretched wings, mounting guard over a fair princess."[96]

The episode suggests that the adult's artistry rests on his ability to take instruction from the naturally imaginative child. Put another way, it asserts that the adult artist needs to view the world with a childlike perception. As such,

Figure 34. Excerpt from Comic Strip by Lyonel Feininger. "Wee Willie Winkie's World." Originally printed in *Chicago Tribune* Comic Supplement.

Figure 35. Excerpt from Comic Strip by Lyonel Feininger. "Wee Willie Winkie's World." Originally printed in *Chicago Tribune* Comic Supplement.

the episode records the development of the cult of childhood among European artists in the early twentieth century. As Higonnet notes, "responding to the models of spontaneity, sincerity, and stylization they found in children's drawings, artists in assorted European movements elaborated 'infantilist' strategies of innovation."[97] Artists such as Paul Klee, Gabriele Münter, and Feininger himself collected children's drawings, driven by the notion that through the appropriation of a child's perception, the artist would find the strange in the mundane, the mysterious in the banal.

The artists' attention to real children was attached to their desire to unlock the child *within* themselves. By observing the child at play, by closely examining the child's artwork, the adult artist was not simply mimicking the child but also attempting to "resurrect" his departed childlike self. Notably, these movements in European art were emerging during a period when Freudian psychoanalysis intertwined and radically reshaped notions of the self and childhood. As Carolyn Steedman argues, in the early twentieth century, "Freudian psychoanalysis . . . summariz[ed] and reformulat[ed] a great many nineteenth-century articulations of the idea that the core of an individual's psychic identity was his or her own lost past, or childhood. The account of infantile sexuality and the process of repression that emerged from Sigmund Freud's writing in this period *theorized* childhood in this sense, gave it another name as 'the unconscious,' or 'the unconscious mind.'"[98] As Feininger implies in this particular episode of *Wee Willie Winkie*, the adult's interaction with the child allows him to access his own "lost" childhood and thus create more spontaneous art. The episode, however, also gestures toward the inherent difference in perception between the child and the adult. While Willie sees a dragon, the figure of Feininger maintains a demarcation between reality and fantasy. He does not see a dragon; rather, he acknowledges that the cliff face *resembles* a dragon. The episode suggests that while the child is immersed fully in a fantasy world, the adult still identifies reality and fantasy as two separate realms.

In another episode of *Wee Willie Winkie*, the strip's presumably adult narrator also draws a line between what is real and what is imagined. The narrator explains that the tongue that is sticking out of the front door of a house is "only a red carpet that Bridget has put out of the window to air."[99] Thus the narrator unmakes the fantasy crafted by the child character. Even while the episode celebrates the wondrous power of Willie's imagination, it also insists that his acts of transformation are ultimately ephemeral and subject to adult dismantling.

But then Willie himself is aware of the distinction between reality and fantasy. After finding himself "face to face with an elephant" as well as "a screaming eagle and a grinning-jawed crocodile," he realizes that "the elephant really is nothing but an old tree trunk and the eagle and the crocodile only tops of trees."[100] He dispels the illusion by exclaiming, "I was really fooled that time!"[101] Overall, the strip delivers ambivalent messages about childhood imagination. The series simultaneously affirms and curtails the power of a child's reverie. It shows that the child whose innocence allows him to conjure strange visions paradoxically possesses the knowledge that enables him to undo these very visions.

"Look What the Artist Has Done to Me!": A Coda via *Little Nemo*

Like Feininger, McCay utilized metacomic elements to make his presence felt in *Little Nemo*. In one episode, the hand of the artist is plainly evoked when Nemo finds the objects and people surrounding him being reduced to stick figures.[102] The increasingly alarmed Nemo announces, "I'm going home before I change into a bad drawing!"[103] Eventually, "bad" artistry catches up with him, and he turns into a simplified sketch. Only upon waking does he find his body restored to its "normal" state.

McCay often broke the fourth wall in his strips and his animated cartoons. In such moments, he frequently played with the notion of characters being at the mercy of their creator. His animated short film *Gertie the Dinosaur* (1914), for example, was designed as a vaudeville act in which McCay, standing onstage, addressed the projected image of Gertie. McCay boasts that the dinosaur will "do everything I tell her to do."[104] For the most part, Gertie does comply with his commands: she bows to the audience, raises her feet one at a time, and catches a pumpkin on his cue. When she gets distracted by a sea serpent, McCay scolds her for being a "bad girl."[105] At the end of the cartoon, McCay declares that "Gertie will now show that she isn't afraid of me and take me for a ride."[106] He disappears from the stage and then reemerges as an animated figure standing on Gertie's ridged back. As Gertie walks offscreen, the cartoon figure of McCay makes one final display of dominance by whipping her.

In *Gertie*, the character's agency is subordinate to the artist's agency: Gertie is subject to McCay's whims. This relationship between character and artist is echoed by Feininger in the advertisement he drew for *Kin-der-kids*, in which he draws himself as the puppeteer controlling the strings attached to his child characters (fig. 36).[107] What is particularly intriguing is that the puppeteer—Feininger's avatar—bears an ear tag labeled "your Uncle Feininger." The signature itself is not so unusual—Feininger signed his strips for children with "your Uncle Feininger," a gesture that asks the child reader to imagine tangible kinship with the adult storyteller. But in the advertisement, the tag suggests that the marionettist-artist is himself a product meant to be possessed, an object subject to the control of the reading public.

In any case, Feininger's pictorial depiction of the artist's control over his characters is reiterated by McCay in a self-referential episode of *Little Nemo*, in which Nemo, Flip, and the Imp are elated to find themselves in a factory full of giant cakes and sweets (fig. 37).[108] To their dismay, the enormous edible delights slowly disappear, until Nemo and his companions are left standing against a blank background. The panel's border begins to collapse. Flip and the Imp fall out of sight, and Nemo, clinging to the bottom of the frame, remarks, "I wonder what is the matter with the artist? He's forgot something."[109] In the penultimate panel, the frame collapses inward, trapping Nemo. He cries out, "Look what the artist has done to me oh!"[110]

Nemo's exclamation invites us to take a closer look at what the artist is doing and, more particularly, what he is doing to the child. As I discuss above, McCay complicates the image of the imaginative, agentic child by showing how the strip's young protagonist has little to no control of the goings-on in Slumberland. Often depicted as helpless, perplexed, and easily swept up by the twists and turns of Slumberland, Nemo sometimes wakes up in relief. "I am glad I am home and in my little bed and not where I dreamed I was," he declares in one episode.[111] With this statement, Nemo indicates that he views home as a space of safety and comfort. Thus the series seems to deliver a contradictory message about childhood autonomy. It champions the child's right to face the unknown and free himself from adult supervision, but at the same time, insists that the child is powerless against forces larger than himself. Nemo exhibits a constant need for a comfortable, stable place where he can cry out for his mother; as such, the strip securely fastens this little dreamer and explorer to his home.

With the statement of "Look what the artist has done to me," McCay calls attention to the artist's role in crafting and constructing the vivid, intricate fantasy realm that is Slumberland. In effect, he reveals that this dream world is not constructed by an imaginative child, but is rather the product of an imaginative, meticulous adult artist. Through his use of metacomic elements, McCay pulls back the curtain to expose Slumberland as an adult's rendering of a child's dream

Figure 36. Illustration by Lyonel Feininger. Promotional Material for *The Kin-der-kids*. In *Chicago Tribune* Comic Supplement, April 29, 1906. SFT 96-1, San Francisco Academy of Comic Art Collection, the Ohio State University Billy Ireland Cartoon Library and Museum.

Figure 37. Excerpt from Comic Strip by Winsor McCay. "Little Nemo in Slumberland." Originally printed in *New York Herald* Comic Supplement.

world. Nemo's exclamation also reveals how he himself is aware that he is a character created by an artist, that he is a *representation* of childhood. Nemo's name itself is a reminder that he is a fiction, a figure of fantasy. In Latin, the name means "no one," and can be evocative of the (Greek) term "utopia," the ideal place that is also "no place." Certainly, as Bukatman suggests, *Little Nemo* could be understood as a "utopic space," in the sense that it depicted a "marvelous place of wonderful adventures" and, at the same time, "offered a utopia to its readers, for whom it constituted a temporary break in the action of the day, a temporary break from the facticity of the newspaper."[112] But perhaps *Little Nemo* was also giving the readers a glimpse of a world—and a child—that was not simply temporary, but rather forever elusive. Like utopia, it could be that a child such as Nemo is the product of dreams, perfect yet nonexistent. The name "Nemo" also alludes to not only the pseudonym that Ulysses uses to trick the Cyclops Polyphemus but also the character of Captain Nemo, the enigmatic antihero of Jules Verne's *Twenty Thousand Leagues under the Sea* (1870). Both Ulysses and Captain Nemo wander the seas in exile. In *Little Nemo*, the child protagonist can also be understood as displaced, cast off into a sea of dreams, a world of imagination, a realm isolated from the world of adults.

Ultimately, the self-referential episodes of *Little Nemo* point to the paradoxes behind the world of Slumberland. McCay's strip depicts the child's mind as mysterious and inaccessible yet also confirms that the supposed secret tracts of childhood are created by the adult. *Little Nemo* evinces that the child's ostensibly private world is freely penetrated by the adult artist (and adult reader). As such, the series calls attention to the fact that behind the fantasy comic strips, children's books, and psychological studies of childhood that insist that the child is a naturally imaginative being, there stands the adult artist, writer, or psychologist who is observing, scrutinizing, and theorizing the child. Fantasy comic strips—as well as literary and psychology texts—exalt the imaginative child. But these comics also remind us that this figure is a figment of the adult imagination, a fantasy constructed and dreamed up by adults.

CHAPTER 5

WHAT WOULD YOU DO WITH GIRLS LIKE THESE?

As I argue in previous chapters, Progressive Era newspaper comics had a penchant for circulating and celebrating the image of the bad boy. When R. F. Outcault posed the question "What would you do with a boy like this?" in an episode of *Buster Brown* (see chapter 2), he implied that one should welcome trouble-making boys, whether fictional or real, with open arms. In *Buster Brown*, the naughty boy is held up as a paragon of ingenuity, vitality, and self-reliance. As I discuss in chapter 3, Buster and his comics peers were descendants of the bad boys that appeared in popular art and literature in the nineteenth century. The young male prankster was a stock character of antebellum genre paintings; in the mid-nineteenth century, novels such as Thomas Bailey Aldrich's *The Story of a Bad Boy* (1869) and Mark Twain's *The Adventures of Tom Sawyer* (1876) and *Adventures of Huckleberry Finn* (1884) were widely read and imitated. The success and influence of Aldrich's and Twain's novels—which both authors claimed to be semiautobiographical accounts of their boyhoods—suggest that audiences, young and old, delighted in reading about narratives of "real" boyish mischief. Moreover, it appears that adults were eager to provide young (male) readers fictional models to emulate.[1]

Cartoonists at the turn of the century continued these visual and literary practices of exalting the bad boy. Numerous strips, including long-running series such as Outcault's *Buster Brown*, Rudolph Dirks's *The Katzenjammer Kids*, and Carl E. "Bunny" Schultze's *Foxy Grandpa* as well as short-lived, lesser-known strips such as Harry Greening's *The Tinkle Brothers* and Charles Forbell's *Naughty Pete*, were headlined by mischief-making boys. Some of these series became the bases of theatrical plays and films, and images of naughty boys were used in advertisements for clothing, food, toys, and other consumer goods. The bad boy, in other words, was an omnipresent figure in Progressive Era consumer culture.

With numerous boys running amok in the pages of the supplements, it may seem as if fictional girls were exiled from newspaper comics, welcomed only if they were in supporting roles. Certainly, as exhibited in series that focused on the exploits of young male characters, girls were typically sweethearts. In *Buster Brown*, young Mary Jane is Buster's muse rather than his prankish peer. In Winsor McCay's *Little Nemo in Slumberland*, the Princess is Nemo's object of desire, the "treasure" that patiently waits for him in the palace. Yet a significant number of Progressive Era newspaper comics did feature young female protagonists, many of whom "made trouble." The apparent lack of fictional girls in Progressive Era comic supplements is not necessarily due to turn-of-the-century cartoonists' disinterest in creating girl-centered strips; rather, twentieth-century historians and scholars have, by and large, failed to acknowledge and highlight such strips.[2] Histories and criticism tend to collect, analyze, and memorialize turn-of-the-century strips about prankish boys, consequently offering an incomplete record of late nineteenth- and early twentieth-century comic strips. Some comics histories note that comic strip girls did not become widely accepted until the 1920s and 1930s, with the publication of Harold Gray's *Little Orphan Annie* (which debuted in 1924), Marjorie Henderson Buell's *Little Lulu* (debuted 1935), and Ernie Bushmiller's *Nancy* (debuted 1938).[3] Yet many strips published in decades previous also imagined the misdeeds, precocities, adventures, and misadventures of girls. Some of the period's most well-known cartoonists published strips headlined by girls: Winsor McCay produced *Hungry Henrietta*, George Herriman drew *Rosy Posy*, and James Swinnerton created *Dear Little Katy*. Other girl-centered titles include Peter Newell's *The Naps of Polly Sleepyhead*, Tom Tucker's *Betsy Bouncer and Her Doll*, Grace Wiederseim's *Dottie Dimple*, and W. O. Wilson's *Madge the Magician's Daughter*. In some cases, strips were headlined by mixed-sex pairs. In his *Buddy and Alice* series, Outcault brazenly appropriates Lewis Carroll's Alice. Accompanied by a young bellhop named Buddy, she continues her adventures in a world much like Wonderland, meeting familiar characters from fairy tales and nursery rhymes. Other girl-and-boy strips included Wiederseim's *Dolly Drake and Bobby Blake* and John Neill's *The Little Journeys of Nip and Tuck*. In short, fictional girls were not completely excised from the pages of the Progressive Era comic supplement. The publication of newspaper comics featuring girls was in fact expressive of growing acknowledgement that young female readers constituted an emergent and vibrant consumer market.

This chapter redresses the scholarly neglect of girl-centered comics, excavating and examining series with young female protagonists. But why do historians and critics tend to overlook these comics about misbehaving girls in the first place? Perhaps girl-centered comics are easy to forget because they did not come close to rivaling the cultural impact of contemporary boy strips. We have yet to uncover evidence of a female character's expansion into a cultural and commercial phenomenon in the manner of the Yellow Kid, Buster Brown, Hans and Fritz Katzenjammer, and Little Nemo. Most series that featured misbehaving girls ran for less than a year, with some disappearing a few weeks after their debut. Of course, girl-centered comics were not the only titles that came and went. The comic supplement was a volatile marketplace; regardless of theme or subject, many series were replaced in a matter of weeks. Successful strips such as *Katzenjammer Kids*, *Buster Brown*, and *Little Nemo* were arguably exceptions to the rule. Furthermore, even as comics producers kept coaxing readers to delight in girls' transgressions, audiences appeared reluctant to fully embrace young female characters who subverted gender norms, especially if these characters were white and middle class.

The tension between production and reception of girl-centered comics ran parallel to the contradictory signals sent to white, middle-class girls who were growing up at the turn of the century. While girls increasingly gained access to educational opportunities that prepared them for public roles, they also were instructed to bind themselves to the home and prepare for "private" roles of wife and mother. The comics figure of the "girl who made trouble" thus expressed contemporary debates about the present and future duties of white, middle-class girls.

This chapter begins by placing newspaper comics about girls in the context of series that lampoon "troublesome" women. Progressive Era comics proved to be a potent tool for undermining women who were perceived to be undesirable or threatening to patriarchal, heteronormative hegemony. Cartoonists often used their work to deride suffragettes, "unfeminine" working-class women, and those who called themselves New Women. Yet comics creators tended to approach mischief-making girls with affection rather than scorn. More specifically, their comics about misbehaving girls expressed uncertainties regarding the business of raising young females at the turn of the century, displaying both enthusiasm for and anxieties about redefining girls' (and implicitly, women's) social roles. This chapter discusses how series such as McCay's *The Story of Hungry Henrietta* and Wiederseim's *Dolly Dimple* instruct readers to delight in the image of the girl who breaks the rules while also reminding them of the limits of girls' misbehavior. In the meantime, Wilson's *Madge the Magician's Daughter* and Tucker's *Betsy Bouncer and Her Doll* suggest that imaginative play allows girls to test social boundaries and practice acts of transgression.

Censuring Women

For girls growing up at the turn of the century, reading the comic supplement may have been a pleasurable yet bewildering experience. The supplement featured many series headlined by girls, which were presumably designed to appeal to young female readers. In these titles, the protagonists played boys' games, upset their parents, and did not behave like "proper" girls. Also prominently featured in the comic supplements were images of troublemaking *women*; these fictional females challenged authority figures, rejected marriage and motherhood, sought to pursue education and professional careers, and demanded the right to vote. While the disorderly girl was meant to elicit delightful, sentimental laughter, the "provocative" woman was created in the vein of derisive humor.

Newspaper cartoons and comic strips in the Progressive Era often ridiculed and diminished figures who allegedly threatened to destabilize or defile Anglo-Saxon, Protestant, middle-class culture. Members of racial and ethnic minority groups, the immigrant class, and the working class were often represented as unruly and witless. As I discuss in previous chapters, caricatures occasionally shook off the shackles of stereotyping, emerging as multifaceted, sympathetic characters. They sometimes came across as heroic underdogs, foils that exposed the ignorance, excess, and corruption of authority figures and members of the dominant culture. Caricatures of women, however, were given very little room to expand into more multidimensional characters. The comic supplement offered up various female "types" as objects of laughter, from "naïve" and "extravagant" society women, to "vulgar" female members of the working and immigrant classes, to "clueless" women who floundered when they tried to get involved in public matters.

The cartoonist T. E. Powers seemed to especially relish the act of ridiculing women. His one-off strip "T. E. Powers' List of Famous Women in History: 18—Count 'Em—18" is a barefaced display of the contempt he held for women who took on public roles (fig. 38).[4] In the title, Powers asserts his "natural" authority to write women's history. He also uses the subtitle to insist that only eighteen women since Creation have made a substantial impact to merit mention in historical records. On the other hand, the subtitle can also be read as Powers's indignant declaration that eighteen famous women is eighteen too many.

Powers's list includes figures from myth and fiction as well as contemporary women activists. He insists that these women should be remembered not for their contributions but for their disruptions: they are temptresses who lead men to their downfall (Eve and Salome); women who commit the sin of being unattractive (Mother Hubbard, whom Powers labels the "inventor of the pinchless corset"); overbearing, hostile presences who threaten male autonomy and virility (the hatchet-wielding temperance activist Carrie Nation and the uptight mother-in-law, whose weapon of choice is a rolling pin). Powers insists that such women emasculate men—as Delilah does when she cuts off Samson's hair—and thus negatively alter the course of history. Powers also uses "List of Famous Women" to affirm that the woman's place is in the home. He chides Louisa Knapp Curtis for her role as "editoress of the *Ladies Never Home Journal*"[5] and suggests that

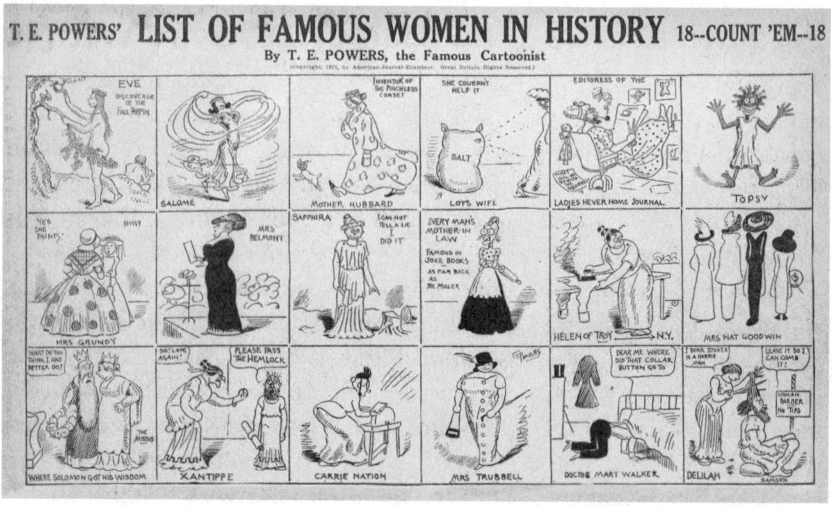

Figure 38. Comic Strip by T. E. Powers. "T. E. Powers' List of Famous Women in History." In *American Journal Examiner*, circa 1911. SFT 71-3, San Francisco Academy of Comic Art Collection, the Ohio State University Billy Ireland Cartoon Library and Museum.

outspoken women such as Mary Walker—a physician, abolitionist, and women's rights advocate—were the antitheses of the ideal woman. Instead of illustrating Walker, Powers highlights her absence; all we see is her husband crawling on the floor, haplessly searching for a collar button. In this panel, the cartoonist condemns women like Walker for "deserting" their husbands. At the same time, Powers also reprimands men for willingly reducing themselves to subservient positions: Mr. Walker's head is under the bed, much like the proverbial ostrich who buries his head in the sand, refusing to acknowledge and confront the "hostile" forces bearing down on him.

Unfortunately, Powers was not unique in expressing such views of women. Many of his male contemporaries shared his negative response to the growing visibility of women in politics, economics, and social reform movements. Women were becoming more spirited participants in traditionally masculine spheres, and in 1895, the *New York World* documented the rise of these New Women. Such New Women, as the *World* put it,

> believe that nature fully intended the female sex to be equal in all respects with the male. . . . They believe that women as a class have a higher, more noble duty in life than the mere bearing and nursing of children and the comforting and encouraging of men. They believe that after the incidental business of the household has been performed women should go out into the world, work side by side with men, fight when they are oppressed, vote, insist upon their rights and make themselves generally agreeable.[6]

The *World* article carefully implied that such women still prioritize the "incidental business of the household"; it also avoided offering any negative commentary on the figure of the New Woman, as the publication hoped to retain and expand its female readership.[7] But many other observers, including leaders of political, civic, and religious groups, denounced women who chose to attend college, work outside the home, and join organizations and social clubs. For some commentators, to be a New Woman was to express a self-centered, perverse refusal of one's "natural" duty to procreate. Theodore Roosevelt, expressing white Americans' racial anxiety, insisted that women's (and men's) postponement or abandonment of reproductive duties was akin to sounding the death knell for Anglo-Saxon, Protestant Americans. In response to the steady influx of immigrants, many of whom were "swarthy" Italians and Jews fleeing pogroms in Russia and Eastern Europe, Roosevelt reproached both white women and men for building careers and amassing fortunes instead of raising families. In a 1905 speech delivered before the National Congress of Mothers, he claimed that white Americans were on the verge of committing "race suicide":

> The man or woman who deliberately foregoes [the supreme blessing of children], whether from viciousness, coldness, shallow-heartedness, self-indulgence, or mere failure to appreciate aright the difference between the all-important and the unimportant—why, such a creature merits contempt as hearty as any visited upon the soldier who runs away in battle, or upon the man who refuses to work for the support of those dependent upon him, and who tho [*sic*] able-bodied is yet content to eat in idleness the bread which others provide.[8]

Roosevelt insisted that women could best exercise patriotism by staying in the home: "The primary duty of the woman is to be the helpmate, the housewife, and mother. The woman should have ample educational advantages; but save in exceptional cases the man must be, and she need not be, and generally ought not to be, trained for a lifelong career as the family breadwinner; and, therefore, after a certain point, the training of the two must normally be different because the duties of the two are normally different."[9] Roosevelt was not alone in raising the alarm. Progressive Era cartoonists were among those who stoked fears about the "dying" Anglo-Saxon race. Two years before Roosevelt's speech, R. F. Outcault weighed in on the "race suicide question" in the episode "Buster Brown Visits the Zoo and Talks to the Stork" (fig. 39).[10] As Buster asks the stork in the zoo for a "nice baby sister," a woman—presumably Mrs. Brown—stands in the background with her back to Buster. Her position and distance signify not only her neglect of her son but also her lack of interest in communicating with the stork—that is, having another child. The stork attempts to fulfill Buster's request. It shows up on the Brown doorstep carrying a bundled-up child. Buster

Figure 39. Comic Strip by R. F. Outcault. "Buster Brown Visits the Zoo and Talks to the Stork." In *New York Herald* Comic Supplement, July 26, 1903. SFS 32-1-4, San Francisco Academy of Comic Art Collection, the Ohio State University Billy Ireland Cartoon Library and Museum.

eagerly throws open the door to their home, but Mrs. Brown prevents the bird and infant from crossing the threshold, shouting, "Shoo! Get out—we don't want it!" Buster then instructs the stork to carry the infant to the Smith household, believing that the Smiths "want one." But Mrs. Smith also rejects the child, and so does every other woman whom the stork visits. Outcault depicts how the infant becomes endangered by repeated rejection: as the narrative progresses, the stork's hold on the child becomes increasingly careless, and the child perilously swings from side to side and, at one point, hangs upside down. The absence of the women's husbands in this episode also gestures to men's similar disinterest in reproduction. But there is no question that the episode primarily means to admonish women who emphatically declare "I don't want it" and who refuse to fulfill their so-called natural and national duty to procreate.

To be clear, the female characters in this episode of *Buster Brown* do not fit June Sochen's definition of New Women: Mrs. Brown and her peers are not women who have "left the home for the factory, a career, and the marketplace."[11] Rather than spurning domesticity, they appear to settle comfortably within the walls of their homes. But they respond "aberrantly" when they treat the bird and the baby as invasive elements that will unsettle rather than stabilize the home. In the episode, the women view the newborn as an object of inconvenience rather than a person to cherish. In contrast to the women, Buster and the animals are the clear-eyed innocents who uphold the joys of motherhood. The stork, for example, tells one of the women that "[children] are the greatest comfort on earth."[12] The woman's poodle agrees, smiling at the sight of the child and stating, "Let us keep it."[13] Both Buster and his pet dog, Tige, grin happily at the prospect of becoming the infant's parents. In his resolution, Buster sarcastically remarks that "society is in a beautiful attitude toward posterity." He writes, "Goodness!! What are we coming to?" But perhaps the strip's depiction of different attitudes toward the infant also exposes the gap between the ideals of motherhood and its lived realities. Buster romanticizes motherhood, yet he himself does not and will never fully comprehend the stresses that come with performing ideal motherhood—stresses that his mother knows only too well.

Framing Indulgent Women

While Outcault does not employ the withering tone that Powers uses in his "List of Famous Women" strip, he does occasionally use the character of Mrs. Brown to mock mothers who were "distracted" by leisurely pursuits. As such, Mrs. Brown fits a particular (and disparaging) description of the New Woman: a "lady of leisure who spent her time and money decadently indulging herself."[14] Focused on shopping, fashion, and tea parties, Mrs. Brown becomes a negligent mother. In one episode, she is so intent on going to a bargain sale that she fails to notice that Buster is stepping on the train of her dress.[15] Here, Buster serves as a figurative anchor, trying to fasten his mother to her domestic obligations. But she rebuffs these duties; when she takes a step forward, Buster falls over, knocking heads with Tige. Preoccupied by the thought of the sale, Mrs. Brown remains oblivious to her son's injury.

Outcault, in drawing Mrs. Brown, referenced the Gibson Girl, a visual representation of womanhood that was ubiquitous during the period. The Gibson Girl, created and popularized by Charles Dana Gibson, has long limbs, an hourglass figure, a small mouth, an upturned nose, and swept-up hair. First appearing in 1894, she quickly became a prevalent figure in visual culture, frequently reproduced by Gibson and appropriated by other illustrators and cartoonists. Her image appeared in cartoons and spot illustrations, adorned the covers of sheet music, and was deployed in numerous advertisements. The Gibson Girl's physical appearance served as evidence of the "natural" beauty of the affluent Anglo-Saxon woman. Even when she engaged in sport and leisure and seemed to value her independence above marriage and motherhood, she remained delicate and graceful. She was also the antithesis of the immigrant, working-class female figures that appeared in cartoons and comic strips. Characters such as Mrs. Katzenjammer and the Duchess lacked the elegance and youthfulness of the Gibson Girl; their vulgarity was made visually apparent by their stocky figures, round noses, and wide mouths as well as their taste for loud prints and cheap hats.

But the Gibson Girl was not an unequivocal expression of male admiration for women; rather, she embodied male ambivalence over women's efforts to change the patriarchal status quo. On the one hand, the Gibson Girl could be understood as a sympathetic attempt to explore the preoccupations and motivations of women who pushed against social boundaries and engaged with the world outside the home. On the other hand, her image also reinforced the lower social status of women. She not only signified the glorification and objectification of "beautiful women," but more important, she frequently served the purpose of satire. The Gibson Girl's creator, for one, typically used her image to belittle women's quest for rights and self-sufficiency.[16] The appellation "girl" was infantilizing, a label that suggested that women who sought autonomy were destined to remain childish and powerless and thus presumably dependent on men. Yet some women embraced the Gibson Girl as a figure who exemplified female independence.[17] The writer and women's rights advocate Charlotte Perkins Gilman was one of her notable admirers. Gilman asserted that "typical" women had much to learn from the Gibson Girl, who was "braver, stronger[,] more healthful and skillful and able and free, more human in all ways."[18]

But the liberating potential of the Gibson Girl was buried under the avalanche of messages that censured women for their "frivolities," "indulgences," and "naïve" and "misguided" efforts at social reform—and newspaper comics actively participated in spreading these deleterious messages. In L. A. Searl's short-lived *Mrs. Timekiller*, the obtuse and helpless protagonist constantly asks men to aid her in chores or leisurely pursuits. In the process, Mrs. Timekiller inconveniences the men and prevents them from completing their jobs, which are implied to be more pressing than Mrs. Timekiller's "trivial" priorities. A contemporary strip titled *Lucy and Sophie Say Goodbye* extends the themes expressed in *Mrs. Timekiller*, overtly claiming that women who interfere with male pursuits are in effect impeding the nation's economic growth. Lucy and Sophie cannot bear to part ways, and as they engage in long, seemingly endless rituals of farewell, they remain oblivious to, and frequently get in the way of, the fast-paced, modernizing world around them. In short, the strip imagines that intense, intimate female relationships can thwart national progress and development.

Gene Carr's character Lady Bountiful was similarly disruptive, but not because she was dependent on men or ignorant of the world around her.[19] Rather, she "made trouble" by aspiring to become self-sufficient and involved in public life. Lady Bountiful declines her suitors, as her passion lies in philanthropy and the "deliverance" of street urchins. She likely reminded Progressive Era readers of upper- and middle-class women who participated in political and social venues through charitable activities and campaigns for social reform. Carr's strip, however, suggests that well-to-do women were often misguided in their attempts to uplift the poor and immigrant classes. The term "lady bountiful," after all, is derogatory, referring to a woman who put her wealth on display through lavish charitable acts.[20] Indeed, Carr's Lady Bountiful is depicted as patronizing and naïve; she is especially incognizant of the street children's imperviousness to reform. In the episode "What Broke Up the Firm of Lady Bountiful and Co.," she encourages a group of street children, consisting of three immigrant boys and an African American boy, to learn independence and responsibility by setting up and running a lemonade stand.[21] Yet her actions preclude lessons in self-reliance: she provides all the supplies and then hands a quarter to "the little colored boy," so he could play a "make believe customer." "Now begin," she states, as if expecting the boys to perform for her. Here, she asserts her purported inherent privilege to manage the children's lives.

But the boys resist Lady Bountiful's efforts to control and "redeem" them. One of the immigrant boys jokes that she is on the pathway to spinsterhood, calling out "Lemminade, made in der shade, by an old maid." The immigrant boys then pick a fight with the black boy. "Look at de coon," says one. The black boy retorts, "Hey white trash, I'se a bad coon, loaded wiv money. Rush up dat lemonade or I'se liable t' tuhn loose wiv ma razzer." But Lady Bountiful appears unfazed by—or oblivious to—the exchange of insults and displays of racial aggressions. She concludes that "[the boys] will do nicely" and turns to leave. In the last panel, her project of reform collapses: the young immigrants throw lemonade at the African American boy and gang up on him. The character of

Lady Bountiful is a declaration that women's efforts at social reform leads to more harm than good.

A contemporary series by T. E. Powers also disparages women's struggles for self-determination and sociopolitical participation. It does so by poking fun at a specific iteration of the New Woman: the suffragette. In some installments of *Ysobel the Suffragette* (circa 1911),[22] Powers appears to announce his support of women's right to vote. He ends one episode with a caption that reads, "My wife is as good as myself. Votes for women."[23] Yet the cartoonist repeatedly caricatures suffragists as elderly, stocky, unfashionable, perpetually frowning women. The one exception is the young and slender Ysobel, who commits herself to the cause after an "unattractive" suffragette chastises her. While Ysobel plays the harp, the suffragette rebukes her: "How can you idle your time away while your sisters are fighting for their rights?" (fig. 40).[24] Ysobel declares, "I'll go right out and help them." Thus begins her earnest effort at recruiting men to the suffragist cause.

At first glance, Ysobel succeeds in softening male resistance toward women's demands for political reform. Most episodes end with the "conversion" of male characters, who become enthusiastic allies of the suffragette movement. But Ysobel's triumphs are undercut by how she is objectified and sexualized by the men she encounters (and, by extension, by Powers). Male characters ogle her and refer to her as a "peach," and they appear more interested in winning Ysobel's affections than supporting women's struggle for equal rights. Powers ridicules the suffragettes as well as the men who are too "feeble" to resist them. The January 17, 1911, episode even suggests that the feminist movement resorts to acts of brutality: Ysobel grabs a potential male "recruit" by his lapels, hoists him in the air, and stomps on him. The man is reduced to stuttering; in the last panel, he refers to himself as a "mere man."[25]

Through the image of pretty Ysobel, Powers also insists that "ladylike" women—rather than "hoydens" and wizened "spinsters"—are more effective representatives of the suffragette movement. The strip also maintains suffragists can only win men to the cause if they prove that the right to vote does not conflict with their domestic obligations. In one episode, John, the husband of one of Ysobel's friends, dismisses Ysobel as a "nice little girl who is on the wrong side of this suffrage business."[26] Later, when John finds out that his cook has left without notice, he cries, "Then who will cook dinner?" Ysobel sees a window of opportunity. She cooks a meal for John and his wife, declaring, "Here's where I win a vote for the cause." The delighted John then proclaims, "Ysobel, you're all right. Me for the cause."[27] Although the episode mocks the hidden helplessness of male authority figures, revealing them to be highly dependent on the women and servants who are meant to attend to them, it also returns the suffragist to her "rightful" place.

Figure 40. Comic Strip by T. E. Powers. "The Suffragette." In *San Francisco Examiner*, January 17, 1911. SFT 71-3, San Francisco Academy of Comic Art Collection, the Ohio State University Billy Ireland Cartoon Library and Museum.

Girl Trouble

Women who transgressed social boundaries, neglected their domestic duties, and sought to participate in the "masculine" spheres of politics, economics, and civil life proved to be easy targets for Progressive Era cartoonists. The proliferation of such images of womanhood might lead one to expect that the strips would also denounce girls who failed to fulfill the ideal of white, middle-class girlhood. Surprisingly, comics producers and readers appeared to welcome and take pleasure in images of girls who broke the rules.

Such affection for naughty girls in the strips reminds us of similar fondness for fictional orphan girls that appeared in contemporary children's books. Kate Douglas Wiggin's *Rebecca of Sunnybrook Farm* (1903) and L. M. Montgomery's *Anne of Green Gables* (1908) were among the most popular children's novels of the period. The eponymous protagonists of both books are imaginative, talkative, high-spirited girls who upend the lives of the adults they interact and live with. They also charm these fictional adults—and warmed the hearts of early twentieth-century readers. Rebecca and Anne were appealing because they made manifest a romantic vision of girlhood: that of the girl who is especially gifted in softening the inflexible adult. But these characters do not simply possess transformative powers; they themselves undergo "necessary" transformations, becoming "respectable" ladies who commit themselves to domestic life. Rebecca gives up a teaching career to attend to her ill mother; later, when she learns of her inheritance, she envisions how it will allow her to help care for her family. Similarly, Anne declines a prestigious scholarship in order to take care of her ailing adoptive mother. In both novels, the girls outgrow their exuberance, becoming demure women who embody so-called feminine virtues of sacrifice and care. It is important to acknowledge, however, that while the orphan girl genre offered reassuring narratives of vexing girls growing up to become disciplined women, it also often questioned the vexing limitations placed upon girls. In short, the women authors who wrote orphan girl novels participated in discourses about girlhood, highlighting tensions between girls' self-abnegation and self-actualization.[28]

Perhaps readers of turn-of-the-century newspaper comics were not threatened by images of troublemaking girls as they might have believed that these characters would, like Rebecca and Anne, eventually mature into "proper" women.[29] Of course, newspaper comics could not offer the same kind of closure that the novels provided. Within the conventions of newspaper comics, most child characters did not age, much less age into adulthood. But the strips did record and call attention to—as well as disseminate—the contradictory messages sent to white, middle-class girls growing up in the Progressive Era. Toward the end of the nineteenth century, white, middle-class girls were, like their mothers before them, trained in the "domestic arts" in preparation for their future lives as wives and mothers. Yet many parents, educators, and psychologists also permitted and championed girls' participation in sports and outdoor activities.[30] Compared to previous generations, white, middle-class girls growing up in the Progressive Era arguably had more opportunities to engage in activities outside the home. Proponents of such outdoor pursuits argued that girls needed to develop "boyish" qualities of resourcefulness, autonomy, and vitality. These tensions regarding girlhood were also apparent in discussions about girls' relationship with consumer culture. In the realm of newspaper comics, cartoonists recognized that girls constituted a viable market not just for comics series but also for products associated with comics. But while cartoonists sought to cultivate and maintain the robust consumerism of girls, they also seemed to hold on to the belief that the comic supplement was not entirely healthful for girls. Like the vaudeville theater, the nickelodeon, the dance hall, and the amusement park, the comic supplement was understood to be a rowdy and bawdy space that threatened the sanctity of white, middle-class girlhood. As a result, while the supplement encouraged young girls to participate in the market, it also often offered warnings about the "dangers" of consumerism, especially as practiced by girls.

Winsor McCay's short-lived *The Story of Hungry Henrietta* encapsulates this very ambivalence over girls' consumption habits. As Katherine Roeder suggests, *Hungry Henrietta* illustrates the "perils of over-consumption."[31] The strip employed what was then a unique conceit in comic strips: its protagonist ages.[32] From January to July 1905, readers witnessed Henrietta's development from infancy to eight years of age. She turns out to be a ravenous child, and her feeding habits interfere with her training to be a "proper" lady. In one episode, she eats ashes from the stove and ends up in blackface (fig. 41).[33] Her appearance shocks her parents, her grandmother, and their guests. Henrietta's mother is so upset with her daughter's blackened appearance that she turns away and buries her face in her hands. In a later episode, Henrietta finishes off the brandy sauce that the maid left unattended on the kitchen table.[34] The intoxicated Henrietta starts singing and dancing with her skirts hiked up. Her father, with arms akimbo, expresses his displeasure by saying, "That's the strangest thing I ever heard of. Well!" The father's response to his daughter's dance recalls contemporary attitudes toward the "bawdiness" of racial/ethnic Others and members of the working class. In both episodes, Henrietta's insatiable hunger is linked to the invasion of the white, middle-class home by so-called foreign elements. It is notable that the latter episode reveals that Henrietta's family employs a black cook, a Mammy figure who speaks in "black" dialect. The strip suggests that the kitchen is not simply a space for women's work, but more particularly, a space reserved for nonwhite, laboring women. In *Hungry Henrietta*, the white, middle-class girl who frequents the kitchen finds herself spoiled by the "dirty" work of women of the underclass.

At first blush, the series is a cautionary tale about the "ungirlish girl," the young female who lacks self-control. Because of her constant hunger, Henrietta

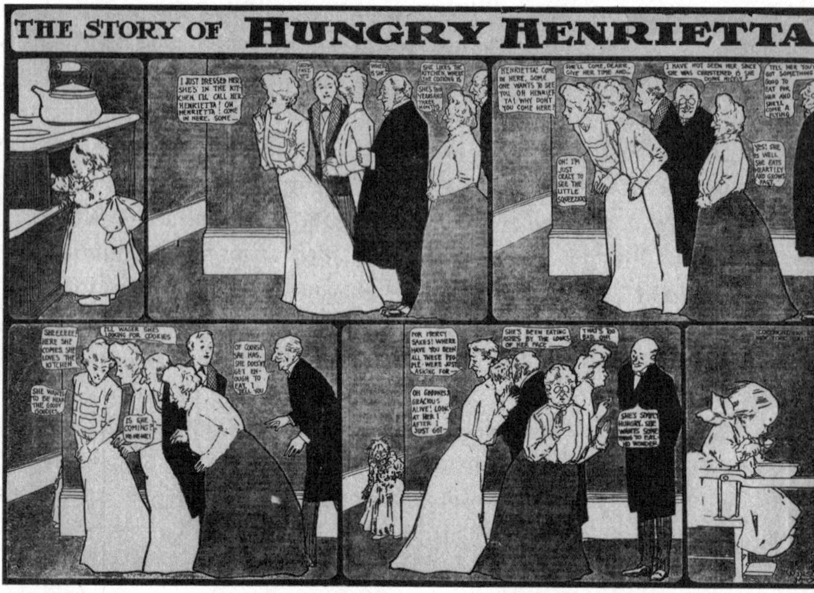

Figure 41. Comic Strip by Winsor McCay. "The Story of Hungry Henrietta." March 3, 1905. SFC 258, San Francisco Academy of Comic Art Collection, the Ohio State University Billy Ireland Cartoon Library and Museum.

behaves badly. She bawls and throws fits until she is fed; she wrestles with another child, all for a cookie; she is called a "selfish" child for refusing to share her peanuts with an elephant.[35] Yet while the strip figuratively wags a finger at the "bad" girl, it also comments on the failures of the adults who raise her. As Roeder suggests, the strip points to "adults' inability to understand or control their offspring."[36] For Roeder, *Hungry Henrietta* is a critique of parental ignorance: "Henrietta's motivations are psychological; her parents consistently fail to meet her emotional needs, and the effects are largely internal—she compensates by overeating and grows larger and larger with each episode."[37] In an early episode, Henrietta's parents call the doctor to help them "satisfy [them]selves she's all right."[38] The mother tells the doctor, "For one so young, we can't understand why she eats so." The grandmother concurs: "She eats entirely too much. Something is wrong." While the doctor claims that "she looks well and her pulse is normal," the parents and grandmother keep fussing over Henrietta. They fail to acknowledge that their overly anxious child-rearing is likely what is upsetting Henrietta.

While Henrietta's father, mother, and grandmother are baffled, aggravated, and even mortified by the child's appetite, one adult character appears sympathetic. The grandfather regards his hungry granddaughter calmly, insisting that nothing is wrong with her. During the doctor's visit, the grandfather maintains that "she's all right":

She does eat a tremendous amount of food for a baby. But—

I don't understand why you worry about her even if she does eat like a wolf. She's hungry thats [*sic*] all—

. . . I'd let her eat if I was boss. She's hungry now too. Let her eat.[39]

Indeed, the last panel of the episode implies that the other adults eventually heed the grandfather's recommendation to "let her eat." Henrietta, her cheeks still wet with tears, has quieted down as she eats milk and porridge. Throughout the series, the grandfather seems to understand food as a source of comfort and healing. When the grandmother worries that Henrietta might be "hurt internally," he runs off to get some cookies. "They'll fix her up. She's hungry," he says.[40] Certainly, the grandfather appears to be a naïve, overindulgent adult, one who tends to pamper rather than discipline children. His style of child-rearing ran counter to contemporary parenting manuals that emphasized restraint. For example, L. Emmett Holt's *The Care and Feeding of Children: A Catechism for the Use of Mothers and Children's Nurses* (1894) advocated strict diets and feeding schedules for the young. For Holt and some of his contemporaries, children needed to learn self-control, especially in environments that were becoming increasingly consumerist and competitive.

Yet Henrietta's grandfather can also be seen as the sensible, "child-friendly" adult who rejects regimentation and austerity. The father, mother, and grandmother keep thinking "something is wrong" with Henrietta, fearing that she is not fulfilling the ideal of disciplined childhood (or, more precisely, disciplined girlhood). The grandfather, however, is able to identify and empathize with the individual needs of his grandchild. While his seniority may make him appear as the doddering fool who offers outdated advice, the strip insists that he is the fount of reason and experience, rightfully rejecting fretful "modern" beliefs about child-rearing. That he gives his granddaughter the freedom to feed and fulfill her desires is significant: here is the family patriarch, giving his female progeny permission to do as she pleases.

Hungry Henrietta also indicates that children may be confused by how their elders simultaneously discipline and mollycoddle them. In the strip, the adults often resort to baby talk, pet names, and exaggerated gestures when they address Henrietta. During a portraiture session, the adults speak in "childish" babble in an effort to make Henrietta look at the camera lens:

FATHER: Look look at the pretty birdie look at the pretty birdie ye ho ye ye upty diddle.

MOTHER: Now look up up petty. See the sugar tree. Up pet. Dey she is deedle dee.

Deedle dee upsy dey upsy dey queenie.

GRANDMOTHER: Di de diddle dee she's a chick a dee ootsy tootsy Dan Ma's pet.

GRANDFATHER: Now see what Dan Pa is going to do. Yehe.[41]

It is quite obvious that Henrietta does not understand a single word uttered by the adults. She appears baffled, then frustrated, by their attempts at "baby talk." But while this episode mocks the image of adults who willingly infantilize themselves in the presence of an infant, the adult characters' use of pet names and baby talk reveals that alongside Holt's prescriptions for parenting ran child-rearing styles that emphasized affection and playfulness. Indeed, the titles of many strips of the period expressed a particular fondness for girls: young female characters were named "dear little Katy," "Rosy Posy," and "Angelic Angelina" and were affectionately called "mama's girl" and "mama's angel child." These labels, of course, were meant to be read ironically: they called attention to the gap between the ideal of sweet, demure girlhood and the girls who did not conform to this ideal. At the same time, these titles suggest that girls who broke (gender) rules could still remain, in the eyes of adults, playful dears and amusing angels.

Little Coquettes

While *Hungry Henrietta* focused on the "disconcerting" image of a girl who could not control her appetite, other series reproduced a related construction of the misbehaving girl: what Gary Cross calls the "innocent coquette," a figure who embodied both sexual innocence and knowledge.[42] The image was certainly a popular trope in contemporary film. Mary Pickford, who was a teenager when she began her acting career in 1909, was, as Cross puts it, "the sensuous woman who turned herself into the cute child."[43] Even when she was in her twenties, Pickford was still occasionally cast to play a young girl, including the titular role of a film adaptation of *Rebecca of Sunnybrook Farm*. Some of her nicknames—"little girl" and "the girl with the curls"—were expressive of a desire to preserve her in youthfulness and girlishness. Decades later, audiences would be similarly captivated by another "girl with curls": Shirley Temple. While Pickford represented the preservation of the child-in-the-adult, Temple teased audiences by suggesting the presence of the adult in the child. As Cross puts it, Temple was marketed as "the innocent who imitated the sensuous woman."[44]

Temple did not appear in films until the 1930s, but she was arguably presaged by the characters of cartoonist Grace Wiederseim.[45] Dottie Dimple, the eponymous protagonist of one of Wiederseim's longest running strips, was a Temple prototype: she had chubby cheeks, blonde ringlets, and plump arms and legs. Much like her male counterparts Buster Brown and Hans and Fritz Katzenjammer, Dottie devises pranks and upends the "normalcy" of daily adult life. But in *Dottie Dimple* (1908–1911), Wiederseim also packages girlish sexuality as amusing. Whenever Dottie trips, falls down, or is punished with a spanking, Wiederseim offers readers a peek of the character's underpants. *Dottie Dimple* assumes that there is no harm in seeing an "innocent" young girl's underclothes. At the same time, the series also titillates readers with a view of garments that are meant to be hidden, of sexuality that is meant to be latent. Wiederseim thus explores the problem of constructing childhood as a sexually innocent space. As James Kincaid provocatively argues, adults' anxious defense of the child's sexual purity has ironically fetishized and eroticized the child.[46] In *Dottie Dimple*, Wiederseim invokes the intertwined feelings of unease and pleasure that could be incited by the image of the coquettish girl. In one episode, Dottie wanders in the park while her older female cousin sits on a bench, distracted by a suitor (fig. 42).[47] When Dottie meets a tearful girl wearing ragged clothes, she takes pity on her new acquaintance. She takes off her clothes and hands them to the destitute girl. Dottie, now in her underclothes, returns to the scene of courtship. The sight of the near-naked Dottie distresses the cousin. Her suitor, on the other hand, seems amused. The child's seminude body perhaps reminds the two adults of the possible outcomes of courtship: marriage, consummation, and offspring. Even as Dottie interrupts a moment of wooing, her babyish, semiexposed body gives the adult characters a picture of their courtship's potential consequence. But the adults' different responses also express contemporary ambivalence regarding girlish sexuality. On the one hand, the scene implies that the (male) gaze on the body of the female child is harmless and permissible. Here, the suitor (and the readers) can take pleasure in Dottie's prepubescent, not-fully-naked body. On the other hand, the scene also insists that the sight of girls' bodies, even if they just *hinted* at sexuality, is still scandalous. For her female

Figure 42. Comic Strip by Grace Wiederseim. "Dottie Dimple Gives Her Nice Dress to a Poor Girl!" In *Los Angeles Examiner* Comic Supplement, May 22, 1910. SFS 85-5-7, San Francisco Academy of Comic Art Collection, the Ohio State University Billy Ireland Cartoon Library and Museum.

cousin, Dottie's "indecent" appearance may represent temptation to perform licentious acts. By responding "appropriately" with shock, the cousin signals her refusal of such temptation. Thus while young Dottie plays the innocent flirt, she paradoxically enables her older cousin to display feminine propriety.

Like *Dottie Dimple*, contemporary strips headlined by girls expressed and explored tensions between desire and discipline, innocence and knowledge, the private and the public. The following pages focus on two comic strips that examined these tensions through depictions of girls' imaginative play. More particularly, these two series—Wilson's *Madge the Magician's Daughter* and Tucker's *Betsy Bouncer and Her Doll*—suggest that fantasy and play were tools that girls used to confront and negotiate the challenges and expectations of growing up female at the turn of the century.

(Mis)management of Magic

W. O. Wilson's *Madge the Magician's Daughter* was a syndicated series that ran for just over a year, from 1906 to 1907. The series, about a young girl who practices magic using her father's wand, evoked contemporary fascination with illusionism and the occult. *Madge* debuted in the same year as Harry Houdini's well-publicized escape from a Washington, D.C., prison. Unlike Houdini, however, Madge is not an illusionist or an escape artist. Rather than performing stunts, sleight-of-hand tricks, or using camera or light effects, she performs "true" magic, invoking the supernatural as she makes something out of nothing.

In their appreciation of *Madge*, comics historians Jenny Robb and Richard D. Olson link Wilson's work to other fantasy comic strips such as Winsor McCay's *Little Nemo in Slumberland* and Lyonel Feininger's *The Kin-der-kids* and *Wee Willie Winkie's World*.[48] *Madge*'s similarity to *Little Nemo* is especially striking. It is likely that Wilson and his publishers were attempting to capitalize on the success of *Little Nemo*. Wilson retained many of the elements that characterized McCay's famous strip. Both series were published in color and took up a full page, and both experimented with panel size and layout. *Madge* also reveals Wilson's particular fondness and talent for drawing animals. His illustrations of cats, bears, elephants, peacocks, dragons, and sea serpents recall McCay's detailed, arresting drawings of domestic, wild, and fantastical creatures.

Robb and Olson contend that *Madge* should be recognized for providing readers a radical female protagonist, pointing out that "Wilson . . . cast [Madge] in stories featuring dinosaurs, dragons, mermaids, pirates and Indians—the adventures usually associated with boys."[49] In aesthetic terms, *Madge* may strike some as a pale imitation of *Little Nemo*, but Wilson's heroine is arguably a more dynamic character than McCay's male protagonist. As I discuss in chapter 4, Nemo may be interpreted as a passive character whose primary function is to bear witness to the wonders of Slumberland. He appears to be more reactive than proactive and he is often subject to the whims of the dream realm's inhabitants and constantly shifting landscape. Madge, on the other hand, is more than a spectator. She is the bearer of enchantments, the girl who attempts to conjure creatures out of thin air. While Nemo is often awed and baffled by the unfamiliar, Madge summons the strange, calling it forth to disrupt the world of the mundane.

Of course, the strip makes clear that Madge is far from being an expert magician. Episode after episode highlights her inability to control spells and her failure to fully comprehend the implications of her use of magic. In depicting Madge's mismanagement of magic, Wilson alludes to Johann Wolfgang von Goethe's *Der Zauberlehrling* (*The Sorcerer's Apprentice*, 1797), a narrative poem whose plot has been popularized by Walt Disney in *Fantasia* (1940). In the poem, the apprentice, tired of cleaning his master's room, enchants a broom to fetch water. As such, he imagines the broom to be *his* apprentice. But the novice magician lacks the knowledge to undo the spell, and the room begins to flood as the broom keeps bringing bucket after bucket of water. The apprentice hacks the broom into pieces, but the splinters "rise like towers," turning into more brooms that set off to fetch more water.[50] The poem ends with the sorcerer restoring order, mending the damage caused by his inept apprentice. In *Madge*, the young protagonist is as uninformed and inexperienced as the sorcerer's apprentice; she constantly attempts to wield power she has no mastery of. Through her, disorder visits the "everyday" world. Her magic acts sometimes put her and her friends in danger. In most cases, her father—a master magician—needs to intervene and reverse her spells.

While Madge can be considered a troublemaker, she is, at the same time, innocent, in the sense that she has no intent to harm. Her primary desire is to entertain and impress her friends. The series also implies that she casts spells in an effort to imitate her father, who appears to be a professional illusionist. Her act of emulation could be understood as transgressive: here is a young girl attempting to wield power associated with the male adult and trying to make a claim to public visibility. While Randall Styers reminds us that in the late nineteenth and early twentieth centuries, "magic [was] attributed primarily to groups on the periphery of social power (primitives, women, children, the disenfranchised)," Wilson's strip establishes magic as the province of the patriarch.[51] By using her father's wand—a stand-in for the phallus—Madge makes an "unnatural" claim to men's creative (and procreative) abilities and privileges. While her father expertly commands the occult, Madge's spells are marked by error and disaster. In one episode, she summons an aberrant creature with the head of a woman and the body of a bird.[52] Although this strange creature appears to be benevolent, introducing herself as the "queen of the lady-birds," she may remind readers of a harpy. In evoking a mythical representation that imagines the female to be destructive and ravenous, the episode implies that Madge's use of her father's wand and her attempts at enchantments have the potential to be emasculating.

But the episode also insists that power remains in the hands of male characters. For one, the queen of the lady birds is depicted as a damsel in distress rather than a femme fatale. The four-legged "wicked king of the zebragoats," who looks nothing more than a brash, juvenile centaur, tries to force her into marriage. Madge and her female friend look on helplessly as the zebragoat attempts to abduct the queen. But Madge's father arrives in time to rescue the queen and put the zebragoat in his place. With a spell, the magician enables the queen to return to her realm. He treats the zebragoat like a misbehaving boy, wagging his finger at him and instructing him to "stay here till I say the word."

"The word," the strip indicates, is the very thing that the father has mastered and that eludes Madge's grasp. In the strip's early episodes, Madge's misenchantments are established as products of linguistic lapses. When she attempts to call forth animals, she recognizes, quite belatedly, that she "[used] the wrong words."[53] When she tries to make butterflies appear from a fountain, her use of the word "gaggley" causes a congregation of alligators to emerge instead.[54] Even when she happens to summon the correct species, the animals appear in overwhelming numbers. Whenever Madge realizes she has made a mistake, she is unable to undo the magic because she "can't remember the right things to say."[55] The strip hints that Madge cannot "make magic" because she is illiterate in this craft. It is worth noting that the incantations are gibberish; the nonsense language references the supposed infantile language of "primitives," uneducated women, members of the lower class, and, of course, children. Ironically, Madge's father—a white, affluent adult male—is the one who is most fluent in this magical gobbledygook.

What is interesting is that Madge's father, established as the series' authoritative figure, apparently has no objections to his daughter's attempts to wield magic. He even encourages her efforts to cast enchantments. While prankish boys in contemporary strips suffer spankings and other forms of punishment, the erring Madge receives tender corrections and instructions from her father. Rather than dissuading Madge, he reminds her that "you ought to know that gaggley means alligator."[56] While the strip makes clear that the father is the "true" master of both natural and supernatural realms, it also shows his desire to train and educate Madge in his craft. While many contemporary strips celebrated boys as the energetic, resourceful heirs to the nation, *Madge* offers the image of a patriarch preparing his female child to inherit his legacy. Moreover, the strip also implies that Madge has, by virtue of being female, an "inherent" connection with magic. When Madge uses her father's phallic wand to summon animals, the creatures emerge from portals associated with the yonic: circular orifices, bodies of water, vases shaped like wombs. The animals that Madge calls forth sometimes invoke the maternal and the fertile, such as a mother bear and her cub and, in another episode, a phalanx of storks that carry bundled-up infants (fig. 43).[57] In "Buster Brown Visits the Zoo," the women slam their doors on the child-bearing

Figure 43. Comic Strip by W. O. Wilson. "Madge the Magician's Daughter." In *San Francisco Call* Comic Supplement, October 28, 1906. SFT 133-5, San Francisco Academy of Comic Art Collection, the Ohio State University Billy Ireland Cartoon Library and Museum.

stork that visits them. In the meantime, Madge opts to rehearse her maternal duties when she encounters the storks and the infants. She recognizes that the babies are crying out of hunger and she tells her friend that "we will go and get some milk for them." Inevitably, the storks take flight when Madge and her friend return with a pitcher of milk. Her father explains that the "wise birds . . . are not going to let you children monkey with those babies who are too young to be fed that way," implying that Madge and her friend are too young and inexperienced to carry—and comprehend—the burden of motherhood.

Overall, *Madge* suggests that its protagonist's constant spell casting troubles the status quo. When Madge waves her father's wand, she turns the parlor and cultivated English gardens into frenzied menageries. She creates havoc in the quiet halls of a museum when she makes dinosaurs come to life. In *Madge*, girls' magic is largely a hazard that upsets domestic, social, and natural orders; it is a force that initiates disruptive collisions between the private and the public, the domestic and the wild, the past and the present, the extinct and the living. As Styers argues, magic was the object of distrust at the turn of the century precisely because it was associated with women and other peripheral figures: "In rhetoric that is often preoccupied with issues of gender and sexuality, magic has been blamed for a broad and contradictory assortment of social ills. The practice of magic is regularly portrayed as a selfish and antisocial preoccupation of those on the fringes of society, with its rebellious practitioners violating a host of natural and societal laws as they seek to disrupt the orderly flow of natural causation for petty, materialistic gain."[58]

In *Madge*, a two-episode sequence featuring mermaids references such anxieties about female magic. More particularly, it implies that magic can awaken female sexuality. Wishing to impress a female friend, Madge tries to make smoke rise out of a pool of water (fig. 44).[59] To their alarm, a pair of mermaids emerges from "the deep." One of the mermaids beckons the girls to dive into the water with them. Madge declines the invitation, and her refusal signals restraint. As a girl being trained to become a "proper" lady, she seems to recognize that she belongs on "dry" land rather than in "sensual" waters. Madge explains to the mermaids that she and her friend "would drown," intimating that she understands that exploration of "the deep" may lead to death—or, in this case, the demise of girlhood innocence.

At one point, a male passerby catches a glimpse of one of the mermaids. Assuming that she is a drowning victim, he jumps headfirst into the pool, hoping that his gallant rescue attempt will result in a "Carnegie medal." But he soon resurfaces and runs off, frightened by what he calls "devil-fish an' octopuses." Unable to believe that the mermaid is no distressed damsel, he concludes that "that poor lady" has been "eaten alive by them devil-fish." Or perhaps what terrifies him is the mermaid's sexual ambivalence. It may be that he is unsettled by the

Figure 44. Comic Strip by W. O. Wilson. "Madge the Magician's Daughter." In *San Francisco Call* Comic Supplement, May 19, 1907. AC-P13-2, Richard D. Olson Collection, the Ohio State University Billy Ireland Cartoon Library and Museum.

fact that she is simultaneously alluring and inaccessible, as she is exposed from the waist up but cold-blooded from the waist down.

The following episode repeats this theme of male bewilderment in the face of the "enigmatic" female. Madge appears to have overcome her wariness of the mermaids and she summons them.[60] A pair of mermaids—a mother and her child—answer her call, but they end up in another pool in which a group of boys are bathing. The boys, believing that the water is "so deep no one has ever been able to find the bottom," swim in the pool as an act of derring-do. But at the sight of the mermaids, they panic. The boys flee from the pool, perhaps fearful of being submerged in female, maternal elements. Madge and her friend, meanwhile, sit close to the edge of the water. Though their interaction with half-naked creatures may prematurely initiate them into knowledge of female sexuality, their engagement with a mermaid mother and her child may be deemed safe, as it reminds the girls to link sexuality with women's reproductive "duties."

Madge's run lasted less than a year. Perhaps its lack of success can be attributed to readers' disinterest in the escapades and preoccupations of a female protagonist. It seems curious that audiences delighted in novels headlined by girls, such as Wiggin's *Rebecca of Sunnybrook Farm*, Montgomery's *Anne of Green Gables*, Lewis Carroll's *Alice's Adventures in Wonderland* (1865), L. Frank Baum's *The Wonderful Wizard of Oz* (1900), and Louisa May Alcott's *Little Women* (1868–1869), while rebuffing the female characters who appeared in the comic supplement. Still, Madge shared something in common with female characters in children's fiction. She performs and entertains to become visible, in much the same way that Jo, Rebecca, and Anne write, stage plays, and tell stories to assert their individuality. *Madge* suggests that girls can hold others in thrall, and in the process, gain acknowledgment and a sense of belonging. While Madge mostly stages her magic acts in domestic/domesticated spaces such as the parlor and the garden and thus does not have as public a venue as her illusionist father's performances, which presumably take place in the theater, her tricks can be understood as rehearsals for a more public role in adulthood, as expressive of her desire to extend her civic duties beyond the home.

Toying with the Boundaries of Girlhood

While Madge's magic tricks are certainly disruptive, she is indisputably a "good girl" who wishes no harm to come to her family and friends. A more disquieting image of girlhood was to be found in *Betsy Bouncer and Her Doll*, a strip by Tom Tucker. *Betsy Bouncer* was published in the *New York Herald* and in sister newspapers that circulated in other cities. Like *Madge*, Tucker's series had a relatively short run, with episodes appearing between August 1904 and May 1905. The strip centers on the playful activities of young Betsy and her sentient doll. But their games are often underpinned by viciousness, as the doll is a devious, sadistic character who dreams up pranks that have the potential to inflict pain on others, including Betsy.

Betsy Bouncer built on the tradition of sentient doll narratives, which emerged and enjoyed immense popularity in the mid-nineteenth century. Twenty-first-century readers may consider *Betsy Bouncer* a precursor to the extremely popular strip *Calvin and Hobbes* (1985–1995) by Bill Watterson. In Watterson's strip, Hobbes is a stuffed toy tiger who appears to Calvin (and readers) as a big cat who breathes, thinks, and feels. In both strips, the toys are the children's "life-sized" playmates and companions.[61] But Hobbes also acts as Calvin's conscience, as he often chides Calvin for his lack of self-restraint. In *Betsy Bouncer*, it is the doll that is impulsive, even wanton. Her tricks are not simply in the spirit of childish mischief; they are often laced with malice. In some ways, this "bad doll" enables the protagonist Betsy to shore up her image as a "good girl." The strip establishes the essential differences between the two female figures through visual means. Betsy is a picture of girlhood innocence; her blonde ringlets, beribboned dress, and flowery bonnet signify primness, purity, and propriety. The doll, on the other hand, is a rag doll fashioned out of cloth straps. She has uneven limbs, a coarse dress, and a tuft of dark hair. The toy, then, is symbolic of rough and vulgar forces that present a threat to "virtuous" girls like Betsy.

But the doll's status as a rag doll ends up complicating the narrative of "good girl" versus her "bad doll." Rag dolls were historically not designated as playthings. In the antebellum period, dolls made of cloth enabled girls to practice and display their sewing skills.[62] At the time, doll play was not yet a common practice, as girls, expected to fulfill many domestic obligations, often had little time for such leisurely pursuits.[63] Only after the Civil War, with the ascendance of consumer culture and the embrace of imaginative play as a healthful and natural activity for children, did the concept of doll play gain traction with middle-class parents. A girl like Betsy, however, would ideally play with a store-bought doll rather than a homemade one. Dolls made of cloth became passé as manufactured dolls, made of porcelain and bisque, became more accessible and fashionable. Playing with "delicate" china and bisque dolls was encouraged in middle-class households in the late nineteenth and early twentieth centuries; the activity was seen as a means for girls to practice consumerism and, more specifically, "[ape] the conspicuous display of consumer goods and social status epitomized by the European bourgeoisie their parents emulated."[64]

The popularity of manufactured dolls in the early twentieth century is revealed by an advertisement that, ironically, appeared on the same page as a *Betsy Bouncer* episode. While the strip shows Betsy and her rag doll at play, the LeMoyne Handkerchief Co.'s below-the-line advertisement, titled "Free to Girls: Two Beautiful Dolls," offered a "Sunday doll" and an "every-day doll" as premiums to girls who were able to sell three dollars and twenty cents worth of handkerchiefs on behalf of the company (fig. 45).[65] The dolls were described as "the

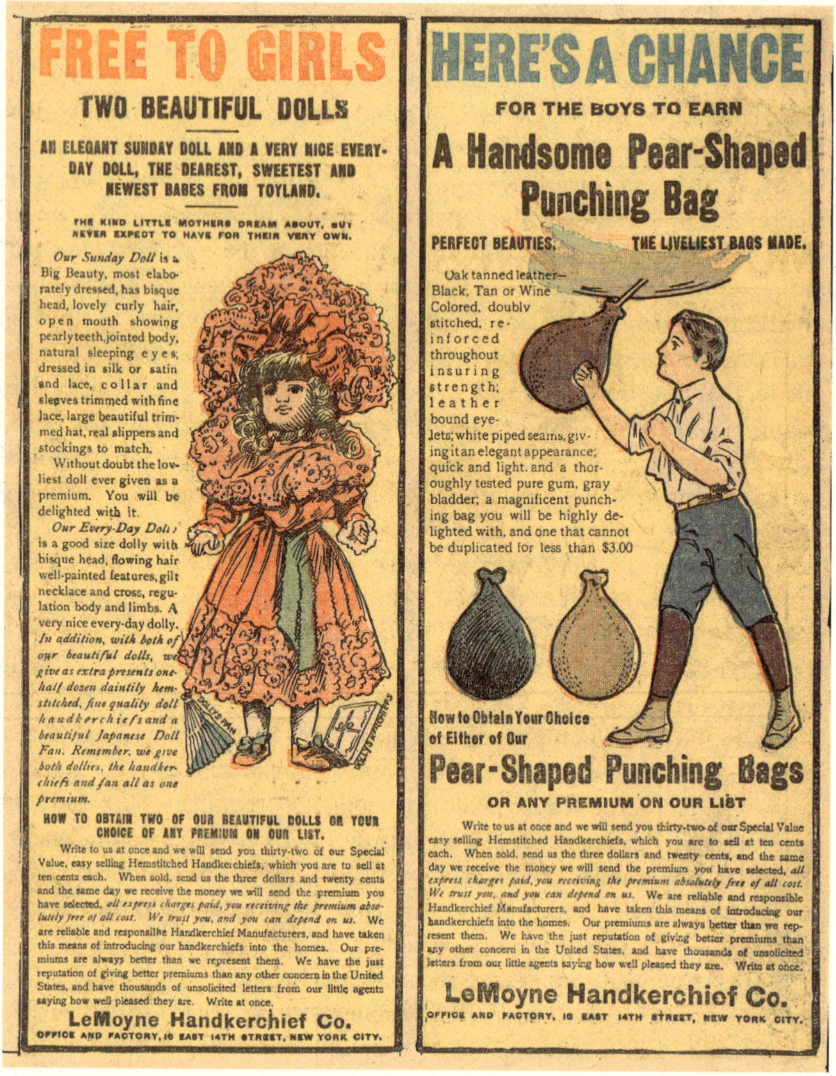

Figure 45. Advertisements by LeMoyne Handkerchief Co. "Free to Girls" and "Here's a Chance." In *Sunday Record Herald* Comic Supplement, October 16, 1904. SFT 2, San Francisco Academy of Comic Art Collection, the Ohio State University Billy Ireland Cartoon Library and Museum.

kind little mothers dream about, but never expect to have for their very own."[66] The Sunday doll—a doll meant to be an accessory for a young girl dressed in her Sunday best—was, at least according to the description, a far cry from the shabby appearance of Betsy's doll: "[It is] most elaborately dressed, has bisque head, lovely curly hair, open mouth showing pearly teeth, jointed body, natural sleeping eyes, dressed in silk or satin and lace, collar and sleeves trimmed with fine lace, large beautiful trimmed hat, real slippers and stockings to match."[67] Even the everyday doll, presumably designed for wear and tear in the hands of young girls, seemed to be an elegant plaything. It was described as a "good size dolly with bisque head, flowing hair, well painted features, gilt necklace and cross, regulation body and limbs."[68]

The advertisement reveals contemporary social prescriptions for doll play and, more broadly, gender play. The dolls are sentimentalized as "dearest, sweetest . . . babes" that girls could use to exercise "little [motherhood]."[69] As documented by Miriam Formanek-Brunell, store-bought dolls were also meant to instruct girls in fashion and socialization, serving as tools that purportedly helped them practice elaborate dress-up as well as host imaginary tea and house-warming parties.[70] It is worth noting that the "Free to Girls" doll advertisement ran alongside another LeMoyne advertisement that further hardened the lines of segregated gender play. The complementary advertisement, aimed toward boys, offered "handsome pear-shaped punching bag[s]" as premiums.[71] While "Free to Girls" encouraged girls to play at being mothers, this accompanying promotion endorsed the notion that boys needed to develop and exercise vigor and masculinity through competitive and aggressive sport. The two advertisements display how children's play at the turn of the century was defined along gender lines.

These promotional materials also coaxed children to actively participate in consumer culture as "little agents." LeMoyne offered the dolls and punching bags as prizes to children who successfully sold "thirty-two of our Special Value, easy selling Hemstiched Handkerchiefs . . . at ten cents each."[72] It is significant, then, that in *Betsy Bouncer*, the titular protagonist remains attached to a coarse cloth doll. The doll signifies Betsy's refusal to participate in the marketplace. Her insistence on playing with an "ugly" homemade doll rather than a manufactured toy is a rejection of the consumerism that swept up and increasingly defined middle-class family life in the Progressive Era.

Of course, Betsy often fulfills the image of the "little mother" prescribed by the "Free to Girls" advertisement. In some episodes, she takes on the role of parent-disciplinarian. She admonishes the doll for tormenting a cat; she sternly warns the toy to stay away from the edge of a cliff. Other episodes depict Betsy as a tender maternal figure. When her doll is injured and torn, Betsy displays her domestic skills by nursing her doll and stitching her up. She is also fiercely protective of her toy. In one episode, Betsy takes dancing lessons from a billy goat who desires to teach her "in a few steps, how to go it in polite society."[73] It seems absurd that Betsy is taking lessons in civility from a farm animal, and the doll exposes this farce. She interrupts the lesson and taunts the goat, calling him "whiskers." In doing so, the doll succeeds in revealing the goat's "inherent" savagery: the goat takes umbrage at the insult and butts the doll with his horns. Instead of reprimanding her toy for teasing her dance instructor, Betsy comes to her doll's defense. She tugs the goat's beard and calls him a "brute." The last panel shows Betsy joyfully waving a fistful of goat hair. By forcibly removing some of the animal's "whiskers," she not only compounds her doll's insult but also upholds the boundary between human and animal.

Although the series exhibits Betsy's maternal, protective instinct toward her doll, it also repeatedly illustrates how Betsy's interaction with her toy falls outside the boundaries of sanctioned doll play. Betsy's games with her doll do not involve dress-up or tea parties in the nursery. Instead, girl and toy spend most of their time outdoors, engaging in "boyish" activities such as sledding, tree-climbing, and playing with domestic and wild animals. While the LeMoyne advertisement imagined doll play to be an exercise in motherhood, *Betsy Bouncer* depicts the doll as an object that facilitates Betsy's practice *and* rebuttal of "little womanhood." Indeed, Thomas Henricks reminds us that play is not simply a rehearsal of future responsibilities; it can also be escapist and subversive. He states that "play as an ideal type of behavior accentuates the two themes of human freedom: In play we are cut off from the customary interferences of the world; in play, we are permitted to do things to that world that we might not otherwise be allowed to do."[74] Through and with her doll, Betsy takes respite from and bucks the rigid requirements of proper girlhood. Betsy's doll could be understood as a plaything that allows a white, middle-class girl to negotiate and toy with the lines between restraint and delight, passivity and autonomy.

In fact, the fictionalized doll play in *Betsy Bouncer* references how real girls at the turn of the century participated in what Formanek-Brunell calls the "politics of dollhood": "If [girls] played with dolls at all, they rejected elaborate dolls for coarse ones. . . . [They] resisted rote prescriptions of play rituals by substituting their own earthy versions and often preferred active 'physical culture' to passive doll culture."[75] Formanek-Brunell also documents how commentators of the period remarked at the sight of "'hoydenish little girls' [who] expressed anger and aggression [toward their dolls] nearly as frequently as love and affection."[76] Similarly, Lois R. Kuznets reminds us that tendencies to sentimentalize children's (and more specifically, girls') doll play obscures the "autobiographical or fictional accounts of intense child-doll relationships [that] frequently depict these relationships degenerating into severe mistreatment of the doll."[77] *Betsy Bouncer* deviates slightly from such narratives of aggressive doll play, in the sense that the doll is the agent of violence as much as she is an object that is repeatedly violated. In one episode, the doll notably compares herself to Buster Brown, the period's most famous fictional troublemaker. After being thrashed by a bear that she taunted, the doll fastens a pillow to her backside. She explains that she is trying to "be in style. Buster Brown always does this after he gets spanked" (fig. 46).[78] This reference to Buster lays bare Tucker's attempt to emulate and capitalize on the success of Outcault's eponymous strip, which had debuted two years earlier. Tucker not only gave his protagonist a similarly alliterative name but also provided her a sentient nonhuman companion, with the doll serving as a stand-in

Figure 46. Comic Strip by Tom Tucker. "Betsy Bouncer and Her Doll." In *Sunday Record Herald* Comic Supplement, September 25, 1904. SFT 2, San Francisco Academy of Comic Art Collection, the Ohio State University Billy Ireland Cartoon Library and Museum.

for Buster's bull terrier, Tige. But while Tige typically functions as Buster's moral center, a pet who tries to curb (in vain) his young master's impulsiveness and puckishness, the doll is a little rogue who goads Betsy to play at being bad. One episode shows how the doll manages to persuade Betsy to disturb a beehive (fig. 47).[79] The doll delights in the thought of upsetting the bees as well as the image of Betsy being stung. "Oh my but won't she suffer," says the toy. "She's such an easy mark." But while Betsy is the one who performs the naughty act, she does not suffer the consequences. The provoked bees end up swarming the doll, not Betsy. The doll is responsible for planting the seed of mischief; consequently, she is also the one who ends up wounded. Upon seeing the doll's face disfigured by bee stings, Betsy cheekily remarks, "Doesn't she look just too swell for anything!" As her body remains unblemished, Betsy is able to revel in the pleasures of unsettling the beehive and mocking her injured doll.

"Good girl" Betsy is thus able to evacuate herself of naughtiness and impetuousness because she projects these qualities on her "ugly" doll. Through her doll, Betsy is able to vicariously engage in bad behavior *and* escape the penalties for misbehaving. The doll climbs and falls from a tree, is inadvertently squashed while sledding, and suffers a tummy ache after stealing and gobbling up apples. The doll is the scapegoat who enables Betsy to maintain the appearance of innocence and virtuous girlhood. Paradoxically, the figure of the battered, suffering

Figure 47. Comic Strip by Tom Tucker. "Betsy Bouncer and Her Doll." In *Chicago Record Herald* Comic Supplement, August 21, 1904. SFS 44-4-3, San Francisco Academy of Comic Art Collection, the Ohio State University Billy Ireland Cartoon Library and Museum.

doll also allows Betsy to try her hand at being a good mother. The doll that allows Betsy to safely engage in misbehavior is also the incorrigible child that she can discipline, the sick child that she can tenderly nurse back to health.

The multifaceted relationship between girl and doll expresses the complex and often contradictory ways girlhood at the turn of the century was conceptualized and experienced. As Kuznets points out, narratives about sentient dolls "embody human anxiety about what it means to be 'real'—an independent subject or self rather than an object or other submitting to the gaze of more powerfully real and potentially rejecting live beings."[80] In *Betsy Bouncer*, the doll represents Betsy's efforts at self-actualization; the toy that comes to life symbolizes Betsy's awakening to her own personhood. But Betsy's claim to subjectivity is necessarily dependent on her doll remaining a "thing." Indeed, the strip locks the doll into the status of object by repeatedly maiming her. The series proposes that it is acceptable to subject the doll to slapstick violence because she is not a "real" girl; she is a nonperson who is presumably immune to suffering. Throughout the series, the doll undergoes gruesome mutilation: she is twisted, flattened, unstuffed, and even beheaded. At first blush, these scenes of violence appear to follow the tradition of morality tales published between the seventeenth and nineteenth centuries, in which fictional bad children receive grisly—but purportedly just—punishments. In *Betsy Bouncer*, however, the doll's mangled state is depicted as comic rather than frightful. Moreover, in accordance with comic strip convention, the doll endures disfigurement and she is restored to her "full" form by the next episode. In insisting that the doll, regardless of its sentience, is ultimately a thing, the strip suggests that doll play is a venue in which girls can practice encounters with a subordinate Other. It is quite telling that the doll remains nameless. Betsy refers to her as "*my* doll" or "*my* dolly" (emphasis mine). For her part, the doll refers to Betsy as "my mistress," signaling her recognition that she is owned, a girl's possession.[81] This hierarchical relationship between girl and doll evokes antebellum doll narratives that, as Robin Bernstein argues, depict "dollness *itself* [as] a racial category that denotes servitude."[82] For Bernstein, "dolls, doll play, and literature about sentient dolls . . . weld childhood to slavery's most foundational, disturbing, and lingering question: What is a person?"[83] *Betsy Bouncer* could thus be understood as an expression of how white supremacy determined the lives of Progressive Era children. More particularly, it demonstrates that a white, middle-class girl's exploration of personhood and autonomy rests on her exploitation of the (racial) Other, who ostensibly cannot make a similar claim to subjectivity.

Madge the Magician's Daughter and *Betsy Bouncer and Her Doll* were two of a number of comics about girls that cartoonists and publishers, eager to maintain their young female readership, launched in the early twentieth century. Both strips built on the template established by popular boy-centered series such as *The Katzenjammer Kids*, *Buster Brown*, and *Little Nemo in Slumberland*. But they also established that girls create trouble because they desire the power and freedom associated with boyhood and manhood. Madge casts spells using her father's wand; with her doll, Betsy engages in and takes delight in boyish pranks and amusements. Both female protagonists use imaginative play to explore the world outside the nursery, the kitchen, and the parlor; both strips approach play as a means to conceive of possibilities outside good girlhood. Yet Madge's and Betsy's misbehavior are also "safe," as their troublesome acts occur largely by proxy: animals cause a riot on Madge's behalf; Betsy's doll takes the lead in engaging in "ungirlish" behavior. By keeping their hands clean of dirty work, both protagonists remain "pure" girls who can help preserve an "untainted" Anglo-Saxon legacy. In effect, *Madge* and *Betsy Bouncer* indicate how the figure of the misbehaving girl could not be a true facsimile of the naughty boy.

The antiauthoritarianism embodied by the comic strip's naughty boy was deeply intertwined with the national values of freedom and equality. However, girl-centered comics, whether intentionally or inadvertently, exposed how some cultural groups were excluded from such visions of independence and egalitarianism. Strips like *Madge* and *Betsy Bouncer* particularly point to the political, economic, and social restrictions placed on women and girls, uncovering the chasm between ideals of democracy and sociopolitical realities. They called attention to the tensions that marked Progressive Era girlhood and the strains placed on girls and women who were pulled in oppositional directions as they confronted the demands of domestic duties and recognized the possibilities of public participation. The strips narrativized the ways girls and women faced restrictions and experienced freedoms. While the strips often reinforced social fantasies about girlhood, they also expressed how girls dreamt about escaping the bonds of normative gender roles.

CONCLUSION

NAUGHTY BOYS IN A NEW MILLENNIUM

R. F. Outcault's retirement of *Buster Brown* in 1921 could be taken as a sign that the naughty child's reign in the newspaper supplements was on the wane. Newspaper comics remained an extremely popular medium, though readers found themselves enthralled with a new format: the continuity strip. With its cliffhangers and "to-be-continued" structure, the continuity strip lent itself to narratives of adventure, crime, romance, and science fiction—and not necessarily to variations on the theme of childhood antics. One of the main stars of Frank King's continuity strip *Gasoline Alley*, which debuted in 1918, did have a notable child character. On February 14, 1921, an infant was left on the doorstep of Walt Wallet. But the boy—whom Walt adopted and nicknamed Skeezix—did not remain a baby for long, as he (and the other characters) aged through the years. By the 1940s, Skeezix was a young soldier, fighting in World War II.

When televisions became fixtures in American households in the 1950s, the continuity strip was rendered obsolete, as it was unable to compete with television serials that offered longer and more complex narratives in one sitting.[1] With continuity strips on the decline, cartoonists returned to the business of comedy. The daily, single-tier, black-and-white strip that offered "a joke a day" emerged as the new standard format. Consisting of three to four panels, the gag-a-day strip typically sets up a joke in the first two or three frames and delivers the punch line in the last panel.[2]

Despite radical changes to the format of newspaper comics, child characters did not altogether disappear from the comics pages. If anything, Buster Brown, the Katzenjammer Kids, and Little Nemo proved that child characters were resilient and able to withstand violent forces of change. In the 1930s, the curly haired, blank-eyed protagonist of Harold Gray's *Little Orphan Annie* (which debuted in 1924) became the most recognizable, beloved comic strip character of the period. Many readers living through the Great Depression responded to the strip's Dickensian theme; audiences took comfort in the figure of Annie, an innocent-yet-plucky child, whose inherent goodness and vitality enabled her to survive and defeat corrupt and criminal forces. The origin of Ernie Bushmiller's *Nancy*, a series headlined by a precocious young girl, also testifies to the lasting appeal of child characters. In 1933, Nancy was introduced as a supporting character in *Fritzi Ritz*; she was the spirited and sometimes acerbic niece of the titular character, a superficial and rather witless flapper. By 1938, Nancy became the star of her own eponymously titled strip.

Nancy also represented a shift in the function of the fictional child in newspaper comics. While Nancy remained mischievous, the series' humor was focused less on physical slapstick and more on young people's keen observations about the incongruities between the ideals and realities of twentieth-century life (and more particularly, twentieth-century childhoods). While visual gags remained a comics staple, cartoonists increasingly utilized verbal jokes. The most popular child-centered comics series of the late twentieth century were proponents of this new practice: in Charles Schulz's *Peanuts* (1950–2000), Berke Breathed's *Bloom County* (1980–1989), and Bill Watterson's *Calvin and Hobbes* (1985–1995), child characters proved to be especially effective vessels for delivering punch lines.

The success of *Calvin and Hobbes* is reminiscent of the popularity of child-centered newspaper comics during the Progressive Era. At its peak, *Calvin and Hobbes* was featured in 2,400 newspapers around the world.[3] Its episodes have been collected and republished in eighteen compilations, forty-five million copies of which have been sold.[4] Debuting almost one hundred years after the Yellow Kid first gazed at the reader, Watterson's strip can be understood as an homage to the child of Progressive Era newspaper comics. For one, it revives the trope of naughty boyhood. Much like *Buster Brown*, *Calvin and Hobbes* disassembles the ideal of the affectionate, democratic household while suggesting that amiable humor can soothe the tensions between child and parent, husband and wife. The character of Hobbes, a toy tiger who "comes to life" and serves as Calvin's playmate and conscience, recalls Buster's pet dog, Tige. Calvin's vivid daydreams also evoke boys' imaginative worlds in *Little Nemo in Slumberland* and *Wee Willie Winkie's World*. As in the case of Nemo and Willie Winkie, Calvin's dream worlds are impenetrable to adults. His reveries are drawn in the mode of realism, in sharp contrast to the cartoonishness of his mundane world. While this realistic style suggests that Calvin lacks a sense of childish whimsy, it also insists on the tangibility and authenticity of his daydreams.

Like its predecessors, *Calvin and Hobbes* plays on anxieties about childhood. In the same way that the Yellow Kid, Hans and Fritz Katzenjammer, and Buster Brown simultaneously resist and revel in modernization, Calvin can be understood as victim, survivor, and abettor of late capitalism. The anarchic Katzenjammer Kids and troublesome Buster undeniably paved the way for Calvin, but their tricks pale in comparison to their descendant's pranks and schemes. In *Calvin and Hobbes*, the child protagonist is not simply a playful jokester; rather, he appears hell-bent on causing injury and ruin. His name alludes to the sixteenth-century theologian John Calvin, who endorsed strict discipline of children in the belief that they were born fallen; the fictional Calvin at once thumbs his nose at his namesake while seemingly affirming the Calvinist view that children are inherently sinful and savage.

Watterson certainly pokes fun at the mismatch between the ideal of the good child and the violent tendencies that underpins Calvin's play and daydreams. In one episode, Calvin imagines his body transforming into a "C-bomb," a weapon that has "the pure destructive force of a million A-bombs" (fig. 48).[5] In another episode, he hands "volume one" of his alphabetized Christmas wish list to his mother, declaring that the list includes items from "atom bomb" to "grenade launcher."[6] *Calvin and Hobbes* ended its run years before Eric Harris and Dylan Klebold orchestrated one of the deadliest school shootings in U.S. history, before Adam Lanza used assault weapons to murder his mother and attack students and teachers in an elementary school, and before Nikolas Cruz opened fire in Marjory Stoneman Douglas High School. After Columbine, Sandy Hook, and Parkland, the image of a boy dreaming up mass destruction is perhaps no longer acceptable fodder for comedy.

To be clear, *Calvin and Hobbes* does not suggest that boys' violent fantasy play should remain unchecked. In fact, the strip emphatically argues that childhood is under siege, targeted by corporate interests and mass media forms that circulate and glorify narratives of aggression and annihilation. Indeed, one of the strip's frequent targets is television. Watterson visually represents the television as a noisy, chaotic presence in Calvin's household: it bounces off the stand, surrounded by whorls, stars, and other emanata. In a sense, *Calvin and Hobbes* reiterates Neil Postman's denunciation of television, as expressed in the influential—and arguably alarmist—*The Disappearance of Childhood* (1982). For Postman, television's encroachment into the lives of children causes what he perceives to be the disconcerting erasure of the boundary between childhood and

Figure 48. Comic Strip by Bill Watterson. "Calvin and Hobbes." Copyright 1992. Distributed by Universal Press Syndicate.

adulthood.[7] The medium, according to Postman, provides children easy access to "adult" knowledge; its objectives to entertain and to sell goods and diversions impede efforts to provide children a sound foundation for their intellectual and moral growth. In *Calvin and Hobbes*, Watterson illustrates television's unparalleled ability to captivate young viewers. Calvin, who is astute enough to recognize how television promoted anti-intellectualism and desensitization, still eagerly basks in its light. In several episodes, Calvin's love for television is equated with religious fervor. He kneels before the television, calling for this "great altar of passive entertainment" to "bestow upon me thy discordant images at such speed as to render linear thought impossible."[8] In another episode, Calvin offers the television a "bowl of lukewarm tapioca [that] represents my brain." Addressing it as "the greatest of the mass media," he offers a prayer of gratitude: "Thank you for elevating emotion, reducing thought, and stifling imagination. Thank you for the artificiality of quick solutions and for the insidious manipulation of human desires for commercial purposes."[9] It is striking that the comic strip, censured by reformers in previous decades as a crass, vacuous commercial form, became, in the late twentieth century, a platform for advocating literacy, intellectualism, and moral standards.

But while *Calvin and Hobbes* echoes Postman's rebuke of television, it notably resists Postman's tendency to construct the child as a passive, defenseless victim of mass media, narratives of violence, and consumer culture. The strip does concede that late capitalism has resulted in the unfortunate "adultification" of children (Watterson clearly resented trends of commercialization, especially as they played out in the newspaper industry. In a 1989 speech, he accused publishers and syndicates of "cheapening" the comics with their single-minded focus on "profit, profit, profit").[10] Yet *Calvin and Hobbes* also performs what Calvin may call a transmogrification, as it takes the disquieting image of the precocious child and turns it into a delightful character. While Postman warns that the adultification of childhood is a portent of society's decline, Watterson offers that children's precocity can be reframed, can be reconsidered as amusing, admirable, and even adorable. Certainly, Calvin may be too distracted by consumer culture that he neglects his childish "duties" such as completing homework. In one episode, he sits in front of the television and explains to his mother that Hobbes is helping him with his assignment: "After I'm done watching TV, he'll tell me what the book was about, I'll tell him what the TV shows were about!"[11] But it is precisely his ingenious-yet-illogical excuses that enables Calvin to remain in the realm of "comfortably cute" childhood.

The strip also implies that Calvin's consumption habits enable his creativity. While television may feed his violent fantasies, it also allows him to access and create elaborate fantasy spaces. As he constructs dream worlds, Calvin appropriates the tropes of soap operas, prehistoric and futuristic fantasies, film noir, nature documentaries, and war stories. While Calvin's daydreams are tinged with lust for mayhem, they also express another desire: to escape from and combat the monotony, scrutiny, and restrictions that characterized late twentieth-century childhood in the United States. These fantasy worlds enable Calvin to retreat and detach from the surveillance and regulation that he faced at home and in school. Moreover, because Calvin's fantasies take place within the bounds of a humorous medium, his reveries of rampage are defanged, rendered harmless. *Calvin and Hobbes* assures readers that Calvin's childish fantasies are expressions of playfulness and creativity, pushbacks against boredom and regimentation. The paradox then is that Calvin's uninnocent dreams confirm his "natural" innocence.

For readers apprehensive about childhood precocity, the image of Calvin finding solace in the natural world perhaps provides further assurance. The boy whose life is defined by consumer culture, it turns out, is far from a couch potato. He happily engages in outdoor games, playing in yards and woods that are, notably, unsullied by commercialism. These outdoor spaces are Calvin's sanctuaries, sites in which he maintains boyish vigor, engages in imaginative play, and performs childhood innocence. The strip undoubtedly indulges in nostalgia for the "good ol' days" when children enjoyed carefree play and were not yet mesmerized by television. As such, *Calvin and Hobbes* recycles a theme that was explored frequently in previous strips: Calvin follows in the footsteps of Buster Brown, who escapes the stresses of city life by vacationing in his uncle's farm; Wee Willie Winkie, who wanders independently around open fields; and Charlie Brown and his gang, who offset their television viewing by playing in the seemingly boundless outdoor spaces of the suburb. As Lois R. Kuznets notes, in *Calvin and Hobbes*, the image of a six-year-old hellion is counterbalanced by pictures of family life, school, and suburban spaces that "hark back to the world of the 1940s and 1950s."[12] These visual images point to Watterson's embrace of the romantic notion of childhood.

Yet the cartoonist also shows that Calvin is often impervious to (adult) efforts that try to return him to Edenic childhood. While on a camping trip with his overenthusiastic father, Calvin sits on a rock with Hobbes, watching the sunset (fig. 49).[13] The episode is framed as a single panel, recalling a panoramic photograph. As the sun sets, the still waters of the lake, the trees, and the rocks become part of a play of light and shadow. Calvin then disrupts the scene with a bitter remark: "I'll bet I'm missing some great TV shows." His comment signifies how consumer culture has irretrievably "spoiled" the child. However, this episode is also part of a multiepisode sequence in which Watterson repeatedly pokes fun at adult nostalgia for a world free of modern, technological conveniences. Calvin's father preaches that camping is good for body and soul, echoing early twentieth-century proponents of outdoor sports and the scouting movement. When Calvin complains about the "nuclear mosquitoes" in their camping site, their ensuing exchange reveals the short-sightedness of both father and son:

Figure 49. Single-panel comics by Bill Watterson. "Calvin and Hobbes." Copyright 1992. Distributed by Universal Press Syndicate.

FATHER: Bug bites build character.
CALVIN: Yeah, and last year you said diarrhea builds character.
FATHER: So think what a fine young man you're growing up to be.
CALVIN: . . . If all this character doesn't kill me first.
FATHER: That reminds me, open the duffel bag and get out the Spam.[14]

While the episode encourages readers to laugh at Calvin's stubborn rejection of a "natural" childhood, it also mocks his father for his misguided sentimentalization of the purported wonders of "communing with nature." The father's last line exposes his paradoxical relationship with modern conveniences. Here, he implies that innovations like canned meat—in particular, a brand whose name is sometimes jokingly referred to as an acronym for "Scientifically Processed Animal Meat"—are harmful to one's health. Yet he obviously remains dependent on such innovations. In another episode in this camping sequence, Calvin's father tries to take photographs of his wife and son, hoping to create mementos to "remember our trip by."[15] But his wife and son not only refuse to be photographed but also forcefully oppose his effort to romanticize the trip. "Ack! Don't take a picture of me! I haven't washed my hair in three days and I'm covered with bug bites!" yells his wife. Calvin cries out, "I don't want to remember this trip! I've been trying to forget it ever since we got here! When are we leaving this dump?" As he walks away, Calvin's father remarks, "The next time I see one of those smarmy Kodak commercials I'm going to put an ax through the TV." His comment reveals that he himself cannot escape the narratives peddled by television. Through television commercials, he crafts an idealized view of a family vacation; on this actual trip, he comes to terms with the incompatibility between his desires and that of his family, between an idealized image and the real stresses of family life.

Such humor of incongruity is recurrently deployed in *Calvin and Hobbes*. In fact, the strip repeats many of the jokes expressed in Progressive Era newspaper comics. *Calvin and Hobbes* pokes fun at the disparities between children's elaborate fantasies and the monotony of their everyday lives; between adults' priorities and children's desires; between the ideal of innocent, natural childhood and the realities of modern/postmodern childhood. And while the strip uses humor to record and assuage (adult) readers' concerns about increasingly monitored, regulated, and commodified childhoods, it also appears to assure readers that the child of the late twentieth century not only had the skill, stamina, and sensibility to survive and thrive in the new millennium but also was quite capable of experiencing a "natural" childhood. Although Calvin is remarkably precocious and observant, he still is largely innocent of "adult" concerns such as sex, economics, and politics; he maintains a link with nature while also displaying an openness to modern technology; his repertoire of play includes outdoor games, indoor play, and fantasy world-building. Of course, that Calvin is a white male child living in the suburbs suggests that newspaper comics in the late twentieth century may have still been preoccupied with representing and exploring a *particular* kind of childhood. Several decades after *Buster Brown*, *Calvin and Hobbes* continued the tradition of celebrating the mischief-making, exuberant, and independent white, middle-class boy.

In 1996, a year after Watterson retired *Calvin and Hobbes*—and a century after the Yellow Kid turned his gaze toward the reader—Aaron McGruder's *The Boondocks* made its debut appearance on the music website Hitlist.com. The strip quickly developed a strong following and was picked up by Universal Press Syndicate in 1999. The strip soon appeared in daily newspapers all over the United States. McGruder's strip is, in many ways, an homage to *Calvin and Hobbes*. In his introduction to *A Right to Be Hostile: The Boondocks Treasury*, McGruder acknowledges he modeled his strip after the work of his "heroes": Watterson, Berke Breathed, and Garry Trudeau.[16] In the same vein as *Calvin and Hobbes*, *The Boondocks* cultivated humor through the figure of the precocious child. Like Calvin, ten-year-old Huey Freeman and his eight-year-old brother Riley are sharp-witted boys who talk back to adults and "make trouble" at home, in school, and in their neighborhood. In a nod to Calvin's inconsistent attitude toward consumer culture, Huey frequently rails against television programming even as he continues to consume it. For his part, Riley engages in role play; his adoption of the alias Riley Escobar may remind readers of Calvin's construction of alter egos such as Spaceman Spiff. There is, however, a stark difference between *Calvin and Hobbes* and *The Boondocks*: the protagonists of the latter strip are young African American boys.

In recasting the "delightfully bad boy" of *Calvin and Hobbes* as black children, McGruder disrupts the overwhelming whiteness of American comic strips. In doing so, he exposes and questions the ease by which narratives of white, middle-class (and suburban) childhoods such as Calvin's are naturalized and universalized. In *The Boondocks*, the residents of the mostly white suburb of Woodcrest are unsettled by Huey and Riley's presence. The appearance of a strip headlined by black characters in the mostly white neighborhood of the newspaper funny pages may have had a similarly disquieting effect. By placing issues of race front and center, *The Boondocks* dismantles the generally accepted notion that the daily newspaper strip must be innocuous and deracialized (read: whitened) to remain "universally" palatable.

McGruder punctures the myth of the apolitical comic strip by performing political resistance. He uses *The Boondocks* as a platform for attacking systemic racism and the complicity of both white and black Americans in maintaining racial injustice. More specifically, McGruder shows how American childhood, just like the comic strip, is not politics-free, but rather has been historically defined by white hegemony. He exposes how the appalling disparities between black and white childhoods that were established or shored up in the Progressive Era—and were expressed in the period's comic supplements—remain unresolved in the new millennium. Headlined by two agentic, distinct African American boys, *The Boondocks* contests the often-undisputed trends that tend to silence and interrupt young black voices. The Freeman boys misbehave, like Calvin. But often they are breaking the rules of racist structures that essentialize and vilify them, that write them out of cultural narratives.

As such, *The Boondocks* was a response to a century-old comics problem. For much of the twentieth century, nonwhite characters were largely excised from the newspaper comics pages. When they did appear, they often fulfilled the role of buffoon or villain. There were some efforts at inclusivity: In 1965, the African American cartoonist Morrie Turner launched *Wee Pals*, a comic strip series about a group of friends of different ethnic backgrounds. In the wake of Martin Luther King Jr.'s assassination, schoolteacher Harriet Glickman wrote to Charles Schulz, suggesting he diversify the European American cast of *Peanuts* and use his strip to promote tolerance and racial integration. In response, Schulz introduced Franklin in July 1968. As Christopher P. Lehman notes, Franklin was mostly a "reactive figure," lacking the nuance that Schulz bestowed on his other characters, both human and nonhuman.[17] Fifteen years after Franklin's debut in *Peanuts*, the child prodigy Oliver Wendell Jones appeared in Berke Breathed's *Bloom County*. While Franklin was a perpetual secondary character in Schulz's strip, Oliver—and his family—were often given distinct storylines. In Oliver, Breathed arguably expressed what was, at that point, the most pronounced repudiation of E. W. Kemble's vacuous, depraved pickaninnies. The very existence of Oliver—a young black scientific genius and inventor who develops a rivalry with physicist and cosmologist Stephen Hawking—would have likely bewildered his namesake, Justice Oliver Wendell Holmes Jr., a former abolitionist who later embraced social Darwinism and eugenics.[18]

Like Oliver, McGruder's Huey Freeman is also prodigious. Huey's expertise, however, lies largely in the fields of African American history, socialism, and racial politics. Huey is committed to living up to his name: he dedicates himself to identifying and undermining modern forms of slavery and segregation as a way of following in the footsteps of Black Panther Party founder Huey P. Newton and of insisting on his status as a "free man." In some ways, Huey disassociates himself from Schulz's Franklin and Breathed's Oliver. As Lehman points out, Franklin was a "good" black boy, whose conformity evinces "successful" racial assimilation.[19] Clean-cut Oliver often wore a white, button-down shirt and a tie, sartorial choices that announce his intelligence and maturity but also establish him as nonthreatening. Huey, on the other hand, uses fashion and appearance to broadcast militancy and champion organized political agitation. He wears an Afro and sometimes dons the dark turtleneck shirts that became associated with the Black Panthers.

Yet Huey may have approved of Oliver. Breathed's black boy genius establishes himself as an enemy of the state, as he sometimes uses his scientific prowess to fight establishment forces: he hacks into the IRS and NASA; he alters the headlines of the *New York Times* in an attempt to undermine Ronald Reagan; he invents, among other things, the "Electro-Photo-Pigment-izer," a machine that could darken skin complexion, as part of his plan to abolish apartheid in South Africa. While Oliver's hacking and inventions often result in unintentional comic consequences, he embodies a refusal to "behave."

Clearly, Huey is a resistor too. Describing the character as a "militant, brainy black boy," Howard Rambsy II locates Huey in the tradition of "intellectually adept young black boys who confront authority figures" and appear in Richard Wright's *Black Boy* and Paul Beatty's *The White Boy Shuffle*.[20] Huey may, at first glance, appear to be a reproduction of the troubling stereotype of the aggressive black boy. But through the figure of Huey, *The Boondocks* strives for dislocation, forcing readers to recognize that the universally embraced construction of innocent childhood is historically shaped by white ideology. In acting hostile rather than obedient, Huey signals his refusal to enter the white realm of childhood innocence. He is not making a plaintive plea to be considered "pure" and playful. On his first day at school, he confronts his teacher, Mr. Petto, with a denunciation of the school system: "Public educational facilities such as this are the cornerstone of the institutionalized racism that continues to oppress black people. Not only will I refuse to succumb to your brainwashing—I will dedicate myself to the eventual elimination of this abomination to the high pursuit of learning."[21] Some may point out that Calvin also expresses antischool sentiments. But the plotlines that show Calvin defying Miss Wormwood and Principal Spittle assume that readers share a collective memory of the tedious, restrictive rituals of school life. Huey's schoolroom resistance, on the other hand, reminds us that black students, subject to enduring racist and segregationist practices in education, may remember school in ways that diverge from so-called universal memories.

The juxtaposition of *Calvin and Hobbes* and *The Boondocks* also reveals the racialization of boys' fantasy-making. *Calvin and Hobbes* presents dreams of destruction as part and parcel of being an "everyboy." Although Calvin's lust for weapons is a commentary on the increasing commodification of—and consequent desensitization toward—violence, his desire for bombs, grenades, and guns is also a comic, hyperbolic expression of "natural" boyhood, a confirmation that "boys will be boys." *The Boondocks*, on the other hand, reminds us that young African American males, burdened by the dominant white belief that they are destined to be "thugs" and "superpredators," do not possess Calvin's privilege to fantasize about violence. When Huey does covet weapons, he does so out of the desire to defend his black body and identity from white supremacist forces that threaten to unmake him. He draws up a wish list similar to Calvin's alphabetized list of weapons, but he explains to his grandfather that the flamethrowers, artillery, armor, and other items on the list are meant not for boyish games, but for arming himself and his family against a possible Klan attack.[22]

Huey's younger brother Riley, for his part, appears eager to fulfill the stereotype of "thug." He plays "gangsta," speaking in "ghetto slang" and cursing in class. In adopting the alias Riley Escobar, he projects an image of himself as a future criminal mastermind. It is interesting that when Riley crowns himself "chief Mafioso thug kingpin," he does so while standing on an isolated hilltop (fig. 50).[23] Like Feininger's Wee Willie Winkie and Watterson's Calvin, McGruder's child turns to the adult-free environment of the outdoors to exercise, and perhaps exorcise, his (violent) fantasies of domination. The episode plays with perceptions that black boys like Riley are perpetually trapped in narratives of "ghetto life" and contaminate spaces that are peaceful and bucolic. Riley's seeming vicious persona, however, is not evidence of his natural aggression; rather, he imagines himself as a crime lord in a vigorous, urgent effort to preserve himself in a society that repeatedly diminishes and demolishes black boys like him. When he vandalizes Woodcrest's street signs (turning his street Timid Deer Lane to Notorious B.I.G. Ave., for example), he explains why he had to take such action: "Any street that I live on has to say 'thug,' and it has to say 'real,' and it has to say 'dangerous.' And it has to say, 'You don't want no parts of nothin' here,' and it has to say, 'Ain't nothin' sweet over here.'"[24] Riley is typically understood as the ignorant, materialistic foil to Huey. But like his older brother, he understands aggression as preemptive, as

Figure 50. Comic Strip by Aaron McGruder. "The Boondocks." Copyright 2003.

necessary to self-preservation. In a way, Riley is much like Calvin: both boys use their imaginations to resist regimentation and the pressures placed on American boys. Yet the chasm between their childhoods is wide. While Calvin typically envisions himself as a hero of a science fiction narrative or comic book, Riley pretends to be a suspect on the run in the show *Cops*. The figure of Riley reminds us that black boys' lives are shaped by particularly damaging narratives.

With its "ghetto" and "gangsta" references, *The Boondocks* proved to be as divisive as it was popular. The strip was no stranger to controversy. A few weeks after the Twin Towers fell, McGruder began using his strip to criticize the Bush administration's "war on terrorism" and promotion of American exceptionalism. He was promptly condemned as unpatriotic by some readers. Other readers repeatedly took issue with *The Boondocks*' representation—and mockery—of African American personalities and black life and culture. As Nancy C. Cornwell and Mark P. Orbe document, some African American readers accused McGruder of committing "black-on-black crime."[25] In their view, his strip replicated negative African American stereotypes. Criticism of *The Boondocks* echoes the denouncements of newspaper comics during the Progressive Era. However, while early twentieth-century critics censured newspaper comics for purportedly poisoning (white) children and befouling Anglo-Saxon culture, *The Boondocks*'s detractors worried that young readers, black and white, would learn to accept, perpetuate, and inhabit, rather than contest, racist stereotypes.

But while *The Boondocks* trades in types, it also actively resists reducing African American identity to one "correct" image. The strip, with its wide array of characters, insists on the nuances and multiplicities of black identities and felt experiences.[26] Moreover, *The Boondocks* shows how black boys can have different responses to a world that constantly polices and maligns their identities, choices, and bodies. Like many other strips about children, *The Boondocks* used the humor of incongruity, finding fun in the gap between ideal childhoods and the real experiences of children. But McGruder's strip is also built on what Terrence T. Tucker calls "comic rage," which synthesizes the funny and the militant.[27] *The Boondocks* invites bitter, angry laughter as it laments and excoriates the discrepancies between black and white childhoods. *The Boondocks* reveals the paradox that shapes the lives of minority children, especially black boys. They are, on the one hand, often rendered invisible, excised from stories about "universal" childhoods. On the other hand, they are persistently surveilled and scrutinized, as they are imagined to be threats to social order. McGruder, through his two child characters, suggests that marginalized children take pains to revise the narratives that erase and distort, to take control of the fictions that keep pushing them to the periphery.

The Boondocks ended its run in 2006, although an animated sitcom version, which debuted in 2005, ran until 2014. McGruder's strip was not present to comment on the election of Barack Obama; the fatal shootings of Trayvon Martin and

Tamir Rice; the astonishing rise of—and ensuing backlash against—the Black Lives Matter movement; and the presidency of Donald Trump, who had vilified the Central Park Five, had fanned the flames of anti-Obama birtherism, and lambasted Colin Kaepernick for taking the knee. In his speeches, Trump repeatedly echoes the barbaric rhetoric employed by many Progressive Era Americans on issues of race, class, immigration, and women's rights. The frightening doctrine and dangerous policies of the Trump administration, ironically, have provided cartoonists a seemingly inexhaustible comedic goldmine. In trying to find the funny in Trump's America, comics creators have refashioned the image of the naughty boy, disassociating this figure from notions of potential and progress. In magazine covers, political cartoons, and web comics, the nation's forty-fifth president is frequently depicted as a petulant child-king, a tantrum-throwing toddler, a spoiled schoolboy, and a hopelessly incorrigible child.

ACKNOWLEDGMENTS

This book is about newspaper comics, also commonly known as the funnies. Ironically, writing this book often felt like a humorless enterprise. I am grateful for the mentors, colleagues, friends, and family members who remained by my side—and often made me laugh—whenever things took an unfunny turn.

I want to thank Lynne Vallone for patiently wading through my murky first drafts. I aspire to become as imaginative, disciplined, and assiduous a scholar as her. Robert Emmons, Nancy Rosoff, and Tanya Sheehan also challenged me, very early on, to raise the stakes of my project. Their guidance and astute feedback gave this book much-needed depth and breadth.

It was a gift to be a part of the vibrant childhood studies community at Rutgers University–Camden. Lynne Vallone, Daniel Cook, and other faculty members gave me the tools I needed to lay the foundation of this book. At Rutgers, I constantly strived to find meaning and pleasure in research and writing, and whenever such meaning and pleasure seemed elusive, Deb Valentine and Nyeema Watson encouraged me to persevere. I am also grateful to Matt Prickett, Neeta Goel, Dianne Fabii, Diane Marano, Marla Wander, and many other peers at Rutgers for the stimulating conversations and uplifting friendships.

The College of Staten Island–The City University of New York has become my intellectual home; I am thankful to be part of an institution that is invested in my professional and moral growth. My colleagues in the English Department, especially Alyson Bardsley, Ashley Dawson, Maria Bellamy, Matt Brim, Christopher Miller, Steve Monte, Lee Papa, Katie Goodland, and Maryann Feola gave me generous advice on research, teaching, and writing. Our motivated, creative, and hardworking students give me a sense of purpose, and I feel honored to be a part of their lives. Special thanks to Jamie Sterner, my stellar undergraduate research assistant.

Many institutions and organizations provided me the time and resources to develop and complete this book. A presidential fellowship and a dissertation writing fellowship from Rutgers University enabled me to conceptualize this book and complete an early draft. A Library of Congress Swann Foundation Fellowship, a Popular Culture Association / American Culture Association Marshall Fishwick Travel Grant, a Hannah Beiter Grant, and a Faculty Research Grant, the last two of which were both administered by the Children's Literature Association, funded my archival research. Various units and offices of the City University of New York supported the completion of this book. I am indebted to the PSC-CUNY Research Foundation, the Office of the University Vice Provost for Research, and CSI's Office of the Provost and Office of the Dean of Humanities and Social Sciences for their generous funding. Special thanks to Lee Papa, Nan Sussman, Gerry Milligan, and Mel Pipe for endorsing my work.

CUNY's Faculty Fellowship Publication Program was instrumental to shaping this book. My workshop group was led by Shelly Eversley, who gave us candid advice and thorough evaluations and was unwavering in her advocacy of junior faculty advancement. My coparticipants—June Kim, Melissa Coss-Aquino, Bill Orchard, Inmaculada Lara Bonilla, and Mary Phillips—were careful, perceptive readers who gave me valuable feedback. I am especially grateful to Mary Phillips, who has become a trustworthy friend and writing partner.

My book rests on the important, exhaustive work of historians and archivists who build and maintain comics archives. My thanks to Martha Kennedy and her colleagues at the Prints and Photographs Division of the Library of Congress, Susan Liberator and Marilynn Scott of the magnificent Billy Ireland Cartoon Library and Museum at the Ohio State University, the digital archive of Barnacle Press, and Allan Holtz of the Stripper's Guide blog.

I challenged myself to craft a nuanced, expansive book on childhood and Progressive Era newspaper comics, prompted by feedback and advice from colleagues from the Children's Literature Association, the Popular Culture Association/American Culture Association's Comics and Comic Art Area, the American Studies Association, and the Comics Studies Society. I single out Charles Hatfield and Philip Nel for being steady supporters and attentive evaluators of my work in its various stages. I also want to thank Lisa Banning of Rutgers University Press for believing in my work. The flaws and gaps that remain are due to my own oversight.

Finally, I want to thank the people dearest to me. The Lachicas of Virginia, the Quintanses on the East Coast, and the Kerns on the West Coast offered me literal and figurative shelter whenever I felt dislocated living in my adopted country. My father, brothers, sisters, and my smart, buoyant nieces and nephews live on the other side of the world, but I have the good fortune of basking in their radiant love every minute of every day. And much love and thanks to Kolson, who kept me steady as I wrote and revised my manuscript.

A shorter version of chapter 3 was previously published in *Children's Literature Association Quarterly* 40, no. 2 (2015). An early version of chapter 4 appeared in the *International Journal of Comic Art* 15, no. 1 (2013). I briefly discuss the lineage of the naughty boy in the comics in my chapter in *Imagining Sameness and Difference in Children's Literature* (2017), edited by Emer O'Sullivan and Andrea Immel. This book expands on that discussion.

NOTES

INTRODUCTION — DRAWING THE LINES

1. In this book, I categorize single-panel cartoons that appeared in newspaper supplements as "comics." Although many practitioners and scholars insist that comics necessarily consist of a series of images/panels, I side with Robert C. Harvey's argument that single-panel cartoons are also comics. These cartoons not only juxtaposed visual and verbal elements but were also often "broken down" into several ongoing actions that readers were meant to put together in some sequence through what Scott McCloud calls "closure." For definitions of comics and for more on breakdown and closure, see Scott McCloud, *Understanding Comics: The Invisible Art* (New York: HarperCollins, 1993); Robert C. Harvey, "Comedy at the Juncture of Word and Image: The Emergence of the Modern Magazine Gag Cartoon Reveals the Vital Blend," in *The Language of Comics: Word and Image*, eds. Robin Varnum and Christina T. Gibbons (Jackson: University Press of Mississippi, 2001), 75–96; and Charles Hatfield, *Alternative Comics: An Emerging Literature* (Jackson: University Press of Mississippi, 2005), 32–67.

2. R. F. Outcault, "Golf—The Great Society Sport as Played in Hogan's Alley," *Hogan's Alley, New York World* Comic Supplement, January 5, 1896, San Francisco Academy of Comic Art Collection, the Ohio State University Billy Ireland Cartoon Library and Museum (hereafter cited as SFA Collection, Ireland Cartoon Library), accessed February 6, 2017, https://cartoons.osu.edu/digital_albums/yellowkid.

3. Thierry Smolderen, *The Origins of Comics: From William Hogarth to Winsor McCay*, trans. Bart Beaty and Nick Nguyen (Jackson: University Press of Mississippi, 2014), 5.

4. Colton Waugh, *The Comics* (1947; repr., Jackson: University Press of Mississippi, 1991), 2. Waugh's *The Comics* has a curious place in the historiography of comics. It is significant because it is the first sustained study of the development of newspaper comic strips but it is also full of inaccuracies and unfounded speculations that other comics scholars sometimes perpetuate. Later historians have worked to check and correct Waugh's claims.

5. Jens Balzer, "'Hully Gee, I'm a Heiroglyphe'—Mobilizing the Gaze and the Invention of the Comics in New York City, 1895," in *Comics and the City: Urban Space in Print, Picture and Sequence*, ed. Jörn Ahrens and Arno Meteling (New York: Continuum International, 2010), 21.

6. Among the most comprehensive studies that consider the Yellow Kid's historical impact are Bill Blackbeard, *R. F. Outcault's The Yellow Kid: A Centennial Celebration of the Kid who Started the Comics* (Northampton: Kitchen Sink Press, 1995), and Mary Wood, *The Yellow*

Kid on the Paper Stage: Acting Out Class Tensions and Racial Divisions in the New Urban Environment, American Studies in the University of Virginia, last modified February 2, 2004, accessed February 7, 2017, http://xroads.virginia.edu/~ma04/wood/ykid/yellowkid2.htm.

7. Although Outcault is commonly considered to be the "inventor" of the American comic strip, some comics historians remind us that his success tends to eclipse the significant contributions of his contemporaries. Frederick Burr Opper (*And Her Name Was Maud!*, *Happy Hooligan*), Rudolph Dirks (*The Katzenjammer Kids*), and James Swinnerton (*The Little Bears*, *Little Jimmy*) were, as Maurice Horn puts it, among the "founding fathers" of the comic strip. Dirks, in particular, popularized the use of sequential panels and recurring characters through his strip, *Katzenjammer Kids*. Maurice Horn, *75 Years of Comics* (Boston: Boston Book and Art, 1971), 8–9; see also Robert C. Harvey, *Children of the Yellow Kid: The Evolution of the American Comic Strip* (Seattle: University of Washington Press, 1999), 85.

8. Ian Gordon, *Kid Comic Strips: A Genre across Four Countries* (New York: Palgrave Macmillan, 2016), 3.

9. Smolderen, *Origins of Comics*, 140–141.

10. Ian Gordon, *Comic Strips and Consumer Culture, 1890–1945* (Washington, D.C.: Smithsonian Institution Press, 1998), 51–58.

11. Although Outcault succeeded in obtaining the copyright to the name "Yellow Kid," he failed to retain rights to the image.

12. Mark D. Winchester, "Hully Gee, It's a War!!! The Yellow Kid and the Coining of 'Yellow Journalism,'" *Inks: Cartoon and Comic Art Studies* 2, no. 3 (1995): 31.

13. W. Joseph Campbell, *Yellow Journalism: Puncturing the Myths, Defining the Legacies* (Westport, Conn.: Praeger, 2001), 31–32.

14. Recent scholarship is beginning to break the silence on childhood's ties to comics. See Gordon's *Kid Comic Strips*; Mark Heimermann and Brittany Tullis, eds., *Picturing Childhood: Youth in Transnational Comics* (Austin: University of Texas Press, 2017); and Michelle Ann Abate and Gwen Athene Tarbox, eds., *Graphic Novels for Children and Young Adults: A Collection of Critical Essays* (Jackson: University Press of Mississippi, 2017). Gordon's *Kid Comic Strips* is of special interest to me, as it focuses exclusively on the genre of "kid strips," or strips headlined by child characters. In this comparative study between comic strips produced in the United States and strips published in Australia, France, and Britain, Gordon focuses on exploring problems of translation and the variations in conceptualizations of humor and race across nations. He also insists that the development of the comic strip must be viewed through an international lens. Overall, Gordon demonstrates that the fixation with childhood was not unique to the American comic strip. Rather, such fascination manifested itself in comics produced in European nations and other Anglophone cultures.

15. See Martha Banta, *Barbaric Intercourse: Caricature and the Culture of Conduct, 1841–1936* (Chicago: University of Chicago Press, 2003); Roger Fischer, *Them Damned Pictures: Explorations in American Political Cartoon Art* (North Haven, Conn.: Archon, 1996); and Henry B. Wonham, *Playing the Races: Ethnic Caricature and American Literary Realism* (Oxford: Oxford University Press, 2004), 3–40.

16. See Steven J. Diner, *A Very Different Age: Americans of the Progressive Era* (New York: Hill and Wang, 1998).

17. See Michael McGerr, *A Fierce Discontent: The Rise and Fall of the Progressive Movement in America, 1870–1920* (New York: Free Press, 2003).

18. See Maureen A. Flanagan, *America Reformed: Progressives and Progressivisms, 1890s–1920s* (New York: Oxford University Press, 2007).

19. McGerr, *A Fierce Discontent*, xv.

20. Flanagan, *America Reformed*, 10.

21. See Thomas C. Leonard, *Illiberal Reformers: Race, Eugenics, and American Economics in the Progressive Era* (Princeton: Princeton University Press, 2016), 129–185.

22. McGerr, *A Fierce Discontent*, 183.

23. McGerr, 79.

24. Paula S. Fass, "Foreword," in *Children and Youth during the Gilded Age and Progressive Era, ed.* James Marten (New York: New York University Press, 2014), vii.

25. Viviana A. Zelizer, *Pricing the Priceless Child: The Changing Social Value of Children* (Princeton: Princeton University Press, 1985), 3.

26. Steven Mintz, *Huck's Raft: A History of American Childhood* (Cambridge, Mass.: Belknap Press of Harvard University Press, 2004), 189.

27. For more on the anxieties surrounding raising white, middle-class boys and girls, see Mintz, *Huck's Raft*, 192–196. Scholars writing in the twentieth and twenty-first centuries have offered important rereadings of "classic" girls' books such as *Rebecca of Sunnybrook Farm* and *Anne of Green Gables.* Complicating the argument that these books "domesticate" girls, this body of scholarship highlights how these texts celebrate girls' creativity, individuality, and independence in the face of tremendous social restraints. See Shirley Foster and Judy Simons, *What Katy Read: Feminist Re-readings of "Classic" Stories for Girls* (London: Palgrave Macmillan, 1995); Holly Blackford, ed., *100 Years of Anne with an "e": The Centennial Study of* Anne of Green Gables (Calgary, Canada: University of Calgary Press, 2009); and Joe Sutliff Sanders, *Disciplining Girls: Understanding the Origins of the Classic Orphan Girl Story* (Baltimore: Johns Hopkins University Press, 2011).

28. Clif Stratton, *Education for Empire: American Schools, Race, and the Paths of Good Citizenship* (Berkeley: University of California Press, 2016), 2–3.

29. See Robin Bernstein, *Racial Innocence: Performing American Childhood from Slavery to Civil Rights* (New York: New York University Press, 2011).

30. In her examination of the play movement in Philadelphia, Deborah S. Valentine discusses reformers' inconsistent and later abandoned efforts to address the needs of African American children. See Deborah S. Valentine, "Playing Progressively? Race, Reform, and Playful Pedagogies in the Origins of Philadelphia's Starr Garden Recreation Park, 1857–1904," in *Children and Youth during the Gilded Age and Progressive Era,* ed. James Marten (New York: New York University Press, 2014), 19–41.

31. Lillian D. Wald, *The House on Henry Street* (1915; repr., New York: Dover, 1971), 67.

32. Wald, 67–68.

33. See Melissa Klapper, *Small Strangers: The Experiences of Immigrant Children in America, 1880–1925* (Chicago: Ivan R. Dee, 2007). Histories of immigrant childhoods typically suggest that parents and children often found themselves at odds in the New World. The younger generation purportedly forsook their parents' (and the Old World's) values, instead embracing the "American" values of freedom and autonomy—alongside consumer goods and entertainments. Klapper complicates this narrative, showing how both parents and children were ambivalent about acculturation. Often, parents believed the United States offered unprecedented opportunities for their children, even as they struggled to comprehend the New World's attitudes toward childhood. Children were themselves wary about some American practices; even as they adopted some "Americanisms," they rejected others. As Klapper puts it, immigrant children "struck a balance between Old World and New World values" (182).

34. See Mintz, *Huck's Raft*, 133–153; Klapper, *Small Strangers.*

35. See Hatfield, *Alternative Comics*, 36–67.

36. Hatfield, 36.

37. Kerry Soper, "From Swarthy Ape to Sympathetic Everyman and Subversive Trickster: The Development of Irish Caricature in American Comic Strips between 1890 and 1920," *Journal of American Studies* 39, no. 2 (2005): 270.

38. For extensive studies of caricatures that appeared in late nineteenth-century magazines, see Banta, *Barbaric Intercourse*; Fischer, *Them Damned Pictures*, 69–120; and Wonham, *Playing the Races*, 3–40.

39. Wonham, 22.

40. Banta, *Barbaric Intercourse*, 17.
41. McCloud, *Understanding Comics*, 37.
42. McCloud, 36.
43. Jared Gardner, "Same Difference: Graphic Alterity in the Work of Gene Luen Yang, Adrian Tomine, and Derek Kirk Kim," in *Multicultural Comics: From Zap to Blue Beetle*, ed. Frederick Luis Aldama (Austin: University of Texas Press, 2010), 135.
44. Gardner, 136.
45. Gardner, 136–138. See also McCloud's discussion of closure in *Understanding Comics*, 63.
46. Gardner, "Same Difference," 138.
47. Jared Gardner, *Projections: Comics and the History of Twenty-First-Century Storytelling* (Redwood: Stanford University Press, 2012), 12–14; Soper, "From Swarthy Ape."
48. Soper, 263.
49. Gardner, *Projections*, 13. Here, Gardner builds on Gordon's observation of how comic strip characters in the Progressive Era became endowed with "personality"; the emergence of comic strip personalities resulted from and secured the commercial success of comic strips. See Gordon, *Comic Strips and Consumer Culture*.
50. Soper, "From Swarthy Ape," 263.
51. Homi Bhabha, *The Location of Culture* (London: Routledge, 2004), 96.
52. Gardner, *Projections*, 14.
53. Here, I build on Anna Mae Duane's proposal that in early America, conceptualizations of race and childhood were often intertwined. But these conceptualizations were not static; rather, they ended up defining and redefining one other. See Anna Mae Duane, *Suffering Childhood in Early America: Violence, Race, and the Making of the Child Victim* (Athens: University of Georgia Press, 2011).
54. For a discussion of the history of conceptualizations of humor, see Gregg Camfield, *Necessary Madness: The Humor of Domesticity in Nineteenth-Century American Literature* (New York: Oxford University Press, 1997), and Daniel Wickberg, *The Senses of Humor: Self and Laughter in Modern America* (Ithaca, N.Y.: Cornell University Press, 1998).
55. Camfield, *Necessary Madness*, viii–ix.
56. Wickberg, *Senses of Humor*, 64–66.
57. Wickberg, 98–107.
58. Gordon, *Comic Strips and Consumer Culture*, 55, 62.
59. Lisa Yaszek, "'Them Damn Pictures': Americanization and the Comic Strip in the Progressive Era," *Journal of American Studies* 28, no. 1 (1994): 25.
60. Yaszek, 30–33.
61. For more on how comic strips created a sense of community among readers, see Gordon, *Comic Strips and Consumer Culture*, and Gardner, *Projections*, 12–17.
62. Campbell, *Yellow Journalism*, 55–59, 61.
63. Mary Wood, "Class Warfare on the Urban Stage: Yellow Kid Readership," in *The Yellow Kid on the Paper Stage: Acting Out Class Tensions and Racial Divisions in the New Urban Environment*, American Studies in the University of Virginia, last modified February 2, 2004, accessed February 13, 2017, http://xroads.virginia.edu/~ma04/wood/ykid/readership.htm.
64. Soper, "From Swarthy Ape," 270.
65. Yaszek, "'Them Damn Pictures,'" 29.
66. Soper, "From Swarthy Ape," 273, 274.
67. Charles Hatfield, "Comic Art, Children's Literature, and the New Comic Studies," *The Lion and the Unicorn* 30, no. 3 (2006): 360–382.
68. Gary Gerstle, *American Crucible: Race and Nation in the Twentieth Century* (Princeton: Princeton University Press, 2001), 3–5.
69. R. F. Outcault, "At the Circus in Hogan's Alley," *Hogan's Alley, New York World* Comic Supplement, May 5, 1895, SFA Collection, Ireland Cartoon Library, accessed February 6, 2017, https://cartoons.osu.edu/digital_albums/yellowkid.

70. Here, I draw on Mikhail Bakhtin's discussion of the carnival and carnivalesque. See Mikhail Bakhtin, *Rabelais and His World*, trans. Hélène Iswolsky (Cambridge: Massachusetts Institute of Technology Press, 1968; repr., Bloomington: Indiana University Press, 1984).

71. Joseph Entin, "'Unhuman Humanity': Bodies of the Urban Poor and the Collapse of Realist Legibility," *Novel: A Forum on Fiction* 34, no. 3 (2001): 319.

72. Maren Stange, *Symbols of Ideal Life: Social Documentary Photography in America, 1890–1950* (Cambridge: Cambridge University Press, 1989), 18.

73. Peter Bacon Hales, *Silver Cities: Photographing American Urbanization, 1839–1939* (Albuquerque: University of New Mexico Press, 2005), 272.

74. Rebecca Zurier, *Picturing the City: Urban Vision and the Ashcan School* (Berkeley: University of California Press, 2006), 183.

75. Zurier, 183.

76. Zurier, 183.

77. R. F. Outcault, "Amateur Circus: The Smallest Show on Earth," *Hogan's Alley*, *New York World* Comic Supplement, April 26, 1896, SFA Collection, Ireland Cartoon Library, accessed February 6, 2017, https://cartoons.osu.edu/digital_albums/yellowkid.

78. As recorded in the Oxford English Dictionary, both meanings of *nipper* were in use by the 1890s.

CHAPTER 1 — FOREIGN YET FAMILIAR

1. In 1849, Samuel George Morton published his findings on the "cranial capacity" of the races. One of his tables ranked "Mongolians" as second in cranial capacity, after Caucasians but ahead of Malays, Americans (North and South American Indians), and Ethiopians. Another table, however, places the "Mongolian Group" near the bottom, ahead only of the "Negro Group." For more on craniometry and a debunking of Morton's methods, see Stephen Jay Gould, *The Mismeasure of Man* (New York: W. W. Norton, 1996).

2. Gould, 144.

3. Approximately 1.5 million immigrant children entered the United States between 1892 and 1910. See Emmy E. Werner, *Passages to America: Oral Histories of Child Immigrants from Ellis Island and Angel Island* (Washington, D.C.: Potomac Books, 2009), 161.

4. In this chapter, I focus on *The Katzenjammer Kids* episodes that Dirks produced as an artist for the Hearst papers between 1897 and 1912. In 1912, Dirks requested a sabbatical from illustrating the strip. Hearst turned down the request, but Dirks went ahead and left for Europe with his wife. Hearst retaliated by handing over *Katzenjammer Kids* to another German American illustrator, Harold H. Knerr, who ended up drawing the strip until 1949. Dirks sued Hearst and eventually, the courts decided that Hearst and his papers could retain the title *Katzenjammer Kids* while Dirks could continue drawing the characters on the condition that he not use the name Katzenjammer. Dirks drew the strip *Hans and Fritz*, later retitled *The Captain and the Kids*, for rival newspapers. Dirks's strip and Knerr's version of *Katzenjammer Kids* were both immensely popular.

5. Melissa R. Klapper, *Small Strangers: The Experiences of Immigrant Children in America, 1880–1925* (Chicago: Ivan R. Dee, 2007).

6. See James Marten, *Childhood and Child Welfare in the Progressive Era: A Brief History with Documents* (Boston: Bedford and St. Martin's, 2005).

7. Charles Loring Brace, *The Dangerous Classes of New York, and Twenty Years' Work among Them* (1872; repr., Washington, D.C.: National Association of Social Workers, 1973), 28.

8. Brace, 28.

9. James Marten, *Childhood and Child Welfare*, 29.

10. Jacob Riis, "How the Other Half Lives: Studies among the Tenements of New York," in *How the Other Half Lives*, ed. Hasia R. Diner (1890; New York: W. W. Norton, 2010), 105.

11. Jane Addams, *The Spirit of Youth and the City Streets* (1909; repr., Urbana: University of Illinois Press, 1972), 16.

12. Steven Mintz, *Huck's Raft: A History of American Childhood* (Cambridge, Mass.: Belknap Press of Harvard University Press, 2004), 184.

13. See John Higham, *Strangers in the Land: Patterns of American Nativism, 1860–1925* (New Brunswick, N.J.: Rutgers University Press, 1994), 131–157.

14. Higham, 151.

15. John Lowe, "Theories of Ethnic Humor: How to Enter, Laughing," *American Quarterly* 38, no. 3 (1986): 439.

16. Roger A. Fischer, *Them Damned Pictures: Explorations in American Political Cartoon Art* (North Haven, Conn.: Archon, 1996), 70.

17. Fischer, 70.

18. Martha Banta, *Barbaric Intercourse: Caricature and the Culture of Conduct, 1841–1936* (Chicago: University of Chicago Press, 2003), 4.

19. Shirley J. Yee, *An Immigrant Neighborhood: Interethnic and Interracial Encounters in New York Before 1930* (Philadelphia: Temple University Press, 2012), 5–6.

20. The term "dago" is an ethnic slur for a person of Italian, and sometimes Spanish and Portuguese, descent.

21. Banta, *Barbaric Intercourse*, 4. Banta defines caricature as "a representation of type that stands alone," while the cartoon is the medium in which such representations are "grouped with like figures arranged in intercourse with one another" (4).

22. Lois Leveen, "Only When I Laugh: Textual Dynamics of Ethnic Humor," *MELUS* 21, no. 4 (1996): 30.

23. Pamela B. Nelson, "From Subhuman to Superhuman: Ethnic Characters in Comics," in *Ethnic Images in the Comics*, ed. Charles Hardy and Gail F. Stern (Philadelphia: Balch Institute for Ethnic Studies, 1986), 12.

24. Joseph Boskin and Joseph Dorinson, "Ethnic Humor: Subversion and Survival," *American Quarterly* 37, no. 1 (1985): 81.

25. John Appel, "Abie the Agent, Gimpl the Matchmaker, Berl Schliemazel, et al.," in *Ethnic Images in the Comics*, ed. Charles Hardy and Gail F. Stern (Philadelphia: Balch Institute for Ethnic Studies, 1986), 18.

26. Quoted in Appel, 17.

27. Appel, 15.

28. Appel, 17.

29. Fischer, *Them Damned Pictures*, 74.

30. Fischer, 74.

31. Fischer, 74, 75.

32. Kerry Soper, "From Swarthy Ape to Sympathetic Everyman and Subversive Trickster: The Development of Irish Caricature in American Comic Strips between 1890 and 1920," *Journal of American Studies* 39, no. 2 (2005): 289.

33. Soper, 289.

34. Soper, 289.

35. Jared Gardner, "Same Difference: Graphic Alterity in the Work of Gene Luen Yang, Adrian Tomine, and Derek Kirk Kim," in *Multicultural Comics: From Zap to Blue Beetle*, ed. Frederick Luis Aldama (Austin: University of Texas Press, 2010), 135–136.

36. In 1907, Nell Brinkley began drawing for Hearst's papers and she quickly became known for her cartoons filled with waifish girls with loose curls, thick eyelashes, and painted lips. The "Brinkley Girl" became an extremely popular figure and turned Brinkley into one of the most famous and successful cartoonists of her time. At first glance, the Brinkley Girl might recall Charles Dana Gibson's "Gibson Girl." But while the Gibson Girl often appeared aristocratic, aloof, and engaged primarily in leisurely activities, the Brinkley Girl was an assertive working-class figure who involved herself in political causes such as the suffrage

movement. For more on the Brinkley Girl, see Trina Robbins, *The Brinkley Girls: The Best of Nell Brinkley's Cartoons from 1913–1940* (Seattle: Fantagraphics, 2009), and Trina Robbins, *Nell Brinkley and the New Woman in the Early 20th Century* (Jefferson, N.C.: McFarland, 2001).

37. Klapper, *Small Strangers*, 16.

38. Sarah E. Chinn, *Inventing Modern Adolescence: The Children of Immigrants in Turn-of-the-Century America* (New Brunswick, N.J.: Rutgers University Press, 2009), 78.

39. Chinn, 78.

40. Fischer, *Them Damned Pictures*, 70.

41. Robert G. Lee, *Orientals: Asian Americans in Popular Culture* (Philadelphia: Temple University Press, 1999), 8–10.

42. Eiichiro Azuma, *Between Two Empires: Race, History, and Transnationalism in Japanese America* (New York: Oxford University Press, 2005), 29–30.

43. Lothrop Stoddard, *The Rising Tide of Color against White World-Supremacy* (New York: Charles Scribner's Sons, 1920), quoted in Lee, *Orientals*, 10.

44. H. Brett Melendy, *The Oriental Americans* (New York: Twayne, 1972).

45. Krystyn R. Moon, *Yellowface: Creating the Chinese in American Popular Music and Performance, 1850s–1920s* (New Brunswick, N.J.: Rutgers University Press, 2004), 8.

46. Sax Rohmer [pseud. Arthur Ward], *The Insidious Dr. Fu Manchu* (New York: McBride, Nast, 1913), 26.

47. Lee, *Orientals*, 117–118.

48. Azuma, *Between Two Empires*, 38–40.

49. For more on the experiences of the Issei in the late nineteenth and early twentieth centuries, see Azuma, *Between Two Empires*, and Yuji Ichioka, *The Issei: The World of the First Generation of Japanese Immigrants, 1885–1924* (New York: Free Press, 1988).

50. John F. Hart, "'It,' the Little Jap, Routs the Enemy with His War Dragon," *Little Jap "It," Chicago Sunday Record-Herald* Comic Supplement, April 24, 1904, SFS 43-8-4, San Francisco Academy of Comic Art Collection, the Ohio State University Billy Ireland Cartoon Library and Museum (hereafter cited as SFA Collection, Ireland Cartoon Library).

51. John F. Hart, "The Russo-Jap War, with 'It' as the Victor," *Little Jap "It," Chicago Sunday Record-Herald* Comic Supplement, April 10, 1904, SFS 43-8-2, SFA Collection, Ireland Cartoon Library.

52. John F. Hart, "'It' Has an Encounter with Foreign Dogs, and Wins," *Little Jap "It," Chicago Sunday Record-Herald* Comic Supplement, April 3, 1904, SFS 43-8-1, SFA Collection, Ireland Cartoon Library.

53. Melendy, *Oriental Americans*.

54. John F. Hart, "A Story of 'Dough' and 'It' in a Rainstorm," *Little Jap "It," Chicago Sunday Record-Herald* Comic Supplement, April 17, 1904, SFS 44-8-3, SFA Collection, Ireland Cartoon Library.

55. Ichioka, *The Issei*, 1–6.

56. The setting for *Little Ah Sid* is vague. The nondescript buildings and the main characters' lack of interaction with characters of other ethnicities create some ambiguity. It is likely that the strip is set in one of the burgeoning Chinatowns on the West Coast or the Northeast. The characters' speech indicates that the strip is set in the United States; the series plays on the contrast between the inarticulate adult and the child who masters the language of his adopted homeland. The absence of characters of other ethnic backgrounds is expressive of Americans' observations that Chinese immigrant communities were insular.

57. At least two versions of this song were published in sheet music form in 1883, and the songs had similar lyrics. See Louis Meyer, *The American Butterfly: A Comic Song with a Point* (Philadelphia: F. A. North, 1883), Library of Congress Performing Arts Databases, accessed January 5, 2015, http://lcweb2.loc.gov/diglib/ihas/loc.music.sm1883.25185; J. P. Skelly, *Little Ah Sid: Great Chinese Song and Dance* (New York: Richard A. Saafield, 1883), Library of Congress

Performing Arts Databases, accessed January 5, 2015, http://lcweb2.loc.gov/diglib/ihas/loc.music.sm1883.11489.

58. Meyer, *American Butterfly.*

59. Meyer.

60. Meyer.

61. Meyer.

62. Meyer.

63. Lee, *Orientals*, 85.

64. Meyer, *American Butterfly.*

65. "Little Ah Sid; or The Chinee Boy and the Japanese Butterfly Bumblebee," *Punch, or the London Charivari* 107, October 20, 1894, Project Gutenberg, accessed January 5, 2015, https://www.gutenberg.org/files/46826/46826-h/46826-h.htm.

66. "Little Ah Sid."

67. "Little Ah Sid."

68. To Westerners, the long fingernails on Chinese males may have appeared comical and/or sinister. In Chinese culture, however, long fingernails signified that one was affluent: they were an indication that one did not perform manual labor.

69. Clarence Rigby, *Little Ah Sid, the Chinese Kid, Courier Journal* Comic Supplement, November 5, 1905, SFS 33-5-1, SFA Collection, Ireland Cartoon Library.

70. Robin Bernstein, *Racial Innocence: Performing American Childhood from Slavery to Civil Rights* (New York: New York University Press, 2011), 20.

71. Iris Chang, *The Chinese in America: A Narrative History* (New York: Penguin, 2003), 176–178.

72. Klapper, *Small Strangers*, 16.

73. Clarence Rigby, *Little Ah Sid, the Chinese Kid, Courier Journal* Comic Supplement, December 10, 1905, SFS 33-6-2, SFA Collection, Ireland Cartoon Library.

74. Rigby.

75. Clarence Rigby, *Little Ah Sid, the Chinese Kid, Courier Journal* Comic Supplement, November 19, 1905, SFS 33-5-3, SFA Collection, Ireland Cartoon Library.

76. Clarence Rigby, *Little Ah Sid, the Chinese Kid, Courier Journal* Comic Supplement, November 12, 1905, SFS 33-5-2, SFA Collection, Ireland Cartoon Library.

77. Rigby.

78. Mintz, *Huck's Raft*, 210.

79. Rigby, *Little Ah Sid*, November 12, 1905.

80. Rigby.

81. Rigby.

82. Clarence Rigby, *Little Ah Sid, the Chinese Kid, Courier Journal* Comic Supplement, January 14, 1906, SFS 33-7-2, SFA Collection, Ireland Cartoon Library.

83. Clarence Rigby, *Little Ah Sid, the Chinese Kid, Courier Journal* Comic Supplement, December 24, 1905, SFS 33-6-4, SFA Collection, Ireland Cartoon Library. The electric thriller was a toy and novelty item produced at the turn of the century and remained popular in the 1920s and 1930s. An advertisement for the Knapp Electric Thriller described the toy as "a shocking machine with a permanent magnet that furnishes its own current. . . . Give the handles to a friend and watch him jump." "Knapp—For Christmas," *Boys' Life*, December 1924, 76.

84. Klapper, *Small Strangers*, 17.

85. Klapper, 17.

86. Maurice Horn, *75 Years of Comics* (Boston: Boston Book and Art, 1971), 8–9.

87. Robert C. Harvey, *Children of the Yellow Kid: The Evolution of the American Comic Strip* (Seattle: University of Washington Press, 1999), 85; Horn, *75 Years*, 9; Ian Gordon, *Comic Strips and Consumer Culture, 1890–1945* (Washington, D.C.: Smithsonian Institution Press, 1998), 34. Gordon notes that *Katzenjammer Kids* was initially a pantomime (or wordless)

strip. Sometimes, narration and dialogue appeared as captions below the panels. Two years after the strip's debut, Dirks began to use word balloons regularly.

88. Bill Blackbeard and Martin Williams, eds., *The Smithsonian Collection of Newspaper Comics* (Washington, D.C.: Smithsonian Institution Press; New York: Abrams, 1977), 19.

89. Gordon, *Comic Strips and Consumer Culture*, 22.

90. Wilhelm Busch, *Max and Moritz: A Juvenile History in Seven Tricks*, trans. C. T. Brooks, ed. H. Arthur Klein (1865; repr., New York: Dover, 1962), 48–49. "Cracknels" here may be referring to hard biscuits, although it can also mean crispy pieces of pork fat. In this "trick," the boys manage to gnaw their way out of the crust into which they are baked. But as the narrator informs us, their next trick is also their last.

91. Rudolph Dirks, "Mrs. Katzenjammer Takes a Week's Vacation, and the Kids Have a Glorious Time," *The Katzenjammer Kids*, *New York Journal*, n.d., SFS 1-1-5, SFA Collection, Ireland Cartoon Library.

92. Dirks.

93. In this sense, Dirks was working in the vein of Heinrich Hoffman's *Struwwelpeter*. *Struwwelpeter*, which Dirks was likely familiar with, has been interpreted as a collection of cautionary tales. However, children's literature scholars argue that Hoffman mocked, rather than reproduced, moralistic and religious tales for children. See Jack Zipes et al., eds., *The Norton Anthology of Children's Literature: The Traditions in English* (New York: W. W. Norton, 2005), C1.

94. Busch, *Max and Moritz*, 56.

95. August Derleth, "Foreword," in *The Katzenjammer Kids: Early Strips in Full Color* (New York: Dover, 1974).

96. Lisa Yaszek, "'Them Damn Pictures': Americanization and the Comic Strip in the Progressive Era," *Journal of American Studies* 28, no. 1 (1994): 37.

97. Yaszek, 37.

98. Quoted in Peter Connolly-Smith, "Casting Teutonic Types from the Nineteenth Century to World War I: German Ethnic Stereotypes in Print, on Stage, and Screen," *Columbia Journal of American Studies*, accessed August 31, 2013, http://www.columbia.edu/cu/cjas/conolly-smith-1.html.

99. Connolly-Smith.

100. Robert C. Allen, Horrible Prettiness: Burlesque and American Culture (Chapel Hill: U of North Carolina P, 1991), quoted in Connolly-Smith.

101. Kevin Grace, Gemutlikeit, Schnitzelbank, and Kitsch: German American Caricature in Vintage Postcards (University of Cincinnati Libraries, 2010), accessed July 6, 2018, http://www.libraries.uc.edu/content/dam/libraries/arb/docs/german-americana/gemutlikeit-schnitzelbank-and-kitsch.pdf.

102. Grace.

103. Fischer, *Them Damned Pictures*, 70.

104. Grace, *Gemutlikeit, Schnitzelbank, and Kitsch.*

105. Connolly-Smith, "Casting Teutonic Types."

106. Frederick C. Luebke, *Germans in the New World: Essays in the History of Immigration* (Urbana: University of Illinois Press, 1990), 112.

107. Luebke, 111. The American psychologist G. Stanley Hall, whose research I discuss in chapter 5, was educated in the University of Berlin.

108. Mary Lynn Stevens Heininger, "Children, Childhood, and Change in America, 1820–1920," in *A Century of Childhood, 1820–1920* (Rochester, N.Y.: Margaret Woodbury Strong Museum, 1984), 27.

109. Rudolph Dirks, "Mamma Katzenjammer Plays a Boomerang Trick," *The Katzenjammer Kids*, *Chicago American* Comic Supplement, March 10, 1901, SFS 1-10-2, SFA Collection, Ireland Cartoon Library.

110. Rudolph Dirks, "Mamma Katzenjammer Makes a New Year's Resolution, and Promptly Breaks It," *The Katzenjammer Kids, San Francisco Examiner* Comic Supplement, December 29, 1901, SFS 1-14-1, SFA Collection, Ireland Cartoon Library.

111. The practice of characters crossing over from one comics series to another was common during the period. Hearst cartoonists, in particular, frequently borrowed characters from one another. They also collaborated with one another on some episodes.

112. Rudolph Dirks, "The Katzenjammer Kids Rob Happy Hooligan's Nephews of their Christmas Pie," *The Katzenjammer Kids*, December 13, 1903. *Barnacle Press*, accessed August 31, 2013, http://www.barnaclepress.com/comic/Katzenjammer%20Kids/kk031213.jpg/.

113. Rudolph Dirks, "The Katzenjammer Kids in School," *The Katzenjammer Kids, New York American and Journal* Comic Supplement, March 12, 1905, SFS 80-3-2, SFA Collection, Ireland Cartoon Library.

114. See Mark Twain, "Chapter XXI," in *The Adventures of Tom Sawyer* (1876; repr., Berkeley: University of California Press, 1980), 153–160.

115. Lillian D. Wald, *The House on Henry Street* (1915; repr., New York: Dover, 1971), 66.

CHAPTER 2 — CROSSING THE COLOR LINE

1. R. F. Outcault, "What Would You Do with a Boy like This?," *Buster Brown, 1906 (Westport, Conn.:* Hyperion, 1977), 47.

2. Outcault, 47.

3. Here, I use the term "racial impersonation" to distinguish it from "passing." Elaine K. Ginsberg defines passing as an act of "assum[ing] a new identity, escaping the subordination and oppression accompanying one identity and accessing the privileges and status of the other." Although the child characters' masquerades that I describe here often give them new advantages, they adopt new guises out of a sense of play rather than survival. Moreover, they put on new identities with the knowledge that these are temporary. See Elaine K. Ginsberg, ed., "Introduction," in *Passing and the Fictions of Identity* (Durham, N.C.: Duke University Press, 1996), 3.

4. Jackson Lears, *Rebirth of a Nation: The Making of Modern America, 1877–1920* (New York: HarperCollins, 2009), 91.

5. Khalil Gibran Muhammad, *The Condemnation of Blackness: Race, Crime, and the Making of Modern Urban America* (Cambridge, Mass.: Harvard University Press, 2010), 7.

6. David W. Southern, *The Progressive Era and Race: Reaction and Reform, 1900–1917* (Wheeling, Ill.: Harlan Davidson, 2005), 46–47.

7. See Thomas C. Leonard, *Illiberal Reformers: Race, Eugenics, and American Economics in the Progressive Era* (Princeton: Princeton University Press, 2016).

8. Elisabeth Lasch-Quinn, *Black Neighbors: Race and the Limits of Reform in the American Settlement House Movement, 1890–1945* (Chapel Hill: University of North Carolina Press, 1993), 1.

9. Lasch-Quinn, 10.

10. As several studies note, popular cultural forms produced from the antebellum period to the Gilded Age were texts in which disdain and desire for blacks and black culture were simultaneously expressed and explored. See Eric Lott, *Love and Theft: Blackface Minstrelsy and the American Working Class* (New York: Oxford University Press, 1993), and Kyla Wazana Tompkins, *Racial Indigestion: Eating Bodies in the 19th Century* (New York: New York University Press, 2012).

11. Steven Mintz, *Huck's Raft: A History of American Childhood* (Cambridge, Mass.: Belknap Press of Harvard University Press, 2006), 185–199.

12. David Pilgrim notes that the term is also spelled "picaninny" and "piccaninny." Kenneth W. Goings speculates that the term originated from the Portuguese word "pequenino," which means "little child," and was subsequently vulgarized by the British, who used the term "pickaninny" to refer to a "small, stupid child." David Pilgrim, "The Picaninny Caricature," Jim Crow Museum of Racist Memorabilia, Ferris State University, 2012, accessed August 31, 2013, https://ferris.edu/HTMLS/news/jimcrow/antiblack/picaninny/homepage.htm; Kenneth W. Goings, *Mammy and Uncle Mose: Black Collectibles and American Stereotyping* (Bloomington: Indiana University Press, 1994), 37.

13. Pilgrim, "The Picaninny Caricature."

14. Goings, *Mammy and Uncle Mose*, 9.

15. Goings, xix, 37.

16. Robin Bernstein, *Racial Innocence: Performing American Childhood from Slavery to Civil Rights* (New York: New York University Press, 2011), 34.

17. Bernstein, 34.

18. Bernstein, 36.

19. Mary Niall Mitchell, "'Rosebloom and Pure White,' Or So It Seemed," *American Quarterly* 54, no. 3 (2002): 381.

20. Goings, *Mammy and Uncle Mose*, 12.

21. Harriet Beecher Stowe, *Uncle Tom's Cabin: Or, Life among the Lowly* (1852; Cambridge, Mass.: Harvard University Press, 2009), 310.

22. For an expanded discussion of how Stowe depicted Topsy as a child who has been "hardened by past abuse," see Bernstein, *Racial Innocence*, 43–68.

23. Pilgrim, "The Picaninny Caricature."

24. Pilgrim.

25. See Lott, *Love and Theft*.

26. For a discussion of the relationship between theater, particularly vaudeville, and comic strips, see Katherine Roeder, *Wide Awake in Slumberland: Fantasy, Mass Culture, and Modernism in the Art of Winsor McCay* (Jackson: University Press of Mississippi, 2014).

27. Kerry Soper, "From Swarthy Ape to Sympathetic Everyman and Subversive Trickster: The Development of Irish Caricature in American Comic Strips between 1890 and 1920," *Journal of American Studies* 39, no. 2 (2005): 273–274.

28. E. W. Kemble, "Illustrating *Huckleberry Finn*," in *Mark Twain in His Times* (Charlottesville: University of Virginia Libraries), accessed July 6, 2018, http://twain.lib.virginia.edu/huckfinn/colophon.html.

29. Kemble.

30. See examples of these illustrations for Stowe's novel in Kemble, "Illustrating *Huckleberry Finn*."

31. Goings, *Mammy and Uncle Mose*, 37.

32. E. W. Kemble, "The Blackberries Leave for the Country," *The Blackberries, New York Journal* Comic Supplement, May 30, 1897, SFS 60-1-5, San Francisco Academy of Comic Art Collection, the Ohio State University Billy Ireland Cartoon Library and Museum (hereafter cited as SFA Collection, Ireland Cartoon Library).

33. See Monica L. Miller, *Slaves to Fashion: Black Dandyism and the Styling of Black Diasporic Identity* (Durham, N.C.: Duke University Press, 2009).

34. Carolyn Dean, "Boys and Girls and 'Boys': Popular Depictions of African-American Children and Childlike Adults in the United States, 1850–1930," *Journal of American and Comparative Cultures* 23, no. 3 (2002): 28.

35. Dean, 25.

36. Cindy S. Aron, *Working at Play: A History of Vacations in the United States* (New York: Oxford University Press, 2001), 5.

37. Kemble, "The Blackberries Leave."

38. E. W. Kemble, "The Blackberry Picnic Is Interrupted by an Uninvited Guest," *The Blackberries, New York Journal* Comic Supplement, October 3, 1897, SFS 60-6-1, SFA Collection, Ireland Cartoon Library.

39. Dean, "Boys and Girls," 22.

40. Dean, 22.

41. E. W. Kemble, "October = A Blackberry Idyll," *The Blackberries, Chicago American* Comic Supplement, circa October 1901, SFS 1-13-5, SFA Collection, Ireland Cartoon Library.

42. Pilgrim, "The Picaninny Caricature." In her analysis of turn-of-the-century trading cards, Kyla Wazana Tompkins notes how a number of these cards relentlessly repeat the motif of black figures—specifically black children—being eaten or about to be eaten. See Tompkins, *Racial Indigestion*, 169–173.

43. *The Ten Little Niggers* (New York: McLoughlin Bros, circa 1878), Baldwin Library of Historical Children's Literature in the Department of Special Collections and Area Studies, George A. Smathers Libraries, University of Florida.

44. Tompkins, *Racial Indigestion*, 170.

45. Tompkins, 169.

46. Rudolph Dirks, "The Katzenjammer Kids Change Clothes with the Blackberry Brothers," *The Katzenjammer Kids, Chicago American* Comic Supplement, September 2, 1900, SFS 1-4-5, SFA Collection, Ireland Cartoon Library.

47. Dean, "Boys and Girls," 28–29.

48. "Dirks's Bad Boys," *Time*, March 4, 1957, 48.

49. In chapter 1, I discuss how *The Katzenjammer Kids* and other strips headlined by immigrant and "ethnic" child characters at once denigrated and celebrated young new arrivals. Dirks himself was a child immigrant: he arrived in the United States at the age of seven. His success as a cartoonist and the popularity of *Katzenjammer Kids* among German Americans could be understood as part of the effort of German immigrants to participate in American society through practices of production and consumption.

50. Dirks, "Katzenjammer Kids Change Clothes."

51. Jean Michel Massing shows how the theme of whitening (and cleaning) black skins was also a common motif in late nineteenth-century soap advertisements in France. See Jean Michel Massing, "From Greek Proverb to Soap Advert: Washing the Ethiopian," *Journal of the Warburg and Courtauld Institutes* 58 (1995): 180–201.

52. Tanya Sheehan, "Comical Conflations: Racial Identity and the Science of Photography," *Photography and Culture* 4, no. 2 (July 2011): 134.

53. Southern, *The Progressive Era*, 24–38.

54. According to Jean Michel Massing, "The Blackamoor" was not written by Aesop but rather by Aphthonius. The first collection of Aphthonius's fables was published in 1597, but his Blackamoor tale was soon absorbed into the Aesop corpus. Massing, "From Greek Proverb," 183.

55. "The Blackamoor," *Aesop's Fables*, accessed January 31, 2015, http://www.fullbooks.com/Aesop-s-Fables2.html.

56. "The Blackamoor."

57. "The Blackamoor."

58. Massing, "From Greek Proverb," 182.

59. From Massing, 183n17.

60. Sheehan, "Comical Conflations," 138.

61. Pilgrim, "The Picaninny Caricature."

62. Pilgrim.

63. Outcault, "What Would You Do."

64. Steven Mintz and Susan Kellogg, *Domestic Revolutions: A Social History of American Family Life* (New York: Free Press, 1998), 116.

65. Dean, "Boys and Girls," 18.

66. Carl E. "Bunny" Schultze, "The Little Rogues Pretend They Are Pickaninnies, but a Good-Sized Darkey Gives Them Quite a Fright," *Foxy Grandpa, St. Louis Republic* Comic Supplement, April 17, 1904, SFS 3-4-3, SFA Collection, Ireland Cartoon Library.

67. David Pilgrim, "The Brute Caricature," Jim Crow Museum of Racist Memorabilia, Ferris State University, 2012, accessed August 31, 2013, https://ferris.edu/jimcrow/brute/.

68. Lott, *Love and Theft*, 4–6.

69. Susan Smulyan, *Popular Ideologies: Mass Culture at Mid-Century* (Philadelphia: University of Pennsylvania Press, 2007), 24.

70. Smulyan, 24.

71. Leslie Paris, *Children's Nature: The Rise of the American Summer Camp* (New York: New York University Press, 2008), 191.

72. Paris, 192.

73. Paris, 191.

74. Paris, 191; Smulyan, *Popular Ideologies*, 39.

75. Smulyan, 39.

76. Smulyan, 20.

77. Edward A. Shannon, "Something Black in the American Psyche: Formal Innovation and Freudian Imagery in the Comics of Winsor McCay and Robert Crumb," *Canadian Review of American Studies* 40, no. 2 (2010): 196.

78. Winsor McCay, *Little Nemo in Slumberland* (West Carrolton, Ohio: Checker Books, 2007), 1:107.

79. McCay, 1:107.

80. In my more extensive discussion of McCay's *Little Nemo in Slumberland* in chapter 5, I consider Nemo's admiration for and fascination with Flip. While Flip appears to be corrupted and antagonistic because he is not able to contain his cross-racial play, Nemo looks to him as a model, one who could help him assert his whiteness and maleness.

81. McCay, *Little Nemo*, 200.

82. McCay, 200.

83. Outcault was inconsistent with the spelling of the title. He interchangeably used "poor" and "pore" and "li'l" and "lil."

84. Mark D. Winchester, "Hully Gee, It's a War!!! The Yellow Kid and the Coining of 'Yellow Journalism,'" *Inks: Cartoon and Comic Art Studies* 2, no. 3 (1995): 31.

85. Goings, *Mammy and Uncle Mose*, xxi–xxiv.

86. The golliwog (or golliwogg) caricature was especially popular in Europe. Florence Kate Upton, who was born in Flushing, New York and later settled in England, introduced the caricature in her children's book *The Adventures of Two Dutch Dolls and a "Golliwogg"* (1895). Her illustration of the golliwog was inspired by a minstrel doll she owned as a child. Her mother, Bertha Upton, wrote the words to the story. Mother and daughter collaborated on twelve more stories that featured the golliwog. The British Bannerman was likely influenced by the Uptons' work.

87. Alan Havig, "Richard F. Outcault's 'Poor Lil' Mose': Variations on the Black Stereotype in American Comic Art," *Journal of American Culture* 11, no. 1 (1988): 33.

88. R. F. Outcault, "Poor Lil Mose on the 7 Ages," *Pore Lil Mose, New York Herald* Comic Supplement, February 3, 1901, SFS 27-2-1, SFA Collection, Ireland Cartoon Library.

89. William Shakespeare, *As You Like It*, ed. Jack R. Crawford (New Haven, Conn.: Yale University Press, 1919), 2.7.139–166.

90. Outcault, "On the 7 Ages."

91. Outcault.

92. Outcault.

93. Shakespeare, *As You Like It*, 2.7.157–158.

94. Outcault, "On the 7 Ages."

95. Outcault.

96. Shakespeare, *As You Like It*, 2.7.166.

97. Outcault, "On the 7 Ages."

98. R. F. Outcault, "He Comes to New York," *Pore Lil Mose, New York Herald* Comic Supplement, June 16, 1901, SFS 27-6-3, SFA Collection, Ireland Cartoon Library.

99. R. F. Outcault, "Pore Lil Mose Talks to the Animals," *Pore Lil Mose, New York Herald* Comic Supplement, February 24, 1901, SFS 27-2-4, SFA Collection, Ireland Cartoon Library.

100. The postcard's copyright date is 1906. It is unclear whether the number "1853," which appears in the bottom left-hand corner of the postcard, is a serial number or the year the image was first produced/circulated. In any case, this visual gag that equates a black child with a pig appears to have been popular in the 1900s. See, for example, a reproduction of a 1907 postcard that bears a version of this motif in Pilgrim, "The Picaninny Caricature."

101. Pilgrim.

102. Outcault, "Talks to the Animals."

103. Outcault.

104. Outcault.

105. Chris Jenks, *Childhood* (London: Routledge, 1996), 62–65.

106. Havig, "Richard F. Outcault's 'Poor Lil' Mose,'" 33.

107. Havig, 33, 39.

108. Havig, 34.

109. Ian Gordon, *Comic Strips and Consumer Culture, 1890–1945* (Washington, D.C.: Smithsonian Institution Press, 1998), 66.

110. Gordon, Comic Strips and Consumer Culture, 66.

111. R. F. Outcault, "He Takes a Ride on the Car," *Pore Lil Mose, New York Herald* Comic Supplement, July 21, 1901, SFS 28-1-3, SFA Collection, Ireland Cartoon Library.

112. R. F. Outcault, "He Visits the Suburbs—and Frightens a Native," *Pore Lil Mose, New York Herald* Comic Supplement, August 18, 1901, SFS 28-2-3, SFA Collection, Ireland Cartoon Library.

113. Outcault.

114. Outcault.

115. Although Outcault remained vague about how Mose supported himself in the city, it is worth noting that he did not depict his protagonist as dependent on white benefactors or engaging in criminal activity.

116. R. F. Outcault, *Pore Lil Mose: His Letters to His Mammy* (Brooklyn: Grand Union Tea Company, 1902).

117. Gordon, *Comic Strips and Consumer Culture*, 67.

118. Ernest Creet, "Three of a Kind Taken on Board the SS New York," *New York Herald* Comic Supplement, October 6, 1901, SFS 28-4-1, SFA Collection, Ireland Cartoon Library.

119. R. Stulmack, "Belle Frye, Who Does the Cake Walk Cleverly," *New York Herald* Comic Supplement, April 21, 1901, SFS 27-4-3, SFA Collection, Ireland Cartoon Library.

120. Stulmack.

121. Dorothy M. Yulee, "Greedy Lil Mose," *New York Herald* Comic Supplement, July 14, 1901, SFS 28-1-2, SFA Collection, Ireland Cartoon Library.

122. R. F. Outcault, "Buster Brown and Pore Lil Mose," *Buster Brown, New York Herald* Comic Supplement, July 20, 1902, SFS 30-1-3a, SFA Collection, Ireland Cartoon Library.

123. Outcault.

124. Jenks, *Childhood*, 62.

CHAPTER 3 — FAMILY AMUSEMENTS

1. Ian Gordon, *Kid Comic Strips: A Genre across Four Countries* (New York: Palgrave Macmillan, 2016), 3–4.

2. Ian Gordon, *Comic Strips and Consumer Culture, 1890–1945* (Washington, D.C.: Smithsonian Institution Press, 1998), 49.

3. "Comic Supplements a Source of Evil," *New York Times*, January 27, 1911, 5, *ProQuest Historical Newspapers*, accessed August 31, 2013.

4. Bill Blackbeard and Martin Williams, eds., *The Smithsonian Collection of Newspaper Comics* (Washington, D.C.: Smithsonian Institution Press; New York: Abrams, 1977), 19.

5. Charles Hatfield, "Redrawing the Comic Strip Child: Charles M. Schulz's *Peanuts* as Cross-Writing," in *The Oxford Handbook of Children's Literature*, ed. Julia L. Mickenberg and Lynne Vallone (New York: Oxford University Press, 2011), 169.

6. Gregg Camfield, *Necessary Madness: The Humor of Domesticity in Nineteenth-Century American Literature* (New York: Oxford University Press, 1997), 3–6.

7. Steven Mintz and Susan Kellogg coined "companionate family" from the term "companionate marriage." The latter phrase was popularized by Ben B. Lindsey and Wainwright Evans in their 1925 book *The Revolt of Modern Youth*. Lindsey and Evans argued that marriage should be founded on sexual attraction, affection, and equal roles in the household. According to Mintz and Kellogg, Lindsey and Evans's ideas were not new, as such "radical" notions about the nature of marriage were part of public discourse well before the 1920s. See Steven Mintz and Susan Kellogg, *Domestic Revolutions: A Social History of American Family Life* (New York: Free Press, 1988), 113–114.

8. Amy Kiste Nyberg, "Percival Chubb and the League for the Improvement of the Children's Comic Supplement," *Inks: Cartoon and Comic Art Studies* 3, no. 3 (1996): 31.

9. Quoted in "Comic Supplements a Source of Evil," 5.

10. Jeet Heer and Kent Worcester, "Introduction," in *Arguing Comics: Literary Masters on a Popular Medium*, ed. Jeet Heer and Kent Worcester (Jackson: University Press of Mississippi, 2004), 1–2.

11. Quoted in "Say Child Must Learn in the Home," *New York Times*, December 16, 1908, 6, *ProQuest Historical Newspapers*, accessed August 31, 2013.

12. "Say Child Must Learn," 6.

13. Quoted in "Comic Supplements a Menace, He Says," *New York Times*, June 10, 1909, 7, *ProQuest Historical Newspapers*, accessed August 31, 2013.

14. "Comic Supplements a Menace," 7.

15. "Comic Supplements a Menace," 7.

16. "Comic Supplements a Menace," 7.

17. Paul S. Moore, *Now Playing: Early Moviegoing and the Regulation of Fun* (Albany: State University of New York Press, 2008), 58, 124.

18. Mintz and Kellogg, *Domestic Revolutions*, 113.

19. Mintz and Kellogg, 114.

20. Joseph M. Hawes and Elizabeth I. Nybakken, eds., "Introduction," in *Family and Society in American History* (Urbana: University of Illinois Press, 2001), 6–7.

21. R. F. Outcault, "Buster Brown Has a Birthday Party," *Buster Brown*, *New York Herald* Comic Supplement, October 19, 1902, SFS 30-4-3a, San Francisco Academy of Comic Art Collection, the Ohio State University Billy Ireland Cartoon Library and Museum (hereafter cited as SFA Collection, Ireland Cartoon Library).

22. Peter G. Filene, *Him/Her/Self: Gender Identities in Modern America* (Baltimore: Johns Hopkins University Press, 1998), 85.

23. Mintz and Kellogg, *Domestic Revolutions*, 116–117.

24. Louis D. Rubin Jr., "The Great American Joke," in *What's So Funny? Humor in American Culture*, ed. Nancy A. Walker (Wilmington, N.C.: Scholarly Resources, 1998), 113.
25. Rubin Jr., "The Great American Joke," 113.
26. Camfield, *Necessary Madness*, 19.
27. Christopher Lasch, *Haven in a Heartless World: The Family Besieged* (New York: Basic Books, 1977), 6–7.
28. Camfield, *Necessary Madness*, 186.
29. Camfield, viii.
30. Camfield, 33.
31. Quoted in Shirley Wajda, "A Room with a Viewer: The Parlor Stereoscope, Comic Stereographs, and the Psychic Role of Play in Victorian America," in *Hard at Play: Leisure in America, 1840–1940*, ed. Kathryn Grover (Amherst: University of Massachusetts Press; Rochester, N.Y.: Margaret Woodbury Strong Museum, 1992), 119–120, emphasis in original.
32. Quoted in Wajda, 131.
33. Daniel Wickberg, *The Senses of Humor: Self and Laughter in Modern America* (Ithaca, N.Y.: Cornell University Press, 1998), 8, emphasis in original.
34. Quoted in "Buster Brown: Creator of Famous Newspaper Comic Visits Salt Lake and Talks of His Work," *Salt Lake Herald*, January 4, 1908, *Chronicling America: Historic American Newspapers*, accessed August 31, 2013.
35. R. F. Outcault, "Buster Brown Suffers, but Doesn't Get a Beating," *Buster Brown, New York Herald* Comic Supplement, October 12, 1902, SFS 30-4-2a, SFA Collection, Ireland Cartoon Library.
36. Outcault.
37. Lisa Yaszek, "'Them Damn Pictures': Americanization and the Comic Strip in the Progressive Era," *Journal of American Studies* 28, no. 1 (1994): 37.
38. Margaret Lynch-Brennan, *The Irish Bridget: Irish Immigrant Women in Domestic Service in America, 1840–1930* (Syracuse, N.Y.: Syracuse University Press, 2009), 70–73.
39. Lynch-Brennan, 72.
40. R. F. Outcault, "Buster Brown—Photographer," *Buster Brown, Chicago Sunday Tribune* Comic Supplement, May 8, 1904, SFS 98-7, SFA Collection, Ireland Cartoon Library.
41. See Jadviga M. Da Costa Nunes, "The Naughty Child in Nineteenth-Century American Art," *Journal of American Studies* 21, no. 2 (1987): 225–247.
42. Nunes, 233.
43. Nunes, 232.
44. David M. Lubin, *Picturing a Nation: Art and Social Change in Nineteenth-Century America* (New Haven, Conn.: Yale University Press, 1994), 194–195.
45. Kenneth Kidd, *Making American Boys: Boyology and the Feral Tale* (Minneapolis: University of Minnesota Press, 2004), 53.
46. Kidd, 55.
47. Kidd, 17, 53.
48. R. F. Outcault, "Buster Brown Plays Another Little Innocent Trick," *Buster Brown, New York Herald* Comic Supplement, June 14, 1903, SFS 31-6-2, SFA Collection, Ireland Cartoon Library.
49. Sarah Burns, *Pastoral Inventions: Rural Life in Nineteenth-Century American Art and Culture* (Philadelphia: Temple University Press, 1989), 302. For more on nineteenth-century images of barefoot country boys, a figure that was closely aligned with the bad boy characters, see Burns, *Pastoral Inventions*, and Claire Perry, *Young America: Childhood in 19th-Century Art and Culture* (New Haven: Yale University Press, 2006), 11–33.
50. Burns, 313.
51. James B. Salazar, *Bodies of Reform: The Rhetoric of Character in Gilded Age America* (New York: New York University Press, 2010), 75.

52. Leslie Paris, *Children's Nature: The Rise of the American Summer Camp* (New York: New York University Press, 2008), 29.

53. Constance Rourke, "The Yankee," in *What's So Funny? Humor in American Culture*, ed. Nancy A. Walker (Wilmington, N.C.: Scholarly Resources, 1998), 88–89; see also Cameron C. Nickels, *New England Humor: From the Revolutionary War to the Civil War* (Knoxville: University of Tennessee Press, 1993), 8–9.

54. In the 1920s and 1930s, plucky female characters, such as Little Orphan Annie, Little Lulu, and Nancy, became extremely popular figures in comic strips. The wide appeal of these characters suggests a shift in attitude toward self-reliant and smart-mouthed girls. The figure of the savvy girl captivated audiences. Readers perhaps delighted in her transgressive nature while remaining assured that she would outgrow such independence and fulfill traditional gender expectations later on.

55. See chapter 5 for a more extensive discussion of the Gibson Girl.

56. R. F. Outcault, "On the Jump!," *Buster Brown, Boston Sunday American* Comic Supplement, March 17, 1907, SFS 83-3-6, SFA Collection, Ireland Cartoon Library.

57. Mary Lynn Stevens Heininger, "Children, Childhood, and Change in America, 1820–1920," in *A Century of Childhood, 1820–1920* (Rochester, N.Y.: Margaret Woodbury Strong Museum, 1984), 27.

58. R. F. Outcault, "Buster Brown's Valentine," *Buster Brown, Chicago Sunday Tribune* Comic Supplement, February 12, 1905, SFS 99-1, SFA Collection, Ireland Cartoon Library.

59. Gary Cross, *The Cute and the Cool: Wondrous Innocence and Modern American Children's Culture* (New York: Oxford University Press, 2004), 65.

60. Lorinda B. Cohoon, *Serialized Citizenships: Periodicals, Books, and American Boys, 1840–1911* (Lanham, Md.: Scarecrow, 2006), 115.

61. Cohoon, 120.

62. Anne Higonnet, *Pictures of Innocence: The History and Crisis of Ideal Childhood* (London: Thames and Hudson, 1998), 47.

63. "Buster Brown: Creator."

64. Kerry Soper, "From Swarthy Ape to Sympathetic Everyman and Subversive Trickster: The Development of Irish Caricature in American Comic Strips between 1890 and 1920," *Journal of American Studies* 39, no. 2 (2005): 273–274.

65. R. F. Outcault, "Buster Brown Helps Santa Claus," *Chicago Sunday Tribune* Comic Supplement, December 25, 1904, SFS 98-10, SFA Collection, Ireland Cartoon Library.

66. Outcault, emphasis in original.

67. R. F. Outcault, "Buster Brown Plays a Trick in a London Hotel," *Buster Brown, Chicago Sunday Tribune* Comic Supplement, December 11, 1904, SFS 98-10, SFA Collection, Ireland Cartoon Library.

68. Outcault.

69. Outcault.

70. R. F. Outcault, "Buster Brown Gives a Party for the Dog Catcher," *Buster Brown, New York Herald* Comic Supplement, August 30, 1903, SFS 32-2-5, SFA Collection, Ireland Cartoon Library.

71. David Rudd, "Animal and Object Stories," in *The Cambridge Companion to Children's Literature*, ed. M. O. Grenby and Andrea Immel (Cambridge: Cambridge University Press, 2009), 242–243.

72. Beverly Lyon Clark, *Kiddie Lit: The Cultural Construction of Children's Literature in America* (Baltimore: Johns Hopkins University Press, 2003), 22.

73. Frances Hodgson Burnett, *Little Lord Fauntleroy* (London: Frederick Warne and Company, 1888), 34.

74. Burnett, 34.

75. Clark, *Kiddie Lit*, 22–23.

76. Cross, *The Cute and the Cool*, 59.

77. R. F. Outcault, "His New Goat Breaks Up Mamma's Tea Party and a Few Other Things," *Buster Brown, New York Herald* Comic Supplement, April 26, 1903, SFS 31-4-4, SFA Collection, Ireland Cartoon Library.

78. Elizabeth Johns, *American Genre Painting: The Politics of Everyday Life* (New Haven, Conn.: Yale University Press, 1991), 153.

79. R. F. Outcault, "Buster Brown and His Faithful Friend Tige," *Buster Brown, Los Angeles Herald* Comic Supplement, January 10, 1904, SFS 70-5-2, SFA Collection, Ireland Cartoon Library.

80. R. F. Outcault, "Buster Brown Gets Another Joke on the Doctor," *Buster Brown, New York Herald* Comic Supplement, May 10, 1903, SFS 31-5-2, SFA Collection, Ireland Cartoon Library.

81. See Melvin P. Earles, "The Introduction of Hydrocyanic Acid into Medicine: A Study in the History of Clinical Pharmacology," *Medical History* 11, no. 3 (1967): 305–313.

82. Outcault, "Another Joke on the Doctor."

83. R. F. Outcault, "Buster Brown Frightens His Parents," *Buster Brown, New York Herald* Comic Supplement, November 23, 1902, SFS 30-5-4a, SFA Collection, Ireland Cartoon Library.

84. Peter N. Stearns, *Anxious Parents: A History of Modern Childrearing in America* (New York: New York University Press, 2004), 21.

85. R. F. Outcault, "Buster Brown Again. His Parents Fool Him," *Buster Brown, Los Angeles Herald* Comic Supplement, no. 126 (1904). SFS 70-6-2, SFA Collection, Ireland Cartoon Library.

86. Gordon, *Comic Strips and Consumer Culture*, 51.

87. Gordon, 49.

88. "Do You Want to Join a Buster Brown Club?," *Chicago Tribune*, February 14, 1904, *Barnacle Press*, accessed August 31, 2013, http://www.barnaclepress.com/comic/Buster%20Brown/buster040214club.jpg/.

89. "Do You Want to Join."

90. "Do You Want to Join."

91. "A Mass Meeting of the Buster Browns," *New York Herald* Second Literary Section, April 5, 1903, SFS 31-4-1, SFA Collection, Ireland Cartoon Library.

92. See "How Mrs. Brown Ties Buster's Tie," May 29, 1905, *Barnacle Press*, accessed August 31, 2013, http://www.barnaclepress.com/comic/Buster%20Brown/buster040529tie.jpg/; "How to Make a Buster Brown Suit," *New York Herald* Children's Supplement, July 19, 1903, SFS 32-1-3, SFA Collection, Ireland Cartoon Library.

93. "Mass Meeting."

94. "Mass Meeting."

95. Quoted in R. F. Outcault, "Circumstantial Evidence Points to Buster Brown," *Chicago Sunday Tribune* Comic Supplement, June 5, 1904, SFS 98-7, SFA Collection, Ireland Cartoon Library.

96. "Mass Meeting."

97. Wajda, "A Room with a Viewer," 113.

CHAPTER 4 — THE "SECRET TRACTS" OF THE CHILD'S MIND

1. Augusti S. Earle, "Kindergarten Light Opera," *Kindergarten Primary Magazine* 21 (1908): 132.

2. Just as comic strips borrowed techniques, jokes, and characters from vaudeville and blackface minstrelsy, theatrical plays, in turn, drew material from the comic supplement. *Little Nemo* was not the only comic strip that inspired a hit play. Popular series such as R. F. Outcault's *Hogan's Alley/McFadden's Row of Flats* and *Buster Brown* as well as Frederick Burr Opper's *Happy Hooligan* were also developed into stage productions.

3. Earle, "Kindergarten Light Opera," 134.

4. Earle, 134.

5. Emily D. Cahan, "Toward a Socially Relevant Science: Notes on the History of Child Development Research," in *When Science Encounters the Child: Education, Parenting and Child Welfare in 20th-Century America*, ed. Barbara Beatty, Emily D. Cahan, and Julia Grant (New York: Teachers College Press, 2006), 17; Holly Blackford, "Apertures in the House of Fiction: Novel Methods and Child Study, 1870–1910," *Children's Literature Association Quarterly* 32, no. 4 (2007): 371.

6. Katherine Roeder, *Wide Awake in Slumberland: Fantasy, Mass Culture, and Modernism in the Art of Winsor McCay* (Jackson: University Press of Mississippi, 2014), 49–54. Further research can also consider the relationship between children's book illustrations and the comic strips. It is worth noting that some artists, such as E. W. Kemble and W. W. Denslow, drew for the comics supplements and also illustrated children's books.

7. Juliet Dusinberre, *Alice to the Lighthouse: Children's Books and Radical Experiments in Art* (New York: St. Martin's Press, 1987), 32.

8. Blackford, "Apertures," 387.

9. Robert Louis Stevenson, "Child's Play," *Virginibus Puerisque and Other Papers* (Boston: Small, Maynard, 1907), 208.

10. Granville Stanley Hall, *The Contents of Children's Minds on Entering School* (New York: E. L. Kellogg, 1893), 13.

11. Hall, 27–28.

12. Hall, 32.

13. Stevenson, "Child's Play," 216.

14. L. Frank Baum, *The Wonderful Wizard of Oz* (Chicago: Geo. M. Hill Company, 1900).

15. Hall, *Contents*, 36.

16. J. M. Barrie, *Peter and Wendy* (New York: Charles Scribner's Sons, 1912), 7–8.

17. Hall was, in effect, building on the work of scientists in Europe, such as Darwin, Perez, and Sully, who argued that the careful observation of children was an effective means of theorizing about the nature of childhood. However, several decades before the emergence of the child study movement, the educator Amos Bronson Alcott embarked on projects in which he observed and recorded children's behavior and speech. *Conversations with Children on the Gospels*, for example, documents the exchanges Alcott had with children on the subject of Jesus and religion. Alcott understood *Conversations* as a "record of [children's] consciousness . . . a revelation of the Divinity in the soul of childhood." He clearly romanticized childhood as a period of innocence, as he argued that "childhood utters sage things, worthy of all note; and he who scoffs at its improvisations, or perverts its simple sayings, proves the corruption of his own being." Alcott's work can be understood as an important antecedent to the child study movement. A. Bronson Alcott, *Conversations with Children on the Gospels* (Boston: James Munroe, 1836), 1:xiii–xiv.

18. Cahan, "Toward a Socially Relevant Science," 18.

19. Cahan, 18.

20. Alice Minnie Herts Heninger, *The Kingdom of the Child* (New York: E. P. Dutton and Company, 1918), 28.

21. Steven Mintz, *Huck's Raft: A History of American Childhood* (Cambridge, Mass.: Belknap Press of Harvard University Press, 2004), 185.

22. This chapter links scientific literature, children's books, and fantasy comic strips that were produced on both sides of the Atlantic over a fifty-year period, from the 1870s to the 1920s. It is thus important to acknowledge that these various texts emerged in different historical and cultural contexts and were responding to specific political and social moments. Yet these texts, when placed in conversation with one another, testify to how the image of the imaginative child was increasingly becoming naturalized and universalized in the late nineteenth and early twentieth centuries.

23. Lewis Carroll, "Through the Looking-Glass, and What Alice Found There," in *Alice in Wonderland*, ed. Donald J. Gray (1871; New York: W. W. Norton, 1992), 209.

24. J. M. Barrie, "Peter Pan; or, The Boy Who Would Not Grow Up," in *The Norton Anthology of Children's Literature: The Traditions in English*, ed. Jack Zipes et al (New York: W. W. Norton, 2005), 1301–1305.

25. James Sully, *Studies of Childhood* (New York: D. Appleton and Company, 1910), 25.

26. This chapter focuses on episodes that appeared in the *New York Herald*.

27. John Canemaker, *Winsor McCay: His Life and Art* (New York: Harry N. Abrams, 2005), 97, 181–182.

28. Winsor McCay, *Little Nemo in Slumberland* (West Carrolton, Ohio: Checker Books, 2007), 1:67.

29. Ralph Bergengren, "The Humor of the Colored Supplement," *The Atlantic*, August 1908, 273.

30. Bergengren, 273.

31. Bergengren, 273.

32. Bergengren, 273.

33. Canemaker, *Winsor McCay*, 79.

34. Winsor *McCay, Dreams of the Rarebi*t Fiend (New York: Dover, 1973), 42.

35. McCay, *Little Nemo*, 64.

36. McCay, 74.

37. Lewis Carroll, "Alice's Adventures in Wonderland," in *Alice in Wonderland*, ed. Donald J. Gray (1865; repr., New York: W. W. Norton, 1992), 98–99.

38. Winsor McCay, *Dreams of the Rarebit Fiend*, *San Francisco Call* Comic Supplement, January 23, 1906, SFC 34, San Francisco Academy of Comic Art Collection, the Ohio State University Billy Ireland Cartoon Library and Museum (hereafter cited as SFA Collection, Ireland Cartoon Library).

39. McCay, *Little Nemo*, 75.

40. Colored editions of *Rarebit Fiend* often used solid colors. Many of the series' episodes lacked the sense of tone and depth present in *Little Nemo* in which McCay employed gradient colors and shading.

41. Sigmund Freud, *The Interpretation of Dreams*, trans. Joyce Crick (1899; repr., Oxford: Oxford University Press, 1999), 102, 140. Although the first English translation of *The Interpretation of Dreams* was not published until 1913, it is possible that Freud's theories on dreams were already influencing American psychologists in the previous decade, as many of them closely followed the development of the fields of psychoanalysis and psychology in Europe. Hall, the leader of the child study movement, was likely already familiar with Freud's theories even before *Interpretation of Dreams* was released in the United States. Hall was educated in Germany and became a close associate of Freud. In 1909, Hall organized a series of lectures at Clark University, with Freud and Carl Jung as featured speakers. The lecture marked Freud's first and only visit to the United States.

42. Katherine Roeder, "Seeing Inside-out in the Funny Pages," *American Art* 25, no. 1 (2011): 25–26.

43. Canemaker, *Winsor McCay*, 34.

44. Canemaker, 39.

45. Scott Bukatman, "Little Utopias of Disorder," *American Art* 25, no. 2 (2011): 12.

46. McCay, *Little Nemo*, 247–253.

47. Hall, *Contents*, 35–36.

48. Granville Stanley Hall, "Preface," in *Aspects of Child Life and Education*, ed. Granville Stanley Hall (Boston: Ginn, 1907), v.

49. I build on Perry Nodelman's discussion of how children's literature teaches young readers to simultaneously recognize their innocence/ignorance and to anticipate the loss of this innocence; therefore, child readers are urged to treasure this "pure" state of childhood.

See Perry Nodelman, *The Hidden Adult: Defining Children's Literature* (Baltimore: Johns Hopkins University Press, 2008), 45–46.

50. Carroll, "Alice's Adventures," 99.

51. Barrie, *Peter and Wendy*, 218.

52. Barrie, 220.

53. Margaret R. Higonnet, "Modernism and Childhood: Violence and Renovation," *The Comparatist* 33 (2009): 86.

54. Higonnet, "Modernism and Childhood," 86.

55. Higonnet, 92.

56. Robert Louis Stevenson, "*Young Night-Thought*," in *A Child's Garden of Verses* (1885; repr., New York: Charles Scribner's Sons, 1905), 4.

57. McCay, *Little Nemo*, 110.

58. "Strange Children to Parade at Fair," *St. Louis Post-Dispatch*, July 31, 1904, 12.

59. For more on how the 1904 World's Fair in St. Louis became a space in which Americans displayed, reinforced, and celebrated expansionism, imperialism, and modernization, see Eric Breitbart, *A World on Display: Photographs from the St. Louis World's Fair, 1904* (Albuquerque: University of New Mexico Press, 1997); Nancy J. Parezo and Don D. Fowler, *Anthropology Goes to the Fair: The 1904 Louisiana Purchase Exposition* (Lincoln: University of Nebraska Press, 2007); and Robert W. Rydell, *All the World's a Fair: Visions of Empire at American International Expositions, 1876–1916* (Chicago: University of Chicago Press, 1984).

60. L. Frank Baum, *The Lost Princess of Oz* (Chicago: Reilly and Lee Company, 1917), 8.

61. Roeder, *Wide Awake in Slumberland*, 75.

62. "Little Nemo *Home with* War Honors," *The Butte Daily Bulletin*, April 19, 1919, *Chronicling America: Historic American Newspapers*, accessed January 22, 2015.

63. The photograph was published in local newspapers in Nevada, Nebraska, Louisiana, and other states.

64. Peter G. Filene, *Him/Her/Self: Gender Identities in Modern America* (Baltimore: Johns Hopkins University Press, 1998), 45; Christopher Lasch, *Haven in a Heartless World: The Family Besieged* (New York: Basic Books, 1977), 8–9.

65. Prototypes of the Imp first appeared in *Tales of the Jungle Imps*, a series that was published in *Cincinnati Enquirer* from February to November 1903.

66. "Holding His End Up," in *Exciting Experiences in our Wars with Spain and the Filipinos*, ed. Marshall Everett (1898; repr., Chicago: The Educational Company, 1900).

67. McCay, *Little Nemo*, 175.

68. McCay, 175.

69. McCay, 175.

70. McCay, 152.

71. Richard Dyer, *White* (London: Routledge, 1997), 74.

72. McCay, *Little Nemo*, 74.

73. McCay, 74.

74. McCay, 181–85.

75. McCay, 182, 184.

76. McCay, 181, 182.

77. McCay, 182–84.

78. McCay, 182.

79. M. Thomas Inge, *Comics as Culture* (Jackson: University Press of Mississippi, 1990), 36.

80. McCay, *Little Nemo*, 182.

81. McCay, 182.

82. Bill Blackbeard, ed., *The Comic Strip Art of Lyonel Feininger* (Seattle: Fantagraphics, 2007).

83. Blackbeard.

84. Feininger would later become a key figure in German expressionism and a prominent member of the Staatliches Bauhaus. See "The Bauhaus, 1919–1933," Metropolitan Museum of Art, accessed January 31, 2015, http://www.metmuseum.org/toah/hd/bauh/hd_bauh.htm.

85. Quoted in Blackbeard, *Comic Strip Art.*

86. Quoted in Blackbeard.

87. Although it can be argued that Willie Winkie's world is a dream realm, the strip does not refer to the act of sleeping or dreaming and thus cues the reader to view Willie as a wide-awake child engaging in reverie and imaginative play.

88. Lyonel Feininger, "Wee Willie Winkie's World," in *The Comic Strip Art of Lyonel Feininger*, ed. Bill Blackbeard (Seattle: Fantagraphics, 2007), 38.

89. Feininger, 44.

90. Feininger, 44.

91. Feininger, 44.

92. Feininger, 51.

93. Hall, "Preface," xi.

94. Feininger, "Wee Willie Winkie's World," 48.

95. Feininger, 48.

96. Feininger, 48.

97. Higonnet, "Modernism and Childhood," 87.

98. Carolyn Steedman, *Strange Dislocations: Childhood and the Idea of Human Interiority, 1780–1930* (Cambridge, Mass.: Harvard University Press, 1995), 4, emphasis in original.

99. Feininger, "Wee Willie Winkie's World," 38.

100. Feininger, 44.

101. Feininger, 44.

102. McCay, *Little Nemo*, 239.

103. McCay, 239.

104. Winsor McCay, *Gertie the Dinosaur* (Box Office Attraction Company, 1914), from YouTube, 12:19, accessed January 22, 2015, http://www.youtube.com/watch?v=ww6zqGHlgsc.

105. McCay.

106. McCay.

107. Lyonel Feininger, Promotional Material for *The Kin-der-kids, Chicago Tribune* Comic Supplement, April 29, 1906, SFT 96-1, SFA Collection, Ireland Cartoon Library.

108. McCay, *Little Nemo*, 214.

109. McCay, 214.

110. McCay, 214.

111. McCay, 247.

112. Bukatman, "Little Utopias," 12.

CHAPTER 5 — WHAT WOULD YOU DO WITH GIRLS LIKE THESE?

1. For extended considerations of the history and functions of literary bad boy narratives in the post–Civil War era, see Kenneth Kidd, *Making American Boys: Boyology and the Feral Tale* (Minneapolis: University of Minnesota Press, 2004), and Lorinda B. Cohoon, *Serialized Citizenships: Periodicals, Books, and American Boys, 1840–1911* (Lanham, Md.: Scarecrow, 2006).

2. For example, see Bill Blackbeard and Martin Williams, eds., *The Smithsonian Collection of Newspaper Comics* (Washington, D.C.: Smithsonian Institution Press, 1977); and Robert C. Harvey, *The Art of the Funnies: An Aesthetic History* (Jackson: University Press of Mississippi, 1994). Comics histories often label young male characters as "naughty kids" or "demon children." By minimizing or eliminating consideration of the characters' gender, these histories

not only fail to highlight the presence of fictional girls in the strips but also suggest that the young male experience is a universal childhood experience.

3. Although *Little Orphan Annie* and *Nancy* are understood to be key texts that redefined the image of girls in the comics, the origin stories of both strips reveal the cartoonists' ambivalence for female protagonists. Harold Gray initially conceived his strip with a young male lead named Otto. His editor, Joseph Patterson, sought to attract more female readers, and Patterson reportedly insisted on changing the character from a boy to a girl. As for the character Nancy, she originally appeared as a minor character in *Fritzi Ritz*, a strip originated by Larry Whittington in 1922 and taken over by Ernie Bushmiller in 1925. *Fritzi Ritz* mocked flapper girls, but it was the precocious Nancy, niece of the titular character, who seemed to appeal more to readers. Over the years, more focus was given to her until the strip was retitled *Nancy* in 1938. Both origin stories suggest that there was a strong desire among publishers to broaden their reach to female readers. The case of *Fritzi Ritz* also suggests that readers rejected a series that mocked women and found more pleasure in a strip about a girl who subverted gender expectations.

4. T. E. Powers, "T. E. Powers' List of Famous Women: 18—Count 'Em—18," *The American Journal Examiner*, circa 1911, SFT 71-3, San Francisco Academy of Comic Art Collection, the Ohio State University Billy Ireland Cartoon Library and Museum (hereafter cited as SFA Collection, Ireland Cartoon Library).

5. At the time of the strip's publication, the *Ladies' Home Journal* was helmed by a man, Edward W. Bok. Powers was most likely referring to Louisa Knapp Curtis, the magazine's founding editor. *Ladies' Home Journal* has been examined as a space that reinforced the notion of essential gender differences and promoted a "feminine" image of womanhood. The magazine, however, also challenged the status quo, as it became a venue for women to publish and make their voices heard. Articles often documented women's professional successes, and the magazine published contributions by women activists and reformers such as Jane Addams. Knapp Curtis was also a strong advocate of women's right to education. See Helen Damon-Moore, *Magazines for Millions: Gender and Commerce in the* Ladies' Home Journal *and the* Saturday Evening Post, *1880–1910* (Albany: State University of New York Press, 1992).

6. "Here Is the New Woman," *New York World*, August 18, 1895, repr. in *The American New Woman Revisited: A Reader, 1894–1930*, ed. Martha H. Patterson (New Brunswick, N.J.: Rutgers University Press, 2008), 47.

7. Martha H. Patterson, ed., *The American New Woman Revisited: A Reader, 1894–1930* (New Brunswick, N.J.: Rutgers University Press, 2008), 46.

8. Theodore Roosevelt, "On American Motherhood," National Congress of Mothers, Washington, D.C., March 13, 1905.

9. Roosevelt.

10. R. F. Outcault, "Buster Brown Visits the Zoo and Talks to the Stork," *Buster Brown*, *New York Herald* Comic Supplement, July 26, 1903, SFS 32-1-4, SFA Collection, Ireland Cartoon Library.

11. June Sochen, *The New Woman: Feminism in Greenwich Village, 1910–1920* (New York: Quadrangle Books, 1972), ix. As Peter Filene reminds us, the New Woman was defined in multiple ways during the Progressive Era. Some of the period's commentators felt that married middle-class women who became active in clubs and organizations or became avid consumers in department stores were disrupting the image of the "true woman" who reigned and remained in the domestic sphere. But Filene also points out that these women were not really "new," as they "remained traditional women in a new locale"; they "did not question the concept of a feminine sphere, only its limits." Filene maintains that it is more fitting to apply the label "New Women" to women who chose to forgo marriage and the younger generation of "New Girls" who pursued college and professional activities. See Peter G. Filene, *Him/Her/Self: Gender Identities in Modern America* (Baltimore: Johns Hopkins University Press, 1998), 16–27.

12. Outcault, "Buster Brown Visits the Zoo."

13. Outcault.

14. Filene, *Him/Her/Self*, 19.

15. R. F. Outcault, "Buster Brown," *Buster Brown*, *Los Angeles Herald* Comic Supplement, December 13, 1903, SFS 70-4-2, SFA Collection, Ireland Cartoon Library.

16. Lois W. Banner, *American Beauty* (New York: Alfred A. Knopf, 1983), 156.

17. Banner, 171.

18. Charlotte Perkins Gilman, *Women and Economics*, ed. Carl N. Degler (1898; repr., New York: Harper and Row, 1996), 148.

19. Although her eponymous series was rather short-lived, running from 1902 to 1905, Lady Bountiful was a frequent recurring character in Carr's other strips until the 1920s.

20. George Farquhar introduced the character Lady Bountiful in his comedy *The Beaux' Stratagem* (1707). In Farquhar's play, Lady Bountiful was a much-admired woman who performed acts of charity and healing. Over time, however, the name Lady Bountiful came to mean a woman who was insincere in and conspicuous with her acts of generosity.

21. Gene Carr, "What Broke Up the Firm of Lady Bountiful and Co.," *Lady Bountiful*, *Chicago Sunday Tribune* Comic Supplement, August 23, 1903, SFS 98-3, SFA Collection, Ireland Cartoon Library.

22. Early episodes of the series were titled *The Suffragette*.

23. T. E. Powers, "Ysobel the Suffragette," *San Francisco Examiner*, March 23, 1911, SFT 71-3, SFA Collection, Ireland Cartoon Library.

24. T. E. Powers, "The Suffragette," *San Francisco Examiner*, January 17, 1911, SFT 71-3, SFA Collection, Ireland Cartoon Library.

25. Powers.

26. Powers, "Ysobel."

27. Powers.

28. See Joe Sutliff Sanders, *Disciplining Girls: Understanding the Origins of the Classic Orphan Girl Story* (Baltimore: Johns Hopkins University Press, 2011).

29. As Anne Scott Macleod points out, narratives about young girls who played rough outdoor games and eventually grow up to become "proper" women were common in the nineteenth century. Louisa May Alcott's *Little Women* is perhaps the most well known of such narratives. See Anne Scott Macleod, *American Childhood: Essays on Children's Literature of the Nineteenth and Twentieth Centuries* (Atlanta: University of Georgia Press, 1994).

30. Steven Mintz, *Huck's Raft: A History of American Childhood* (Cambridge, Mass.: Belknap Press of Harvard University Press, 2004), 193–194.

31. Katherine Roeder, *Wide Awake in Slumberland: Fantasy, Mass Culture, and Modernism in the Art of Winsor McCay* (Jackson: University Press of Mississippi, 2014), 39.

32. The conceit of an aging character was unique during McCay's time and remains a rare practice in newspaper comics. Frank King's *Gasoline Alley*, which first appeared in 1918, is perhaps the first significant long-running strip to use "real-time" continuity.

33. Winsor McCay, *The Story of Hungry Henrietta*, March 3, 1905, SFC 258, SFA Collection, Ireland Cartoon Library.

34. Winsor McCay, "The Story of Hungry Henrietta: Chapter Thirteen," in *Little Sammy Sneeze: The Complete Color Sunday Comics 1904–1905*, ed. Peter Maresca (Palo Alto: Sunday Press Books, 2007).

35. Winsor McCay, "The Story of Hungry Henrietta: Chapter Seventeen," *Little Sammy Sneeze*.

36. Roeder, *Wide Awake in Slumberland*, 42.

37. Roeder, 42.

38. Winsor McCay, "The Story of Hungry Henrietta: Chapter Six," *Little Sammy Sneeze*.

39. McCay.

40. Winsor McCay, "The Story of Hungry Henrietta: Chapter Seven," *Little Sammy Sneeze*.

41. Winsor McCay, "The Story of Hungry Henrietta: Chapter One," *Little Sammy Sneeze.*

42. Gary Cross, *The Cute and the Cool: Wondrous Innocence and Modern American Children's Culture* (New York: Oxford University Press, 2004), 66.

43. Cross, 65.

44. Cross, 65.

45. When *Dottie Dimple* debuted in the supplements of William Randolph Hearst's newspapers in 1908, its cartoonist, then married to Theodore Wiederseim, published under the name "Grace Wiederseim." In 1911, she divorced Wiederseim and married W. Drayton. She subsequently changed her pen name to "Grace Drayton." Drayton, along with Nell Brinkley and Rose O'Neill, is one of the few women who established successful cartooning careers in the early twentieth century. Her success is remarkable, given that comics publishing (both mainstream and alternative) remains a male-dominated industry today.

46. See James Kincaid, *Child-Loving: The Erotic Child and Victorian Culture* (New York: Routledge, 1992).

47. Grace Wiederseim, "Dottie Dimple Gives Her Dress to a Poor Girl!," *Los Angeles Examiner* Comic Supplement, May 22, 1910, SFS 85-5-7, SFA Collection, Ireland Cartoon Library.

48. Jenny Robb and Richard D. Olson, "Madge's Magic: A Look at a Forgotten Graphic Masterpiece," *Hogan's Alley: The Magazine of the Cartoon Arts*, April 9, 2013, accessed January 22, 2015, http://cartoonician.com/madges-magic-a-look-at-a-forgotten-graphic-masterpiece/.

49. Robb and Olson.

50. Johann Wolfgang von Goethe, *The Sorcerer's Apprentice*, 1797, trans. Edwin Zeydel (Richmond: Department of Foreign Languages, Virginia Commonwealth University, 1955), accessed January 31, 2015, https://germanstories.vcu.edu/goethe/zauber_e3.html.

51. Randall Styers, "Mana and Mystification: Magic and Religion at the Turn of the Twentieth Century," *Women's Studies Quarterly* 40, no. 3 and 4 (2012): 229.

52. W. O. Wilson, *Madge the Magician's Daughter, Courier Journal* Comic Supplement, September 16, 1906, SFS 33-13-3, SFA Collection, Ireland Cartoon Library.

53. W. O. Wilson, *Madge, Courier Journal* Comic Supplement, September 2, 1906, SFS 33-13-1, SFA Collection, Ireland Cartoon Library.

54. W. O. Wilson, *Madge, Courier Journal* Comic Supplement, October 7, 1906, SFS 33-14-1, SFA Collection, Ireland Cartoon Library.

55. Wilson.

56. Wilson.

57. W. O. Wilson, *Madge the Magician's Daughter, San Francisco Call* Comic Supplement, October 28, 1906, SFT 133-5, SFA Collection, Ireland Cartoon Library.

58. Styers, "Mana and Mystification," 229.

59. W. O. Wilson, *Madge the Magician's Daughter, San Francisco Call* Comic Supplement, May 19, 1907, AC-P13-2, Richard D. Olson Collection, Ireland Cartoon Library.

60. W. O. Wilson, *Madge the Magician's Daughter, San Francisco Call* Comic Supplement, May 26, 1907, SFT 133-9, SFA Collection, Ireland Cartoon Library.

61. Hobbes shifts between inanimate toy and living creature in *Calvin and Hobbes*; the series suggests that only Calvin recognizes (or enables) the toy tiger's sentience. In *Betsy Bouncer*, Betsy's doll is conscious and "girl-sized" even in the presence of other characters.

62. Miriam Formanek-Brunell, "The Politics of Dollhood in Nineteenth-Century America," in *The Children's Culture Reader*, ed. Henry Jenkins (New York: New York University Press, 1998), 364.

63. Formanek-Brunell, 364.

64. Formanek-Brunell, 376.

65. "Free to Girls: Two Beautiful Dolls," *Sunday Record Herald* Comic Supplement, October 16, 1904, SFT-2, SFA Collection, Ireland Cartoon Library.

66. "Free to Girls."

67. "Free to Girls."

68. "Free to Girls."
69. "Free to Girls."
70. Formanek-Brunell, "The Politics of Dollhood," 369.
71. "Here's a Chance for the Boys to Earn a Handsome Pear-Shaped Punching Bag," *Sunday Record Herald* Comic Supplement, October 16, 1904, SFA Collection, Ireland Cartoon Library.
72. "Free to Girls."
73. Tom Tucker, *Betsy Bouncer and Her Doll, Sunday Record Herald* Comic Supplement, September 11, 1904, SFT-2, SFA Collection, Ireland Cartoon Library.
74. Thomas Henricks, "The Nature of Play: An Overview," *American Journal of Play* 1, no. 2 (2008): 177.
75. Formanek-Brunell, "The Politics of Dollhood," 376.
76. Formanek-Brunell, 374.
77. Lois R. Kuznets, *When Toys Come Alive: Narratives of Animation, Metamorphosis, and Development* (New Haven, Conn.: Yale University Press, 1994), 108.
78. Tom Tucker, *Betsy Bouncer and Her Doll, Sunday Record Herald* Comic Supplement, September 25, 1904, SFT-2, SFA Collection, Ireland Cartoon Library.
79. Tom Tucker, *Betsy Bouncer and Her Doll, Chicago Record Herald* Comic Supplement, August 21, 1904, SFS 44-4-3, SFA Collection, Ireland Cartoon Library.
80. Kuznets, *When Toys Come Alive*, 2.
81. Tom Tucker, *Betsy Bouncer and Her Doll, New York Herald* Comic Supplement, February 12, 1905, SFT-3, SFA Collection, Ireland Cartoon Library.
82. Robin Bernstein, *Racial Innocence: Performing American Childhood from Slavery to Civil Rights* (New York: New York University Press, 2011), 17, emphasis in original.
83. Bernstein, 16–17.

CONCLUSION — NAUGHTY BOYS IN A NEW MILLENNIUM

1. Robert C. Harvey, *The Art of the Funnies: An Aesthetic History* (Jackson: University Press of Mississippi, 1994), 203.
2. This format was first utilized by cartoonist Bud Fisher in 1907 in a strip titled *A. Mutt*, which appeared in the sports pages of *San Francisco Call*. *A. Mutt*, later retitled *Mutt and Jeff*, became one of the most widely syndicated strips of the twentieth century; the format that Fisher "invented" was resurrected in the mid-twentieth century and endured in the early decades of the twenty-first century. For more on the history and development of newspaper comic strips, see Harvey, *The Art of the Funnies*, and Robert C. Harvey, *Children of the Yellow Kid: The Evolution of the American Comic Strip* (Seattle: University of Washington Press, 1998).
3. John Campanelli, "'Calvin and Hobbes' Fans Still Pine 15 Years after Its Exit," *Plain Dealer*, February 1, 2010, accessed January 31, 2015. https://www.cleveland.com/living/index.ssf/2010/02/fans_still_pine_for_calvin_and.html.
4. Campanelli.
5. Bill Watterson, *The Indispensable Calvin and Hobbes: A Calvin and Hobbes Treasury* (Kansas City, Mich.: Andrews and McMeel, 1992), 27.
6. Watterson, 14.
7. See Neil Postman, *The Disappearance of Childhood* (New York: Delacorte, 1982).
8. Bill Watterson, *Calvin and Hobbes*, October 13, 1990.
9. Bill Watterson, *Calvin and Hobbes*, August 10, 1992.
10. Bill Watterson, "The Cheapening of the Comics," Festival of Cartoon Art, Ohio State University, October 27, 1989.
11. Watterson, *The Indispensable Calvin and Hobbes*, 205.

12. Lois R. Kuznets, *When Toys Come Alive: Narratives of Animation, Metamorphosis, and Development* (New Haven, Conn.: Yale University Press, 1994), 57–58.

13. Watterson, *The Indispensable Calvin and Hobbes*, 109.

14. Watterson, 107.

15. Watterson, 110.

16. Aaron McGruder, "Introduction," in *A Right to Be Hostile: The Boondocks Treasury* (New York: Three Rivers, 2003).

17. Christopher P. Lehman, "Franklin and the Early 1970s," in *The Comics of Charles Schulz: The Good Grief of Modern Life*, ed. Jared Gardner and Ian Gordon (Jackson: University Press of Mississippi, 2017), 137.

18. Justice Oliver Wendell Holmes Jr. has long been celebrated for his progressive views. But as Albert W. Alschuler reveals, Holmes often despised reformers and had very little sympathy for the social underclass. See Albert W. Alschuler, *Law without Values: The Life, Work, and Legacy of Justice Holmes* (Chicago: University of Chicago Press, 2000).

19. Lehman, "Franklin," 137.

20. Howard Rambsy II, "The Vengeance of Black Boys: How Richard Wright, Paul Beatty, and Aaron McGruder Strike Back," *Mississippi Quarterly: The Journal of Southern Cultures* 61, no. 4 (2008): 650, 656.

21. McGruder, *A Right to Be Hostile: The Boondocks Treasury* (New York: Three Rivers, 2003), 27.

22. McGruder, 20.

23. McGruder, 18.

24. McGruder, 29.

25. Nancy C. Cornwell and Mark P. Orbe, "'Keepin' It Real' and/or 'Sellin' Out to the Man': African-American Responses to Aaron McGruder's *The Boondocks*," in *Say It Loud! African-American Audiences, Media and Identity*, ed. Robin R. Means Coleman (New York: Routledge, 2002), 35.

26. See Rambsy, "Vengeance of Black Boys." Also see Terrence T. Tucker, "Blackness We Can Believe In: Authentic Blackness and the Evolution of Aaron McGruder's *The Boondocks*," in *Post-Soul Satire: Black Identity after Civil Rights*, ed. Derek C. Maus and James J. Donahue (Jackson: University Press of Mississippi, 2014), 22–37.

27. Tucker, "Blackness We Can Believe In," 23.

BIBLIOGRAPHY

ARCHIVES

Barnacle Press.
Chronicling America: Historic American Newspapers.
ProQuest Historical Newspapers.
San Francisco Academy of Comic Art Collection, the Ohio State University Billy Ireland Cartoon Library and Museum.

NEWSPAPER COMICS SERIES

Breathed, Berke, *Bloom County.*
Bushmiller, Ernie, *Nancy.*
Carr, Gene, *Lady Bountiful.*
Dirks, Rudolph, *The Katzenjammer Kids.*
Feininger, Lyonel, *The Kin-der-kids.*
———, *Wee Willie Winkie's World.*
Gray, Harold, *Little Orphan Annie.*
Hart, John F., *Little Jap "It."*
Kemble, E. W., *The Blackberries.*
King, Frank, *Gasoline Alley.*
Lucy and Sophie Say Goodbye.
McCay, Winsor, *Dreams of the Rarebit Fiend.*
———, *Little Nemo in Slumberland.*
———, *The Story of Hungry Henrietta.*
McGruder, Aaron, *The Boondocks.*
McManus, George, *Bringing Up Father.*
Opper, Frederick Burr, *Happy Hooligan.*
Outcault, R. F., *Buster Brown.*
———, *Hogan's Alley.*
———, *Pore Lil Mose.*
Powers, T. E., *Ysobel the Suffragette* [*The Suffragette*].
Rigby, Clarence, *Little Ah Sid, the Chinese Kid.*
Schultze, Carl E. "Bunny," *Foxy Grandpa.*
Schulz, Charles, *Peanuts.*

Searl, L. A., *Mrs. Timekiller.*
Tucker, Tom, *Betsy Bouncer and Her Doll.*
Watterson, Bill, *Calvin and Hobbes.*
Whittington, Larry, *Fritzi Ritz.*
Wiederseim, Grace, *Dottie Dimple.*
Wilson, W. O., *Madge the Magician's Daughter.*

PRIMARY SOURCES

Addams, Jane. *The Spirit of Youth and the City Streets.* 1909. Urbana: University of Illinois Press, 1972.

Alcott, A. Bronson. *Conversations with Children on the Gospels.* Vol. 1. Boston: James Munroe, 1836.

Barrie, J. M. *Peter and Wendy.* New York: Charles Scribner's and Sons, 1912.

———. "Peter Pan; or, The Boy Who Would Not Grow Up." In *The Norton Anthology of Children's Literature: The Traditions in English*, edited by Jack Zipes, Lissa Paul, Lynne Vallone, Peter Hunt, and Gillian Avery, 1300–1356. New York: W. W. Norton, 2005.

Baum, L. Frank. *The Lost Princess of Oz.* Chicago: Reilly and Lee, 1917.

———. *The Wonderful Wizard of Oz.* Chicago: Geo. M. Hill, 1900.

Bergengren, Ralph. "The Humor of the Colored Supplement." *Atlantic*, August 1908, 269–273.

"The Blackamoor." *Aesop's Fables.* Accessed January 31, 2015. http://www.fullbooks.com/Aesop-s-Fables2.html.

Blackbeard, Bill, ed. *The Comic Strip Art of Lyonel Feininger.* Seattle: Fantagraphics, 2007.

Brace, Charles Loring. *The Dangerous Classes of New York, and Twenty Years' Work among Them.* 1872. Washington, D.C.: National Association of Social Workers, 1973.

Burnett, Frances Hodgson. *Little Lord Fauntleroy.* London: Frederick Warne, 1888.

Busch, Wilhelm. *Max and Moritz: A Juvenile History in Seven Tricks.* 1865. Translated by C. T. Brooks. Edited by H. Arthur Klein. New York: Dover, 1962.

Carroll, Lewis. "Alice's Adventures in Wonderland." 1865. In *Alice in Wonderland*, edited by Donald J. Gray, 1–99. New York: W. W. Norton, 1992.

———. "Through the Looking-Glass, and What Alice Found There." 1871. In *Alice in Wonderland*, edited by Donald J. Gray, 101–209. New York: W. W. Norton, 1992.

"Dirks's Bad Boys." *Time*, March 4, 1957, 48.

Earle, Augusti S. "Kindergarten Light Opera." *Kindergarten Primary Magazine*, September/October 1908, 132–134.

Freud, Sigmund. *The Interpretation of Dreams.* 1899. Translated by Joyce Crick. Oxford: Oxford University Press, 1999.

Goethe, Johann Wolfgang von. *The Sorcerer's Apprentice.* 1797. Translated by Edwin Zeydel. Richmond: Department of Foreign Languages, Virginia Commonwealth University, 1955. Accessed January 31, 2015. https://germanstories.vcu.edu/goethe/zauber_e3.html.

Hall, Granville Stanley, ed. *Aspects of Child Life and Education.* Boston: Ginn, 1907.

———. *The Contents of Children's Minds on Entering School.* New York: E. L. Kellogg, 1893.

Heninger, Alice Minnie Herts. *The Kingdom of the Child.* New York: E. P. Dutton, 1918.

"Holding His End Up." 1898. In *Exciting Experiences in Our Wars with Spain and the Filipinos*, edited by Marshall Everett, 551. Chicago: The Educational Company, 1900.

Kemble, E. W. "Illustrating *Huckleberry Finn*." In *Mark Twain in His Times.* Charlottesville: University of Virginia Libraries. Accessed July 6, 2018. http://twain.lib.virginia.edu/huckfinn/colophon.html.

"Knapp—for Christmas." *Boys' Life*, December 1924, 76.

"Little Ah Sid; or The Chinee Boy and the Japanese Butterfly Bumblebee." *Punch, or the London Charivari* 107, October 20, 1894. Project Gutenberg. Accessed January 5, 2015. https://www.gutenberg.org/files/46826/46826-h/46826-h.htm.

McCay, Winsor. *Dreams of the Rarebit Fiend*. New York: Dover, 1973.

———. *Gertie the Dinosaur*. Box Office Attraction Company, 1914. YouTube, 12:19. Accessed January 22, 2015. http://www.youtube.com/watch?v=ww6zqGHlgsc.

———. *Little Nemo in Slumberland*. Vol. 1. West Carrolton, Ohio: Checker Books, 2007.

———. "The Story of Hungry Henrietta." In *Little Sammy Sneeze: The Complete Color Sunday Comics 1904–1905*, edited by Peter Maresca. Palo Alto: Sunday Press Books, 2007.

McGruder, Aaron. *A Right to Be Hostile: The Boondocks Treasury*. New York: Three Rivers, 2003.

Meyer, Louis. *The American Butterfly: A Comic Song with a Point*. Philadelphia: F. A. North, 1883. Library of Congress Performing Arts Databases. Accessed January 5, 2015. http://lcweb2.loc.gov/diglib/ihas/loc.music.sm1883.25185.

Outcault, R. F. *Buster Brown, 1906*. Westport, Conn.: Hyperion, 1977.

———. *Pore Lil Mose: His Letters to His Mammy*. Brooklyn: Grand Union Tea, 1902.

Riis, Jacob. "How the Other Half Lives: Studies among the Tenements of New York." 1890. In *How the Other Half Lives*, edited by Hasia R. Diner, 1–165. New York: W. W. Norton, 2010.

Rohmer, Sax [pseud. Arthur Ward]. *The Insidious Dr. Fu Manchu*. New York: McBride, Nast, 1913.

Roosevelt, Theodore. "On American Motherhood." National Congress of Mothers. Washington, D.C. March 13, 1905.

Shakespeare, William. *As You Like It*. Edited by Jack R. Crawford. New Haven, Conn.: Yale University Press, 1919.

Skelly, J. P. *Little Ah Sid: Great Chinese Song and Dance*. New York: Richard A. Saafield, 1883. Library of Congress Performing Arts Databases. Accessed January 5, 2015. http://lcweb2.loc.gov/diglib/ihas/loc.music.sm1883.11489.

Stevenson, Robert Louis. *A Child's Garden of Verses*. 1885. New York: Charles Scribner's Sons, 1905.

———. *Virginibus Puerisque and Other Papers*. Boston: Small, Maynard, 1907.

Stowe, Harriet Beecher. *Uncle Tom's Cabin: Or, Life among the Lowly*. 1852. Cambridge, Mass.: Harvard University Press, 2009.

"Strange Children to Parade at Fair." *St. Louis Post-Dispatch*, July 31, 1904, 12.

Sully, James. *Studies of Childhood*. New York: D. Appleton, 1910.

The Ten Little Niggers. New York: McLoughlin Bros, circa 1878. Baldwin Library of Historical Children's Literature in the Department of Special Collections and Area Studies, George A. Smathers Libraries, University of Florida.

Twain, Mark. *The Adventures of Tom Sawyer*. 1876. Berkeley: University of California Press, 1980.

Wald, Lillian D. *The House on Henry Street*. 1915. New York: Dover, 1971.

Watterson, Bill. "The Cheapening of the Comics." Festival of Cartoon Art. Ohio State University, October 27, 1989.

———. *The Indispensable Calvin and Hobbes: A Calvin and Hobbes Treasury*. Kansas City, Mich.: Andrews and McMeel, 1992.

SECONDARY SOURCES

Abate, Michelle Ann, and Gwen Athene Tarbox, eds. *Graphic Novels for Children and Young Adults: A Collection of Critical Essays*. Jackson: University Press of Mississippi, 2017.

Alschuler, Albert W. *Law without Values: The Life, Work, and Legacy of Justice Holmes*. Chicago: University of Chicago Press, 2000.

Appel, John. "Abie the Agent, Gimpl the Matchmaker, Berl Schliemazel, et al." In *Ethnic Images in the Comics*, edited by Charles Hardy and Gail F. Stern, 15–20. Philadelphia: Balch Institute for Ethnic Studies, 1986.

Aron, Cindy S. *Working at Play: A History of Vacations in the United States*. New York: Oxford University Press, 2001.

Azuma, Eiichiro. *Between Two Empires: Race, History, and Transnationalism in Japanese America*. New York: Oxford University Press, 2005.

Bakhtin, Mikhail. *Rabelais and His World*. Translated by Hélène Iswolsky. 1968. Reprint. Bloomington: Indiana University Press, 1984.

Balzer, Jens. "'Hully Gee, I'm a Heiroglyphe'—Mobilizing the Gaze and the Invention of the Comics in New York City, 1895." In *Comics and the City: Urban Space in Print, Picture and Sequence*, edited by Jörn Ahrens and Arno Meteling, 19–31. New York: Continuum International, 2010.

Banner, Lois W. *American Beauty*. New York: Alfred A. Knopf, 1983.

Banta, Martha. *Barbaric Intercourse: Caricature and the Culture of Conduct, 1841–1936*. Chicago: University of Chicago Press, 2003.

"The Bauhaus, 1919–1933." Metropolitan Museum of Art. Accessed January 31, 2015. http://www.metmuseum.org/toah/hd/bauh/hd_bauh.htm.

Bernstein, Robin. *Racial Innocence: Performing American Childhood from Slavery to Civil Rights*. New York: New York University Press, 2011.

Bhabha, Homi. *The Location of Culture*. Oxford: Routledge, 2005.

Blackbeard, Bill. *R. F. Outcault's The Yellow Kid: A Centennial Celebration of the Kid Who Started the Comics*. Northampton: Kitchen Sink Press, 1995.

Blackbeard, Bill, and Martin Williams, eds. *The Smithsonian Collection of Newspaper Comics*. Washington, D.C.: Smithsonian Institution Press, 1977.

Blackford, Holly. "Apertures in the House of Fiction: Novel Methods and Child Study, 1870–1910." *Children's Literature Association Quarterly* 32, no. 4 (2007): 368–389.

Blackford, Holly, ed. *100 Years of Anne with an "e": The Centennial Study of* Anne of Green Gables. Calgary: University of Calgary Press, 2009.

Boskin, Joseph, and Joseph Dorinson. "Ethnic Humor: Subversion and Survival." *American Quarterly* 37, no. 1 (1985): 81–97.

Breitbart, Eric. *A World on Display: Photographs from the St. Louis World's Fair, 1904*. Albuquerque: University of New Mexico Press, 1997.

Bukatman, Scott. "Little Utopias of Disorder." *American Art* 25, no. 2 (2011): 11–14.

Burns, Sarah. *Pastoral Inventions: Rural Life in Nineteenth-Century American Art and Culture*. Philadelphia: Temple University Press, 1989.

Cahan, Emily D. "Toward a Socially Relevant Science: Notes on the History of Child Development Research." In *When Science Encounters the Child: Education, Parenting and Child Welfare in 20th-Century America*, edited by Barbara Beatty, Emily D. Cahan, and Julia Grant, 16–34. New York: Teachers College Press, 2006.

Camfield, Gregg. *Necessary Madness: The Humor of Domesticity in Nineteenth-Century American Literature*. New York: Oxford University Press, 1997.

Campanelli, John. "'Calvin and Hobbes' Fans Still Pine 15 Years after Its Exit." *Plain Dealer*, February 1, 2010. Accessed January 31, 2015. https://www.cleveland.com/living/index.ssf/2010/02/fans_still_pine_for_calvin_and.html.

Campbell, W. Joseph. *Yellow Journalism: Puncturing the Myths, Defining the Legacies*. Westport, Conn.: Praeger, 2001.

Canemaker, John. *Winsor McCay: His Life and Art*. New York: Harry N. Abrams, 2005.

Chang, Iris. *The Chinese in America: A Narrative History*. New York: Penguin, 2003.

Chinn, Sarah E. *Inventing Modern Adolescence: The Children of Immigrants in Turn-of-the-Century America*. New Brunswick, N.J.: Rutgers University Press, 2009.

Clark, Beverly Lyon. *Kiddie Lit: The Cultural Construction of Children's Literature in America*. Baltimore: Johns Hopkins University Press, 2003.

Cohoon, Lorinda B. *Serialized Citizenships: Periodicals, Books, and American Boys, 1840–1911*. Lanham, Md.: Scarecrow, 2006.

Connolly-Smith, Peter. "Casting Teutonic Types from the Nineteenth Century to World War I: German Ethnic Stereotypes in Print, on Stage, and Screen." *Columbia Journal of American Studies*. Accessed August 31, 2013. http://www.columbia.edu/cu/cjas/conolly-smith-1.html.

Cornwell, Nancy C., and Mark P. Orbe. "'Keepin' It Real' and/or 'Sellin' Out to the Man': African-American Responses to Aaron McGruder's *The Boondocks*." In *Say It Loud! African-American Audiences, Media and Identity*, edited by Robin R. Means Coleman, 27–43. New York: Routledge, 2002.

Cross, Gary. *The Cute and the Cool: Wondrous Innocence and Modern American Children's Culture*. New York: Oxford University Press, 2004.

Damon-Moore, Helen. *Magazines for Millions: Gender and Commerce in the* Ladies' Home Journal *and the* Saturday Evening Post, *1880–1910*. Albany: State University of New York Press, 1992.

Dean, Carolyn. "Boys and Girls and 'Boys': Popular Depictions of African-American Children and Childlike Adults in the United States, 1850–1930." *Journal of American and Comparative Cultures* 23, no. 3 (2002): 17–35.

Derleth, August, ed. *The Katzenjammer Kids: Early Strips in Full Color*. New York: Dover, 1974.

Diner, Steven J. *A Very Different Age: Americans of the Progressive Era*. New York: Hill and Wang, 1998.

Duane, Anna Mae. *Suffering Childhood in Early America: Violence, Race, and the Making of the Child Victim*. Athens: University of Georgia Press, 2011.

Dusinberre, Juliet. *Alice to the Lighthouse: Children's Books and Radical Experiments in Art*. New York: St. Martin's, 1987.

Dyer, Richard. *White*. London: Routledge, 1997.

Earles, Melvin P. "The Introduction of Hydrocyanic Acid into Medicine: A Study in the History of Clinical Pharmacology." *Medical History* 11, no. 3 (1967): 305–313.

Entin, Joseph. "'Unhuman Humanity': Bodies of the Urban Poor and the Collapse of Realist Legibility." *Novel: A Forum on Fiction* 34, no. 3 (2001): 313–337.

Fass, Paula S. "Foreword." In *Children and Youth during the Gilded Age and Progressive Era*, edited by James Marten, vii–ix. New York: New York University Press, 2014.

Filene, Peter G. *Him/Her/Self: Gender Identities in Modern America*. Baltimore: Johns Hopkins University Press, 1998.

Fischer, Roger A. *Them Damned Pictures: Explorations in American Political Cartoon Art*. North Haven, Conn.: Archon, 1996.

Flanagan, Maureen A. *America Reformed: Progressives and Progressivisms, 1890s-1920s*. New York: Oxford University Press, 2007.

Formanek-Brunell, Miriam. "The Politics of Dollhood in Nineteenth-Century America." In *The Children's Culture Reader*, edited by Henry Jenkins, 363–381. New York: New York University Press, 1998.

Foster, Shirley, and Judy Simons. *What Katy Read: Feminist Re-readings of "Classic" Stories for Girls*. London: Palgrave Macmillan, 1995.

Gardner, Jared. *Projections: Comics and the History of Twenty-First-Century Storytelling*. Redwood: Stanford University Press, 2012.

———. "Same Difference: Graphic Alterity in the Work of Gene Luen Yang, Adrian Tomine, and Derek Kirk Kim." In *Multicultural Comics: From Zap to Blue Beetle*, edited by Frederick Luis Aldama, 132–147. Austin: University of Texas Press, 2010.

Gerstle, Gary. *American Crucible: Race and Nation in the Twentieth Century*. Princeton: Princeton University Press, 2001.

Gilman, Charlotte Perkins. *Women and Economics*. Edited by Carl N. Degler. 1898. New York: Harper and Row, 1996.

Ginsberg, Elaine K. "Introduction." In *Passing and the Fictions of Identity*, edited by Elaine K. Ginsberg, 1–18. Durham: Duke University Press, 1996.

Goings, Kenneth W. *Mammy and Uncle Mose: Black Collectibles and American Stereotyping*. Bloomington: Indiana University Press, 1994.

Gordon, Ian. *Comic Strips and Consumer Culture, 1890–1945*. Washington, D.C.: Smithsonian Institution Press, 1998.

———. *Kid Comic Strips: A Genre Across Four Countries*. New York: Palgrave Macmillan, 2016.

Gould, Stephen Jay. *The Mismeasure of Man*. New York: W. W. Norton, 1996.

Grace, Kevin. *Gemutlikeit, Schnitzelbank, and Kitsch: German American Caricature in Vintage Postcards*. University of Cincinnati Libraries, 2010. Accessed July 6, 2018. http://www.libraries.uc.edu/content/dam/libraries/arb/docs/german-americana/gemutlikeit-schnitzelbank-and-kitsch.pdf.

Hales, Peter Bacon. *Silver Cities: Photographing American Urbanization, 1839–1939*. Albuquerque: University of New Mexico Press, 2005.

Harvey, Robert C. *The Art of the Funnies: An Aesthetic History*. Jackson: University Press of Mississippi, 1994.

———. *Children of the Yellow Kid: The Evolution of the American Comic Strip*. Seattle: University of Washington Press, 1999.

———. "Comedy at the Juncture of Word and Image: The Emergence of the Modern Magazine Gag Cartoon Reveals the Vital Blend." In *The Language of Comics: Word and Image*, edited by Robin Varnum and Christina T. Gibbons, 75–96. Jackson: University Press of Mississippi, 2001.

Hatfield, Charles. *Alternative Comics: An Emerging Literature*. Jackson: University Press of Mississippi, 2005.

———. "Comic Art, Children's Literature, and the New Comic Studies." *The Lion and the Unicorn* 30, no. 3 (2006): 360–382.

———. "Redrawing the Comic Strip Child: Charles M. Schulz's *Peanuts* as Cross-Writing." In *The Oxford Handbook of Children's Literature*, edited by Julia L. Mickenberg and Lynne Vallone, 165–187. New York: Oxford University Press, 2011.

Havig, Alan. "Richard F. Outcault's 'Poor Lil' Mose': Variations on the Black Stereotype in American Comic Art." *Journal of American Culture* 11, no. 1 (1988): 33–41.

Hawes, Joseph M., and Elizabeth I. Nybakken, eds. *Family and Society in American History*. Urbana: University of Illinois Press, 2001.

Heer, Jeet, and Kent Worcester, eds. *Arguing Comics: Literary Masters on a Popular Medium*. Jackson: University Press of Mississippi, 2004.

Heimermann, Mark, and Brittany Tullis, eds. *Picturing Childhood: Youth in Transnational Comics*. Austin: University of Texas Press, 2017.

Heininger, Mary Lynn Stevens. "Children, Childhood, and Change in America, 1820–1920." In *A Century of Childhood, 1820–1920*, 1–32. Rochester: Margaret Woodbury Strong Museum, 1984.

Henricks, Thomas. "The Nature of Play: An Overview." *American Journal of Play* 1, no. 2 (2008): 157–180.

Higham, John. *Strangers in the Land: Patterns of American Nativism, 1860–1925*. New Brunswick, N.J.: Rutgers University Press, 1983.

Higonnet, Anne. *Pictures of Innocence: The History and Crisis of Ideal Childhood*. London: Thames and Hudson, 1998.

Higonnet, Margaret R. "Modernism and Childhood: Violence and Renovation." *The Comparatist* 33 (2009): 86–108.

Horn, Maurice. *75 Years of Comics*. Boston: Boston Book and Art, 1971.

Ichioka, Yuji. *The Issei: The World of the First Generation of Japanese Immigrants, 1885–1924*. New York: Free Press, 1988.

Inge, M. Thomas. *Comics as Culture*. Jackson: University Press of Mississippi, 1990.

Jenks, Chris. *Childhood*. London: Routledge, 1996.

Johns, Elizabeth. *American Genre Painting: The Politics of Everyday Life*. New Haven: Yale University Press, 1991.

Kidd, Kenneth. *Making American Boys: Boyology and the Feral Tale*. Minneapolis: University of Minnesota Press, 2004.

Kincaid, James. *Child-Loving: The Erotic Child and Victorian Culture*. New York: Routledge, 1992.

Klapper, Melissa R. *Small Strangers: The Experiences of Immigrant Children in America, 1880–1925*. Chicago: Ivan R. Dee, 2007.

Kuznets, Lois R. *When Toys Come Alive: Narratives of Animation, Metamorphosis, and Development*. New Haven, Conn.: Yale University Press, 1994.

Lasch, Christopher. *Haven in a Heartless World: The Family Besieged*. New York: Basic Books, 1977.

Lasch-Quinn, Elisabeth. *Black Neighbors: Race and the Limits of Reform in the American Settlement House Movement, 1890–1945*. Chapel Hill: University of North Carolina Press, 1993.

Lears, Jackson. *Rebirth of a Nation: The Making of Modern America, 1877–1920*. New York: HarperCollins, 2009.

Lee, Robert G. *Orientals: Asian Americans in Popular Culture*. Philadelphia: Temple University Press, 1999.

Lehman, Christopher P. "Franklin and the Early 1970s." In *The Comics of Charles Schulz: The Good Grief of Modern Life*, edited by Jared Gardner and Ian Gordon, 133–147. Jackson: University Press of Mississippi, 2017.

Leonard, Thomas C. *Illiberal Reformers: Race, Eugenics, and American Economics in the Progressive Era*. Princeton: Princeton University Press, 2016.

Leveen, Lois. "Only When I Laugh: Textual Dynamics of Ethnic Humor." *MELUS* 21, no. 4 (1996): 29–55.

Lott, Eric. *Love and Theft: Blackface Minstrelsy and the American Working Class*. New York: Oxford University Press, 1993.

Lowe, John. "Theories of Ethnic Humor: How to Enter, Laughing." *American Quarterly* 38, no. 3 (1986): 439–460.

Lubin, David M. *Picturing a Nation: Art and Social Change in Nineteenth-Century America*. New Haven, Conn.: Yale University Press, 1994.

Luebke, Frederick C. *Germans in the New World: Essays in the History of Immigration*. Urbana: University of Illinois Press, 1990.

Lynch-Brennan, Margaret. *The Irish Bridget: Irish Immigrant Women in Domestic Service in America, 1840–1930*. Syracuse, N.Y.: Syracuse University Press, 2009.

Macleod, Anne Scott. *American Childhood: Essays on Children's Literature of the Nineteenth and Twentieth Centuries*. Atlanta: University of Georgia Press, 1994.

Marten, James. *Childhood and Child Welfare in the Progressive Era: A Brief History with Documents*. Boston: Bedford and St. Martin's, 2005.

Massing, Jean Michel. "From Greek Proverb to Soap Advert: Washing the Ethiopian." *Journal of the Warburg and Courtauld Institutes* 58 (1995): 180–201.

McCloud, Scott. *Understanding Comics: The Invisible Art*. New York: HarperCollins, 1993.

McGerr, Michael. *A Fierce Discontent: The Rise and Fall of the Progressive Movement in America, 1870–1920*. New York: Free Press, 2003.

Melendy, H. Brett. *The Oriental Americans*. New York: Twayne, 1972.
Miller, Monica L. *Slaves to Fashion: Black Dandyism and the Styling of Black Diasporic Identity*. Durham: Duke University Press, 2009.
Mintz, Steven. *Huck's Raft: A History of American Childhood*. Cambridge, Mass.: Belknap Press of Harvard University Press, 2004.
Mintz, Steven, and Susan Kellogg. *Domestic Revolutions: A Social History of American Family Life*. New York: Free Press, 1988.
Mitchell, Mary Niall. "'Rosebloom and Pure White,' Or So It Seemed." *American Quarterly* 54, no. 3 (2002): 369–410.
Moon, Krystyn R. *Yellowface: Creating the Chinese in American Popular Music and Performance, 1850s–1920s*. New Brunswick, N.J.: Rutgers University Press, 2004.
Moore, Paul S. *Now Playing: Early Moviegoing and the Regulation of Fun*. Albany: State University of New York Press, 2008.
Muhammad, Khalil Gibran. *The Condemnation of Blackness: Race, Crime, and the Making of Modern Urban America*. Cambridge, Mass.: Harvard University Press, 2010.
Nelson, Pamela B. "From Subhuman to Superhuman: Ethnic Characters in Comics." In *Ethnic Images in the Comics*, edited by Charles Hardy and Gail F. Stern, 11–14. Philadelphia: Balch Institute for Ethnic Studies, 1986.
Nickels, Cameron C. *New England Humor: From the Revolutionary War to the Civil War*. Knoxville: University of Tennessee Press, 1993.
Nodelman, Perry. *The Hidden Adult: Defining Children's Literature*. Baltimore: Johns Hopkins University Press, 2008.
Nunes, Jadviga M. Da Costa. "The Naughty Child in Nineteenth-Century American Art." *Journal of American Studies* 21, no. 2 (1987): 225–247.
Nyberg, Amy Kiste. "Percival Chubb and the League for the Improvement of the Children's Comic Supplement." *Inks: Cartoon and Comic Art Studies* 3, no. 3 (1996): 31–34.
Parezo, Nancy J., and Don D. Fowler. *Anthropology Goes to the Fair: The 1904 Louisiana Purchase Exposition*. Lincoln: University of Nebraska Press, 2007.
Paris, Leslie. *Children's Nature: The Rise of the American Summer Camp*. New York: New York University Press, 2008.
Patterson, Martha H., ed. *The American New Woman Revisited: A Reader, 1894–1930*. New Brunswick, N.J.: Rutgers University Press, 2008.
Perry, Claire. *Young America: Childhood in 19th-Century Art and Culture*. New Haven: Yale University Press, 2006.
Pilgrim, David. "The Brute Caricature." Jim Crow Museum of Racist Memorabilia. Ferris State University. 2012. Accessed August 31, 2013. https://ferris.edu/jimcrow/brute/.
———. "The Picaninny Caricature." Jim Crow Museum of Racist Memorabilia. Ferris State University. 2012. Accessed August 31, 2013. https://ferris.edu/HTMLS/news/jimcrow/antiblack/picaninny/homepage.htm.
Postman, Neil. *The Disappearance of Childhood*. New York: Delacorte, 1982.
Rambsy, Howard, II. "The Vengeance of Black Boys: How Richard Wright, Paul Beatty, and Aaron McGruder Strike Back." *Mississippi Quarterly: The Journal of Southern Cultures* 61, no. 4 (2008): 643–657.
Robb, Jenny, and Richard D. Olson. "Madge's Magic: A Look at a Forgotten Graphic Masterpiece." *Hogan's Alley: The Magazine of the Cartoon Arts*, April 9, 2013. Accessed January 22, 2015. http://cartoonician.com/madges-magic-a-look-at-a-forgotten-graphic-masterpiece/.
Robbins, Trina. *The Brinkley Girls: The Best of Nell Brinkley's Cartoons from 1913–1940*. Seattle: Fantagraphics, 2009.
———. *Nell Brinkley and the New Woman in the Early 20th Century*. Jefferson, N.C.: McFarland, 2001.
Roeder, Katherine. "Seeing Inside-out in the Funny Pages." *American Art* 25, no. 1 (2011): 24–27.

———. *Wide Awake in Slumberland: Fantasy, Mass Culture, and Modernism in the Art of Winsor McCay*. Jackson: University Press of Mississippi, 2014.

Rourke, Constance. "The Yankee." In *What's So Funny? Humor in American Culture*, edited by Nancy A. Walker, 83–89. Wilmington: Scholarly Resources, 1998.

Rubin, Louis D., Jr. "The Great American Joke." In *What's So Funny? Humor in American Culture*, edited by Nancy A. Walker, 107–119. Wilmington: Scholarly Resources, 1998.

Rudd, David. "Animal and Object Stories." In *The Cambridge Companion to Children's Literature*, edited by M. O. Grenby and Andrea Immel, 242–257. Cambridge: Cambridge University Press, 2009.

Rydell, Robert W. *All the World's a Fair: Visions of Empire at American International Expositions, 1876–1916*. Chicago: University of Chicago Press, 1984.

Salazar, James B. *Bodies of Reform: The Rhetoric of Character in Gilded Age America*. New York: New York University Press, 2010.

Sanders, Joe Sutliff. *Disciplining Girls: Understanding the Origins of the Classic Orphan Girl Story*. Baltimore: Johns Hopkins University Press, 2011.

Shannon, Edward A. "Something Black in the American Psyche: Formal Innovation and Freudian Imagery in the Comics of Winsor McCay and Robert Crumb." *Canadian Review of American Studies* 40, no. 2 (2010): 187–211.

Sheehan, Tanya. "Comical Conflations: Racial Identity and the Science of Photography." *Photography and Culture* 4, no. 2 (July 2011): 133–156.

Smolderen, Thierry. *The Origins of Comics: From William Hogarth to Winsor McCay*. Translated by Bart Beaty and Nick Nguyen. Jackson: University Press of Mississippi, 2014.

Smulyan, Susan. *Popular Ideologies: Mass Culture at Mid-Century*. Philadelphia: University of Pennsylvania Press, 2007.

Sochen, June. *The New Woman: Feminism in Greenwich Village, 1910–1920*. New York: Quadrangle Books, 1972.

Soper, Kerry. "From Swarthy Ape to Sympathetic Everyman and Subversive Trickster: The Development of Irish Caricature in American Comic Strips between 1890 and 1920." *Journal of American Studies* 39, no. 2 (2005): 257–296.

Southern, David W. *The Progressive Era and Race: Reaction and Reform, 1900–1917*. Wheeling, Ill.: Harlan Davidson, 2005.

Stange, Maren. *Symbols of Ideal Life: Social Documentary Photography in America, 1890–1950*. Cambridge: Cambridge University Press, 1989.

Stearns, Peter N. *Anxious Parents: A History of Modern Childrearing in America*. New York: New York University Press, 2004.

Steedman, Carolyn. *Strange Dislocations: Childhood and the Idea of Human Interiority, 1780–1930*. Cambridge, Mass.: Harvard University Press, 1995.

Stratton, Clif. *Education for Empire: American Schools, Race, and the Paths of Good Citizenship*. Berkeley: University of California Press, 2016.

Styers, Randall. "Mana and Mystification: Magic and Religion at the Turn of the Twentieth Century." *Women's Studies Quarterly* 40, no. 3 and 4 (2012): 226–243.

Tompkins, Kyla Wazana. *Racial Indigestion: Eating Bodies in the 19th Century*. New York: New York University Press, 2012.

Tucker, Terrence T. "Blackness We Can Believe In: Authentic Blackness and the Evolution of Aaron McGruder's *The Boondocks*." In *Post-Soul Satire: Black Identity after Civil Rights*, edited by Derek C. Maus and James J. Donahue, 22–37. Jackson: University Press of Mississippi, 2014.

Valentine, Deborah S. "Playing Progressively? Race, Reform, and Playful Pedagogies in the Origins of Philadelphia's Starr Garden Recreation Park, 1857–1904." In *Children and Youth during the Gilded Age and Progressive Era*, edited by James Marten, 19–41. New York: New York University Press, 2014.

Wajda, Shirley. "A Room with a Viewer: The Parlor Stereoscope, Comic Stereographs, and the Psychic Role of Play in Victorian America." In *Hard at Play: Leisure in America, 1840–1940*, edited by Kathryn Grover, 112–138. Amherst: University of Massachusetts Press; Rochester, N.Y.: Strong Museum, 1992.

Waugh, Colton. *The Comics*. 1947. Jackson: University Press of Mississippi, 1991.

Werner, Emmy E. *Passages to America: Oral Histories of Child Immigrants from Ellis Island and Angel Island*. Washington, D.C.: Potomac Books, 2009.

Wickberg, Daniel. *The Senses of Humor: Self and Laughter in Modern America*. Ithaca, N.Y.: Cornell University Press, 1998.

Winchester, Mark D. "Hully Gee, It's a War!!! The Yellow Kid and the Coining of 'Yellow Journalism.'" *Inks: Cartoon and Comic Art Studies* 2, no. 3 (1995): 22–37.

Wonham, Henry B. *Playing the Races: Ethnic Caricature and American Literary Realism*. Oxford: Oxford University Press, 2004.

Wood, Mary. *The Yellow Kid on the Paper Stage: Acting Out Class Tensions and Racial Divisions in the New Urban Environment*. American Studies in the University of Virginia. February 2, 2004. Accessed February 7, 2017. http://xroads.virginia.edu/~ma04/wood/ykid/yellowkid2.htm.

Yaszek, Lisa. "'Them Damn Pictures': Americanization and the Comic Strip in the Progressive Era." *Journal of American Studies* 28, no. 1 (1994): 23–38.

Yee, Shirley J. *An Immigrant Neighborhood: Interethnic and Interracial Encounters in New York Before 1930*. Philadelphia: Temple University Press, 2012.

Zelizer, Viviana A. *Pricing the Priceless Child: The Changing Social Value of Children*. Princeton: Princeton University Press, 1985.

Zipes, Jack, Lissa Paul, Lynne Vallone, Peter Hunt, and Gillian Avery, eds. *The Norton Anthology of Children's Literature: The Traditions in English*. New York: W. W. Norton, 2005.

Zurier, Rebecca. *Picturing the City: Urban Vision and the Ashcan School*. Berkeley: University of California Press, 2006.

INDEX

Page numbers in *italics* refer to figures.

Abie the Agent, 28, 29
acculturation, 31, 39–41, 43
Addams, Jane, 26, 88
adolescence, 8
adults: and dreams, 120–122; as observing children, 117–118, 136, 141; and perception, 116, 135–136; and race, 53, 68
Adventures of Huckleberry Finn, The, 58–59
advertisements, 91–92, 138, *139*, 167–169, *168*
African Americans: ambivalence toward, 55, 61, 75; as animal-like, 59, 76, 78; as childlike, 59–60; children, as consumable, 61, 202n42; children, potential of, 5, 68; as comics characters, 18, 53, 58–65, 73–76, 78–82, 181–185; marginalization of, 53–55, 74; and progressivism, 9–10; representations of, 17–18; sexualizing of, 67; as threat, 54. *See also under* caricatures; stereotypes
Ah Sid (*Little Ah Sid* character), 36, *39*, *42*, 51
Alice's Adventures in Wonderland, 121, 125–126
"Amateur Circus: The Smallest Show on Earth," 21–23, *22*
American Butterfly: A Comic Song with a Point, The, 36
Americanization, 32, 36, 39–41
Americanness, 31–32, 46
Anne of Green Gables, 9, 154
antiauthoritarianism, 46, 93, 173
Appel, John, 29
Around the World with the Yellow Kid, 3
Asians: as comics characters, 33–36, 37–41; representations of, 24–25, 32–33, 36–37, 197n56; as threat, 33. *See also under* caricatures; stereotypes
assimilation, 25, 27, 30, 36, 39–41, 51
"At the Circus in Hogan's Alley," 19–21, *20*
Aunt Jim-jam (*Kin-der-kids* character), 133
autonomy, 82, 89, 115, 134, 138
awakening, from dreams, 121, 124, 138

Balzer, Jens, 3
Banta, Martha, 12, 27, 28, 196n21
Barrie, J. M., 117, 118
Baum, L. Frank, 117, 128
Bergengren, Ralph, 86, 120
Bernstein, Robin, 57, 173
Betsy Bouncer (*Betsy Bouncer* character), 166–167, 169–173, *171*, *172*
Betsy Bouncer and Her Doll, 18, 166–167, 169–173, *171*, *172*, 215n61
Bhabha, Homi, 13
Billie Bear (*Buster Brown* character), 79, 80
"Blackamoor, The," 66
Blackbeard, Bill, 43, 84–85
Blackberries, The, 53, 58–65, *60*, *62*
"Blackberries Leave for the Country, The," 59–60, *60*
Blackberry children (*Blackberries* characters), 59–65, *60*, *62*, *65*, *73*
"Blackberry Picnic Is Interrupted by an Uninvited Guest, The," 61
blackface, 69–72, 155
Blackford, Holly, 116
blackness, 52, 55, 66–67; as dirty, 66; metaphors of, 61, 63
Bloom County, 182
Boondocks, The, 181–185, *184*
Boskin, Joseph, 28–29
boyhood, 46, 53, 85, 97, 102, 131
boys: and masculinity, 9; naughty, 43, 46, 85, 96–98, 100, 102–103, 142–143, 176

Brace, Charles Loring, 26
Breathed, Berkeley, 182
Bringing Up Father, 28, 29–31, *31*
Brinkley, Nell, 196–197n36
Brinkley Girl, 31, 196–197n36
Buddy and Alice, 143
Bukatman, Scott, 124, 140
Burns, Sarah, 97
Busch, Wilhelm, 43–44
Bushmiller, Ernie, 176
Buster Brown (*Buster Brown* character), 18, 52–53, 55, *55*, 68–69, 82, *83*, 84–85, *89*, 89–110, *95*, *104*, *107*, *111*, 147, *148*, 149, 179; commercialization of, 84, 106, 108; as compassionate, 100–101
Buster Brown, 18, 28, 52–53, 55, *55*, 68–69, 82, *83*, 85–113, *89*, *95*, *99*, *104*, *107*, *111*, 142, 147, *148*, 149; as boy work, 97; as conservative, 85; and gender, 98, 100, 110; and immigrants, 94, 96; as inspiration, 170–171; secondary characters, 28; as subversive, 84–85; success of, 106; as teaching, 92–93
"Buster Brown Again. His Parents Fool Him," 106, *107*
"Buster Brown and His Faithful Friend Tige," 103
"Buster Brown and Pore Lil Mose," *83*
"Buster Brown Frightens His Parents," 105
"Buster Brown Gets Another Joke on the Doctor," 103, *104*, 105
"Buster Brown Has a Birthday Party," 89–90, *89*
"Buster Brown Helps Santa Claus," 101
"Buster Brown Helps the New Cook to Bake a Cake," 110
"Buster Brown Just Fixes Up His Mama's Hair Tonic," 110, *111*
"Buster Brown—Photographer," 94, *95*, 96
"Buster Brown Plays a Trick in a London Hotel," 101
"Buster Brown Suffers, but Doesn't Get a Beating," 93, 103
"Buster Brown's Valentine," 100
"Buster Brown Visits the Zoo and Talks to the Stork," 147, *148*, 164

Cahan, Emily, 117
Calvin (*Calvin and Hobbes* character), 167, 176–181, *177*, *180*, 183–184, 185, 215n61
Calvin and Hobbes, 167, 176–181, *177*, *180*, 183, 215n61
Camfield, Gregg, 14, 90–91
Canemaker, John, 122
capitalism, 6, 7, 97, 178
caricatures, 5, 11–13, 17, 27–28, 35, 39, 196n21; African American, 53, 56–59, 73; Asian, 33, 37–38, 133; female, 145; German, 45–46; as infantilizing, 5, 13, 24, 25, 60, 129; Irish, 29–30, 94
Carr, Gene, 151
Carroll, Lewis, 118, 121
cartoons. *See* comics
Cedric Errol (*Little Lord Fauntleroy* character), 100, 101–102
Chang, Iris, 38
characters: development of, 58; individuality of, 3, 80; as interactive, 3, 35–36, 135, 137; polysemic, 15; recurring, 3, 43, 58, 122; secondary, 28; tricksters, 30
Charlie Brown (*Peanuts* character), 179
Chicago Tribune, 108, 132–133
childhood: black vs. white, 52–53, 55–56, 57, 69, 181–182, 185; and comics development, 1, 4, 16–17; as ephemeral, 125–126; government involvement, 8; healthy, 56; ideal vs. reality, 180–181; as innocent, 5, 8, 19, 26, 183; as male, 212; markers of, 8; as metaphor, 13–14; modern, 179, 181; pure, 18; theorizing, 115, 136; as threatened, 177–178; universality of, 52–53, 68–69
child labor, 9, 10–11
child psychology. *See* developmental psychology
child-rearing, 9, 106, 156–157
children: and animals, 76, 78, 101, 169–170; as comics focus, 4, 13–14; as creative, 5, 178–179; and culture norms, 31–32; imaginative, 114–116, 128, 135, 141; as impressionable, 87; as inspiration, 108, 118, 119, 136; as misbehaving, 5, 18, 87; and perception, 116–117, 135–136; potential of, 17, 98; as primitive adults, 24–25; and race, 52–53, 55–56, 67, 80, 81, 127; response to comics, 110, 112; roles of, 16. *See also* boys; girls
children's literature, 16–17, 116–119; on boys, 97, 142; fantasy, 114–115; German, 43; on girls, 9, 154, 166, 193n27; modernist, 126
child-savers, 8, 9, 10, 26
Child's Garden of Verses, A, 127
child's kingdom, 129
"Child's Play," 116
child study, 9, 115, 117–118; and race, 127. *See also* developmental psychology
Chinese Exclusion Act of 1882, 27, 33
Chinn, Sarah E., 31–32
Chubb, Percival, 19, 84, 86–88
cities, 2, 7, 73, 75, 79–80, 97

citizenship, 5, 8; and African Americans, 54, 61; defining, 17; ineligibility for, 36; narratives of, 10
Clark, Beverly Lyon, 101–102
Cohoon, Lorinda B., 100
comic rage, 185
comics: and caricature, 12–13; child-centered, 1–6, 13–14, 176; color use, 3, 122; as containing threats, 55; disapproval of, 19, 84, 86–88, 185; and ethnicity, 27–32; fantasy, 115–116, 118–122, 132; formats, 175; functions of, 4, 12, 93; girl-centered, 143–144, 173; gutter spaces, 12; literary influences, 16–17, 43; misreadings of, 28; multiple readings of, 15–16; panel layout, 12–13, 43, 58, 124, 138; as political, 182; and race, 24, 33–41, 181; and realism, 21; sequential, 12; social relevance of, 19–23; tensions in, 11; and visibility, 56. *See also* *individual comics*
commercialization, 3, 178
Connolly-Smith, Peter, 45
consumer culture, 3–4, 6, 39–41, 169, 178; and African Americans, 59–60; and girls, 155
consumerism, 60, 167; rejection of, 169
Contents of Children's Minds on Entering School, The, 116–117
Coon Alphabet, A, 59
coquettes, 158–160
Cornwell, Nancy C., 185
Cousin Gussie (*Kin-der-kids* character), 133
Creet, Ernest, 80–81
Cross, Gary, 100, 158

Dangerous Classes of New York, and Twenty Years' Work among Them, The, 26
daydreams, 134–137, 176, 178–179
Dean, Carolyn, 60, 61, 65
Delia (*Buster Brown* character), 94, *95*, 96
Derleth, August, 44
developmental psychology, 18, 115, 116–119
dialect, 66, 73, 75, 81, 132
Dirks, Rudolph, 25, 28, 43–44, 46, 64–66, 202n49. See also *Katzenjammer Kids, The*
Disappearance of Childhood, The, 177–178
distancing, 20, 30
Dixon, Thomas, Jr., 54
dolls, 167–173
domestic ideology, 88–91
Dorinson, Joseph, 28–29
Dottie Dimple, 158, *159*
"Dottie Dimple Gives Her Nice Dress to a Poor Girl!," *159*
"Do You Want to Join a Buster Brown Club?," 108, 110
dreams, 115–116, 119–122, 125, 126–127, 131–132, 183–184; of adults, 120–122; realms of, 119, 121, 124–125, 129, 178. *See also* daydreams
Dreams of the Rarebit Fiend, 120–122, *123*
Dusinberre, Juliet, 116
Dutch Act, 45

Earle, Augusti S., 114
education, 86
empathy, 25, 56, 73
Entin, Joseph, 20–21
equality, 17
eugenics, 9–10, 27
Evening Telegram, 120

family, 84–85, 180; companionate, 85, 88–89, 90, 112; crisis in, 86–88; dynamics, 8, 71, 87–88; redefining, 88–89; resilience of, 93–94; threats to, 147
fantasy, 114–116, 118–119, 178–179, 184; and race, 183–184; vs. reality, 136–137
Fass, Paula S., 8
fathers, 90; as comics characters, 161–162, 179–180. *See also* Mr. Brown
Feininger, Lyonel, 133, 138, 211n84. See also *Kin-der-kids, The*; *Wee Willie Winkie's World*
Filene, Peter, 90, 213n11
Fischer, Roger A., 27
Flanagan, Maureen A., 7
Flip (*Little Nemo* character), 71–72, *130*, 131, *140*, 203n80
Formanek-Brunell, Miriam, 169, 170
Foxy Grandpa, *69*, 69–71
Franklin (*Peanuts* character), 182–183
Freud, Sigmund, 122, 136
Fritzi Ritz, 212–213n3
Fu Manchu (Sax Rohmer character), 33

Gardner, Jared, 12–13, 31
Gasoline Alley, 175
Gassaway, Katharine, 76
gender, 9, 23, 37, 59, 110, 164, 212–213n2–3; expectations, 18, 100
generation gap, 31
genre painting, 96–97, 100
gentrification, of comics, 15, 18–19
German Americans, 44–46, 65–66, 132–133, 202n49
Gerstle, Gary, 17
Gertie the Dinosaur, 137–138
Gibson, Charles Dana, 150
Gibson Girl, 103, 150, 196–197n36

Gilman, Charlotte Perkins, 150
girlhood, 154–155; vs. boyhood, 100; contradictions of, 172; ideals of, 157, 158; as innocent, 167
girls: and *Buster Brown*, 110; as comics characters, 18, 23, 98, 143–144, 155–162, 164, 166–167, 169–174, 206–207n54, 212–213n2–3; as comics readers, 144–145; as good, 100, 130, 167; opportunities for, 9, 155; orphan, 154; roles of, 144
Goings, Kenneth W., 59
Gold Dust Twins, 67
"Golf—The Great Society Sport as Played in Hogan's Alley," 2, 2–3, 13–14
Gordon, Ian, 4, 15, 43, 79, 80–81, 106, 108
Grace, Kevin, 45
grandfathers, in comics, 38–41, 69–71, 156–157
Grandpa Lee (*Little Ah Sid* character), 36, *39*, 39–41, *42*
graphic alterity, 12
Gray, Harold, 175, 212–213n3
"Greedy Lil Mose," 81
Greening, Harry, 43

Hales, Peter Bacon, 21
Hall, G. Stanley, 8–9, 116–117, 125, 135
Hans and Fritz Katzenjammer (*Katzenjammer Kids* characters), 43, 44–51, *47*, *48*, *50*, 64–66, *65*
Happy Hooligan, 28, 29, 30–31, 48, 49
Hart, John F., 24, 33–34. See also *Little Jap "It"*
Hatfield, Charles, 11, 16, 85
Havig, Alan, 73, 79
Hawes, Joseph M., 89
Hearst, William Randolph, 4, 119
"He Buys His Mammy a Hat," 79
"He Comes to New York," 75
Heer, Jeet, 86
Heininger, Mary Lynn Stevens, 100
Heniger, Alice Minnie Herts, 118
Henricks, Thomas, 170
Henrietta (*Story of Hungry Henrietta* character), 155–158, *156*
Hershfield, Harry, 28, 29
"He Visits the Suburbs—and Frightens a Native," 79–80
hierarchies: familial, 85; racial, 33, 71; social, 29
Higonnet, Anne, 100
Higonnet, Margaret, 126, 136
"His New Goat Breaks Up Mamma's Tea Party and a Few Other Things," 102
Hobbes (*Calvin and Hobbes* character), 167, 176, *180*, 215n61
Hoffman, Heinrich, 199n93
Hogan's Alley, 2, 2–4, 19–23, *20*, *22*
Hogarth, William, 2
Holt, L. Emmett, 157
House on Henry Street, The, 51
Howarth, F. M., 43
How the Other Half Lives: Studies among the Tenements of New York, 14, 20–21, 26
Huey Freeman (*Boondocks* character), 181, 182–184, *184*
humanizing, 75
humor, 11, 21, 90; as bonding, 85, 91–93, 94, 96, 176; as denigrating, 27; domestic, 85, 90–91; ethnic, 27–32; functions of, 14–16, 27; literary, 85, 91; sympathetic, 85

Ichioka, Yuji, 36
imagination, 115–116, 126, 134, 185; of adults, 141; as natural, 135; vs. reality, 137; as redemptive, 131–132
immigrants: adult, 26, 28, 39–41; caricature responses, 28–29; as cartoonists, 28–31, 202n49; children, defense of, 10, 51; children, potential of, 5, 10, 25, 26, 51; as comics characters, 43–51; conflicts between, 33, 35, 48–49; as dangerous, 26, 28, 147; and ethnic humor, 27–30; family dynamics, 32, 40–41, 41, 46–48, 49, 193n33; marginalization of, 94; and progressivism, 9–10; representations of, 2–3, 13–14, 17, 24–25, 94, 96
Imp (*Little Nemo* character), 129–130, *130*, *140*
imperialism, 127–129
impersonation, racial, 52–53, 64–72, 200n3
individualism, 6, 80, 89
Inge, M. Thomas, 131
innocence, 5–6, 38; and African Americans, 10, 57; universality of, 14, 19; as white, 53, 82, 183
Interpretation of Dreams, The, 122
In the Land of Wonderful Dreams. See *Little Nemo in Slumberland*
Irish Americans, 30–32
Issei, 33, 36
"'It,' the Little Jap, Routs the Enemy with His War Dragon," 34, *34*
"'It' Has an Encounter with Foreign Dogs, and Wins," 34–35

Japanese Americans. *See* Issei
Jap It (*Little* Jap "It" character), 24–25, 33–36, *34*
Jenks, Chris, 78, 82
Jiggs (*Bringing Up Father* character), 30–31

Johns, Elizabeth, 102
Judge, 43

Katzenjammer Kids, The, 25, 43–51, *47*, *48*, *50*, 65, 93, 202; and race, 64–66
"Katzenjammer Kids Change Clothes with the Blackberry Brothers, The," 64–66, *65*, 66–68, 69–70
"Katzenjammer Kids in School, The," 49, *50*, 51
"Katzenjammer Kids Rob Happy Hooligan's Nephews of Their Christmas Pie, The," 48–49
Kellogg, Susan, 85, 88, 112
Kemble, E. W., 58–59. See also *Blackberries, The*
Keppler, Joseph, 29–30
Kidd, Kenneth, 97
Kincaid, James, 159
Kin-der-kids, The, 133; advertisement for, 138, *139*
King, Frank, 175
Kingdom of the Child, The, 118
Klapper, Melissa, 25, 31, 41, 43, 193n33
Kuznets, Lois R., 170, 172, 179

Lady Bountiful (Gene Carr character), 151–152
Lasch, Christopher, 90
Lasch-Quinn, Elisabeth, 54
League for the Improvement of the Children's Comic Supplement, 88
Lehman, Christopher P., 182–183
Leveen, Lois, 28
liminality, 24–25, 51, 53, 76
Little Ah Sid, the Chinese Kid, 25, 32, 36–41, *39*, *42*, 51, 197n56
Little Jap "It," 24–25, 32, 33–36, *34*
Little Lord Fauntleroy, 100
Little Nemo in Slumberland, 18, 115–116, 119–122, *124*, 124–128, *128*, 129–132, *130*, *132*, *140*; influences on, 119–120; as inspiration, 160; and minstrelsy, 71–72; as nostalgic, 125–126; as self-reflexive, 137, 138; as utopic, 140–141
Little Orphan Annie, 175–176, 212–213n3
"Little Rogues Pretend They Are Pickaninnies, but a Good-Sized Darkey Gives Them Quite a Fright, The," *69*, 69–71
Lost Princess of Oz, The, 128
Lott, Eric, 57–58, 70
Lowe, John, 27
Lubin, David M., 96
Lucy and Sophie Say Goodbye, 151
Luks, George, 4
Lynch-Brennan, Margaret, 94

Madge the Magician's Daughter, 18, 160–162, *163*, 164, *165*
magazines, 5, 11–12, 27, 29, 91
Maggie (*Bringing Up Father* character), 30–31
magic, 160, 161–162, 164
malleability, of children, 5, 10, 23, 25, 32
Mamma Katzenjammer (*Katzenjammer Kids* character), 44, 46–48, *47*, *48*, 49, 65, 66–68, 103, 150
"Mamma Katzenjammer Makes a New Year's Resolution," *48*
"Mamma Katzenjammer Plays a Boomerang Trick," 46–47, *47*
Mammy (*Blackberries* character), 59–60, *60*, 65, 67
Marble, Annie Russell, 86
marginalization, 94, 185
Marten, James, 26
Mary Jane (*Buster Brown* character), 98, *99*, 143
masculinity, 9, 100, 101–102
Massing, Jean Michel, 66
"Mass Meeting of the Buster Browns, A," 108, *109*, 110
Max und Moritz: Eine Bubengeschichte in sieben Streichen (*Max and Moritz: A Juvenile History in Seven Tricks*), 43–44
Mayer, Henry "Hy," 120
McCay, Robert, 119, 128–129
McCay, Winsor, 119, 122, 137, 138. See also *Dreams of the Rarebit Fiend*; *Gertie the Dinosaur*; *Little Nemo in Slumberland*; *Story of Hungry Henrietta, The*
McCloud, Scott, 12
McFadden's Row of Flats, 3
McGerr, Michael, 7–8
McGruder, Aaron, 181–182, 185. See also *Boondocks, The*
McManus, George, 28, 29
Melendy, H. Brett, 33
metacomedy, 115–116, 137, 138
middle class, 7–8, 9–11, 26, 90–94; in comics, 21–23, 85, 97, 119; markers of, 60
minstrelsy, 57–58, 70–71, 81
Mintz, Steven, 9, 40, 85, 88, 112, 118
Mitchell, Mary Niall, 57
molding, of children, 5, 7, 14, 25
Morton, Samuel George, 24
Mose (*Pore Lil Mose* character), 18, 53, 73–76, *74*, *76*, 77–82, *83*, 204n115
motherhood, 147, 149, 164; ideal of, 68, 102
mothers, 90, 117–118; as comics characters, 22, 46, 52, 68, 102–103; as ineffective, 22, 102–103. *See also* Mamma Katzenjammer; Mammy; Mrs. Brown

Mr. Brown (*Buster Brown* character), 82, *83*, *89*, 89–90, 105–106, *107*
Mrs. Brown (*Buster Brown* character), 68, *89*, 90, 95, 102–103, *104*, 105–106, *107*, *111*, 147, *148*, 149–150
Mrs. Katzenjammer. *See* Mamma Katzenjammer
"Mrs. Katzenjammer Takes a Week's Vacation and the Kids Have a Glorious Time," 44
Mrs. Timekiller, 151
Muhammad, Khalil Gibran, 54

Nancy, 176, 212–213n3
Nast, Thomas, 29–30
nationalism, 17
nationhood, 17
nativism, 28, 30; racial, 27
naughtiness, 23, 85, 96–98; and gender, 98, 171
Nemo (*Little Nemo* character), 119, 121–122, *124*, *128*, 129–132, *130*, *132*, 138, *140*; name of, 140–141; as passive, 124–128
New Woman, 146–147, 213n11
New York American and Journal, 119
New Yorker Staats-Zeitung, 44–45
New York Herald, 73, 81–82, 108, 119, 120, 132, 166
New York Journal, 3, 4, 43
New York World, 2, 4, 19, 146–147
Nora (*Bringing Up Father* character), 31–32
norms: childhood, 9; cultural, 6, 31; gender, 144; social, 23, 41
nostalgia, 56, 70, 97, 98, 125–126, 134, 179
Nunes, Jadviga M. Da Costa, 96
Nybakken, Elizabeth I., 89

"October = A Blackberry Idyll," 61–63
Oliver Wendell Jones (*Bloom County* character), 182–183
Olson, Richard D., 160
"On the Jump!," 98, *99*
Opper, Frederick Burr, 28, 29, 48
Orbe, Mark P., 185
Other, 129, 155, 173; ambivalence toward, 13; comic, 59; ethnic, 48–49, 94; potential of, 14; racial, 38, 53, 71; representations of, 45; visibility of, 56
Outcault, R. F., 2–4, 19, 73–76, 82, 120; on *Buster Brown*, 92, 100; children as subject, 14, 16; city as subject, 2, 21; as comic strip originator, 43; and commercialization, 84, 106; on *Pore Lil Mose*, 80; and race, 52–53. See also *Buddy and Alice*; *Buster Brown*; *Hogan's Alley*; *Pore Lil Mose*

parents, 106; as permissive, 87, 156. *See also* fathers; mothers
Paris, Leslie, 71, 98
Peanuts, 182
Peter and Wendy, 117, 126
phallic metaphors, 74, 161, 162
photography, 91–92
pickaninny, 17, 53, 56–58, 64, 200–201n12
Pickford, Mary, 158
Pilgrim, David, 67
play, 112, 118, 193n30; cross-racial, 71; with dolls, 167–170, 173; encouragement of, 128; and gender, 169; imaginative, 115, 117, 160, 173; as subversive, 170
Pore Lil Mose, 53, 73–76, *74*, *76*, 77–82
"Pore Lil Mose on the 7 Ages," 73–74, *74*
"Pore Lil Mose Talks to the Animals," *76*, 76–77, 78
Postman, Neil, 177–178
Powers, T. E., 145–146, 152
precocity, 178–179
Princess (*Little Nemo* character), 130, 143
prodigal son, 105
Progressive Era, 6–11, 16–17; and boyhood, 131; and childhood, 5, 129; conflicts in, 1; and consumerism, 59; and family, 86–96; and gender, 154–155, 174; and immigration, 25–27, 40; and inequality, 9–10; and race, 54–56, 58, 173
progressivism, 7–11, 54
psychoanalysis, 136
Pulitzer, Joseph, 4
Punch, 29, 37

race, 17–18, 127, 181–185; and caricature, 11–13; markers of, 37; similarities between, 67, 75. *See also* African Americans; Asians
racism, 27, 38, 65, 80–81, 182
Rambsy, Howard, II, 183
readership, 56, 87, 132; cross-generational, 112; diversity of, 15, 16, 28; female, 173; white middle-class, 15–16, 27
Rebecca of Sunnybrook Farm, 9, 154
recapitulation theory, 24–25, 125
recreation, 60–61, 64
reformers, progressive, 7–8, 54, 131; and comics, 19, 86–89
religion, 131–132
"Revenge of the Persecuted Baker, The," 43
Rigby, Clarence, 25, 36, 37–38. See also *Little Ah Sid, the Chinese Kid*
Riis, Jacob, 14, 20–21, 26
Riley Freeman (*Boondocks* character), 181, *184*, 184–185

Robb, Jenny, 160
Roeder, Katherine, 115, 122, 128, 155, 156
Rohmer, Sax, 33
Roosevelt, Archie, 108
Roosevelt, Theodore, 147
Rubin, Louis D., 90
Rudd, David, 101
rural settings, 56, 63–64, 97–98, 134
Ryan's Arcade, 3

Salazar, James B., 97
schrecklichkinder, 43, 44
Schultze, Carl E. "Bunny," 69
Schulz, Charles, 182
Sears, Roebuck and Company, 91–92
segregation, 7, 54, 56
self-referentiality, 138, 141
sequentiality, 12
seriality, 58
serialization, 13
sexuality: and girls, 158–160, 166; and magic, 164, 166; and race, 33, 37, 72
Shakespeare, William, 73–75
Shannon, Edward A., 71
Shantytown, 131–132
Sheehan, Tanya, 66
Slumberland, 119, 124–125, 126
"smart kids," 87
Smolderen, Thierry, 2
Smulyan, Susan, 70, 71
Sochen, June, 149
Soper, Kerry, 13, 15–16, 30
Southern, David W., 54
Spencer, Lilly Martin, 96–97
Stange, Maren, 21
Steedman, Carolyn, 136
stereographs, 91–92
stereotypes, 12–13, 28; African American, 64, 184–185; appropriation of, 28–29; Asian, 24, 32–33; German, 45–46; Irish, 94; redefining, 29
Stevenson, Robert Louis, 116, 127
Stoddard, Lothrop, 33
"Story of 'Dough' and 'It' in a Rainstorm, A," 35–36
Story of Hungry Henrietta, The, 155–158, *156*
Story of Little Black Sambo, The, 73
Stowe, Harriet Beecher, 57
Stratton, Clif, 10
Struwwelpeter, Der, 43, 199n93
Styers, Randall, 161, 164
suburbs, 179, 181
suffragettes, 152
Sully, James, 118
sympathy: and caricature, 12, 13; and children, 5, 23, 38; and humor, 14–15, 85, 91, 92
syndication, 15

television, 175, 177–178, 179, 180
Temple, Shirley, 158
tenements, 2, 14, 19–20
Ten Little Niggers, The, 62–63
Tenniel, John, 29
tensions: in comics, 11; cultural, 31, 36, 112; dispelling, 85, 91, 97; ethnic, 27, 29; family, 94, 176; generational, 46, 193n33; and girlhood, 154–155, 160, 174; racial, 80
"T. E. Powers' List of Famous Women in History: 18—Count 'Em—18," 145–146, *146*
theater, 122
"Three of a Kind Taken on Board the S.S. New York," *81*, 81
Tige (*Buster Brown* character), 101
Tinkle Brothers, The, 43
Tompkins, Kyla Wazana, 63, 202n42
Topsy (*Uncle Tom's Cabin* character), 57–58
Trump, Donald, 186
Tucker, Terrence T., 185
Tucker, Tom, 166, 170
Twain, Mark, 142
typographies, 13, 27, 45; racial, 24–25, 53, 55, 73–74, 80

Uncle Tom's Cabin, 57, 59
urbanization: as feminizing, 9, 98; and race, 63–64, 79
utopia, 140

violence, in comics, 62, 93, 170–171, 172, 177, 183–184

Wajda, Shirley, 112
Wald, Lillian D., 10, 51
Wardman, Ervin, 4
Watterson, Bill, 176. See also *Calvin and Hobbes*
Waugh, Colton, 3
Wee Pals, 182
Wee Willie Winkie's World, 18, 115–116, 133–137, *135*, *136*
"What Broke Up the Firm of Lady Bountiful and Co.," 151–152
"What Would You Do with a Boy like This?," 52–53, 55, *55*, 68–69
whiteness, 52, 59, 65–66, 80; in comics, 181
"Whose Baby Is Oo?," 76–77, *77*, *78*
Wickberg, Daniel, 14, 92

Wiederseim, Grace, 158, 214n45. See also *Dottie Dimple*
Williams, Martin, 43, 84–85
Willie (*Wee Willie Winkie's World* character), 134–137, *135*, *136*, 179
Will O' Dreams and the Sandman, 120
Wilson, W. O., 160–161
women: African American, 59, 75, 79; ambivalence toward, 150; representations of, 150–152; roles of, 147; as troublemaking, 145, 151
Wonderful Wizard of Oz, The, 117
Wonham, Henry B., 11–12
Worcester, Kent, 86
word balloons, 3, 43, 198–199n87
working class, representations of, 2–3, 13–14, 80
World's Fair (1904), 127

xenophobia, 27, 28, 97; of immigrants, 33

Yankee, 98
Yaszek, Lisa, 15–16, 44, 93
yellow journalism, 4
Yellow Kid (*Hogan's Alley* character), 2, 3–4, 13, 15, 21–23, *22*, 36, 73
"Yellow Kid Takes a Hand at Golf, The," 15
yellow peril, 32–33, 37
yonic metaphors, 162
"Young Night-Thought," 127
Ysobel the Suffragette, 152, *153*
Yulee, Dorothy M., 81

Zelizer, Viviana A., 8
Zurier, Rebecca, 21

ABOUT THE AUTHOR

LARA SAGUISAG is assistant professor of English at the College of Staten Island–City University of New York.